EXPRESSED EMOTION IN FAMILIES

EXPRESSED EMOTION IN FAMILIES

Its Significance for Mental Illness

JULIAN LEFF

*Medical Research Council Social Psychiatry Unit
and Friern Hospital*

CHRISTINE VAUGHN

Department of Clinical Psychology, Prestwich Hospital

THE GUILFORD PRESS
New York   London

© 1985 The Guilford Press
A Division of Guilford Publications, Inc.
200 Park Avenue South, New York, N.Y. 10003

Printed in the United States of America

LIBRARY OF CONGRESS CATALOGING IN PUBLICATION DATA

Leff, Julian
  Expressed emotion in families.

  Includes bibliographical references.
  1. Schizophrenics—Family relationships.
2. Expression. I. Vaughn, Christine.
II. Title.
RC514.L37 1984   616.89′82   84-549
ISBN 0-89862-058-9

Acknowledgments

We are particularly indebted to a number of colleagues for their permission to quote data from work in progress. They include Professor Gerard Hogarty of the University of Pittsburgh; Professor Narendra Wig of the India Council of Medical Research; Dr. Tim Crow of the Clinical Research Centre, London; Dr. George Szmukler of the Institute of Psychiatry, London; and Professor George Brown of Bedford College, London.

The California replication of the naturalistic EE studies reported in Chapter 7 was funded by National Institute of Mental Health Research Grant No. MH 30911, and was conducted at the Mental Health Clinical Research Center for the Study of Schizophrenia (Chief, R. P. Liberman) in collaboration with Karen Snyder, Simon Jones, William Freeman, and Ian Falloon.

Our gratitude is due Mrs. Linda Sharon and Mrs. Kathleen MacKenzie for their careful typing and numerous other tasks involved in the production of the manuscript.

Contents

II. STUDIES OF THE ASSOCIATION BETWEEN RELATIVES' EXPRESSED EMOTION AND RELAPSE OF PSYCHIATRIC ILLNESS

III. STUDIES OF INTERVENTION IN FAMILIES OF SCHIZOPHRENIC PATIENTS

EXPRESSED EMOTION IN FAMILIES

Introduction

The great majority of people throughout the world live in families, and so do most individuals who develop psychiatric illnesses, at least at the time of the first episode. It is universally recognized that the family not only provides a supportive environment, but is also a potent source of psychological tensions. It is hardly surprising that theorists have put two and two together and have implicated psychological pressures from family members in the etiology of most psychiatric conditions. Although this may appear to be no more than common sense, there are many obstacles in the way of determining the truth of this assertion. Many of the theoretical and practical contributions to this endeavor have focused on schizophrenia, one of the most severe and enigmatic of mental illnesses. A major problem in studying family influences on the origin of schizophrenia, and indeed of virtually all other psychiatric conditions, is that there is no way of identifying precisely those individuals who are susceptible to the illness prior to the development of symptoms. Hence nearly every study in this area has been either retrospective in nature, starting from the point of illness and looking backward in time, or cross-sectional. Both approaches involve the assumption that relationships assessed after the onset of the illness are indicative of those that existed beforehand. The fallacies and biases that are implicit in these strategies have been fully explored by Hirsch and Leff (1975). In reviewing a large number of relevant studies, these authors identified a handful that avoided such biases by drawing on child guidance clinic and school records. The findings from these are presented at an appropriate point in this book (see Chapter 15). In addition, there are a few ongoing studies in which cohorts of children identified as being at high risk for developing schizophrenia are followed up prospectively. However, it will be some years before these far-sighted projects begin to yield definitive findings.

It is perhaps surprising that the theories of the family's role in the origin of schizophrenia that have been most influential either are based on cross-sectional studies (R. W. Lidz & Lidz, 1949; Singer & Wynne, 1963) or are supported by little or no scientific evidence (Bateson, Jackson, Haley, & Weakand, 1956; Laing & Esterson, 1964). Despite these handicaps, such theories have led to the development of therapeutic methods of working with

1

the families of schizophrenic patients, particularly in the United States. These innovations were introduced in the 1950s and 1960s in an atmosphere of considerable enthusiasm, but this subsequently waned as the difficulties of altering the constellations in such families became apparent (Leff, 1979). Attention shifted to families of patients with other conditions, such as adolescent behavior disorders and anorexia nervosa, and schizophrenia ceased to dominate the family therapy arena for some years. The recent revival of interest owes much to the work described in this book.

Although no convincing evidence was forthcoming for the family theories of the genesis of schizophrenia or for the effectiveness of the therapeutic methods that developed from them, nevertheless they strongly influenced a generation of clinicians. It is regrettable that this often resulted in the indiscriminate apportioning of blame to parents of schizophrenic patients, and, paradoxically, in their exclusion from any therapeutic program. This attitude toward the parents of schizophrenic patients was never as pervasive in the United Kingdom, where its main proponent, R. D. Laing, remained a controversial figure. Instead, a different approach was adopted, which grew out of the revolutionary change in the care of psychiatric patients that took place in the early 1950s.

From the start of record keeping, the number of psychiatric beds occupied by patients in the United Kingdom climbed steadily until 1954, when it reached a peak of 152,000. Since then there has been a steady decline; the number of beds recorded in 1977 was 90,000. This turnaround cannot be ascribed solely to the effects of the major tranquilizers, since it began before these drugs came into general use, both in the United Kingdom and the United States. Even before the dramatic change in national bed-occupancy figures became apparent, alterations in the duration of stay of patients were detected prior to the introduction of the new drugs (Lewis, 1959). In particular hospitals, the reduction in the inpatient population began much earlier than the national trend did. For example, in Mapperley Hospital, Nottingham, in the United Kingdom, the decline began in 1948, while in Vermont Hospital in the United States, it also started in the late 1940s. These harbingers of a movement that was to sweep irresistibly through the mental hospitals of North America and Europe were the consequence of a radical change in the attitudes of professionals toward the psychiatric patients in their care. The deleterious effects of institutional living were being publicized (Barton, 1959; Martin, 1955), while sociologists like Goffman (1961) and Etzioni (1960) were analyzing the political structure of institutions and questioning the assumptions underlying custodial care.

The trickle of discharges from psychiatric institutions swelled to a flood as the new enlightenment created enthusiasts, but even then a few sober individuals doubted the capacity of the community to absorb so many erstwhile long-term inmates. The realities of community care soon began to assert themselves as discharged patients started to shuttle back and forth between institutions and the community, and led to the coining of the cynical term "the revolving-door policy." There were, however, undoubted and striking successes in deinstitutionalizing patients, so that the issue of what contributed to the failures became the focus of considerable interest.

This interest was fostered in the Medical Research Council (MRC) Social Psychiatry Unit in London and led to a series of follow-up studies of schizophrenic patients discharged from psychiatric institutions. Readmission of patients in these cohorts was found to be significantly related to the type of living group to which they were discharged. In general, patients who left the hospital to live with parents or spouses had a worse outcome than those living on their own, in terms of readmission rates and reports of severely disturbed behavior. These findings are subject to more than one interpretation. It could be argued, for example, that relatives living with patients are more intolerant of disturbed behavior and more likely to push for readmission than the friends, neighbors, or landlords of solitary patients. Hence the difference recorded in respect to readmission rates and severely disturbed behavior might reflect more on the attitudes of the relatives than on the patients' clinical state or actual behavior.

These strands can only be untangled by a study that combines the epidemiological approach of the initial follow-up studies with an in-depth inquiry into the minutiae of patients' behavior and of the relationships between patients and relatives. The particular aspect of these relationships that became the focus of further research was their emotional quality. The way in which thinking about this area developed is described in Chapter 1, but, before moving on, it is worth reflecting on a methodological issue.

The approach to family influences on schizophrenic patients that underlies the work presented in this book grew directly out of the follow-up studies referred to above. The starting point of these enquiries is the person who has already developed a schizophrenic illness. The question dictated by this situation is "Given that this individual suffers from schizophrenia, what factors make his or her illness worse or improve it?" This question can be answered in a relatively short period of time, using standard research techniques. In this respect, it differs markedly from the question asked by the family theorists referred to at the beginning of this introduction, namely, "What factors are responsible for the first appearance of schizophrenia?" For the reasons given above, the answer to this question is exceedingly difficult to establish, requires innovatory strategies, and will necessarily consume a great deal of time. The contrast between these two questions and their implications explains why the line of reasoning pursued in this volume has been so much more productive to date than the work on the etiology of schizophrenia.

THE CONCEPT OF EXPRESSED EMOTION AND ITS MEASUREMENT

1

The Discovery of Expressed Emotion: Induction or Deduction?

GEORGE W. BROWN
Bedford College

INDUCTION

It is unusual for a research worker to be asked to make a how-was-it-done statement about his or her work, and I find it difficult to break from such restraint. To give a straightforward account of how "expressed emotion" was discovered seems somewhat intemperate, and I have therefore interspersed an account of what occurred with a discussion of the problem of induction in scientific research.

Medawar (1969) points out that for more than 100 years the English-speaking world was dominated by the opinion that scientific reasoning was inductive. At its simplest, induction is a scheme of reasoning that empowers us to pass from statements expressing particular "facts" to general statements that comprehend them (Medawar, 1969). The core idea is that one starts by looking at data. Medawar has an excellent account of why this will not do, and goes on to present the hypothetical–deductive view that the initiative for the kind of activity that is "distinctively scientific is held to come not from apprehension of 'facts', but from an imaginative preconception of what might be true" (p. 51). The emphasis is on hypotheses, and through its impressive promulgation by Karl Popper, it was the view of science that held sway when I began research. Statisticians also, I have found, in their puritanical way, often cast doubt on the wisdom of just looking at data. If we heed too much how data just happens to turn out, and pick out something of interest from an array of tabulations or divide a series of categories at certain points rather than others, we risk capitalizing on chance associations. Tests of significance are of doubtful help: In surveying many findings, some results will be bound to be statistically significant on the grounds of chance alone, and we may well set off fruitlessly in pursuit of some social-science or psychiatric equivalent of Don Quixote's windmills.

And yet I was, and still am, unhappy with such caution. It has seemed clear to me that "facts" without prior hypotheses have on a number of occasions played a critical role in my own research. Indeed, I have come to believe that too strict an adherence to a hypothetico–deductive view will be bound to weaken the chance of new ideas emerging. Hypotheses and their testing are only one part of what has to be done. There is the equally important task of getting ideas, and it would be short-sighted to rule out that these can come from contemplating "facts" and choosing to pursue certain results rather than others.

On the assumption that we are never dealing with totally unfounded observations, I think something like the reverse of the hypothetico–deductive formulation will often be relevant. Given that there is at least some broad purpose — say, understanding of what happens to discharged schizophrenic patients — contemplation of mere "facts," or how things happen to turn out, can lead to important insights. Moreover, the risk of pursuing chimeras in analyzing data that is not circumscribed by hypotheses formulated before we begin is probably greatly exaggerated. In any analysis of data, it is, of course, necessary to do what is possible to rule out sources of bias and invalidity; standard accounts of research design and analysis tell us a good deal about this. But once this is done, the success of any mere looking at data, on what in the analysis happens to come to our notice, will depend on whether or not we have really latched on to something of importance. If so, then searching through our data for further relevant evidence is unlikely to mislead us.

Insofar as there is a dispute here between different visions of scientific activity, it is likely to turn on the issue of preparedness. Quite correctly, proponents of the hypothetico–deductive view of research will emphasize that success comes to the prepared mind, and the well-known example of the discovery of penicillin will be cited. While there is no denying the correctness of the general point, it is essential to recognize that the preparation may fall a good deal short of what most appear to intend by the term. The kind of critical achievement I have in mind may be no more than the ability to sense the presence of something puzzling in the data, which, if it could be understood, would contribute to an understanding of the broader problem. This sense of being puzzled will often occur without the investigator's having anything approaching formally stated hypotheses or orienting theory. There is simply a sense that certain "facts" are puzzling and are worth pursuing.

Although I was not aware of it during the early years of research, Znaniecki had argued for the importance of induction in field research — termed "analytical induction" — as long ago as 1934. The most impressive exponents of such a view have been Glaser and Strauss (1967) in their influential book *The Discovery of Grounded Theory*. Again, they are largely concerned with field research and are least convincing when they extend their argument to "quantitative" survey analysis. Their suggestion that the core variables are related to every other item in the survey that seems remotely of interest is particularly likely to raise the specter of chasing will-o'-the-wisps.

While I would not rule out the usefulness of such data dredging in some desperate situation, I suspect that a more prudent approach is required — one in which the investigator has at least had an intimate role in collecting the data (Glaser and Strauss suggest using someone else's material for their exercise), and in which this is allowed to guide the search to some degree, rather than the scanning of the innumerable class tabulations involved in data dredging.

However, whatever degree of preparedness the investigator brings to the data, it is easy to see how the course of the research is bound to be closely caught up with the level of personal confidence the investigator has in the significance of the sense of puzzlement I have emphasized. This is not the confidence that comes from meeting formal methodological or statistical criteria, though these may contribute to it; it is a much more personal belief about whether or not the anomaly is worth pursuing. Moreover, confidence is likely to center on an essentially economic issue: Should scarce time and money be spent in pursuing the anomaly, or should resources be allocated elsewhere? The issue of truth may at this point play a quite subsidiary role.

The fact that the initial research dealing with expressed emotion and schizophrenia spanned a 12-year period and involved three substantial projects, employing a number of workers, underlines the importance of the straightforward issue of the cost. An issue highlighted by the tradition of the MRC Social Psychiatry Unit to which I belonged was that all research workers, whatever their seniority, should be intimately involved in collecting research material, whether in the laboratory or in the field. The first study was of discharged chronic male patients who happened, against all odds, to have left the hospital, was begun in 1956, and was carried out in collaboration with Morris Carstairs and Gillian Topping. The second, begun in 1959 with Morris Carstairs, Elizabeth Monck, and John Wing, looked at what happened to schizophrenic male patients who left the hospital after any length of stay; in terms of such an economic perspective, it was the most critical of the three projects. It was by no means a foregone conclusion that the resources for an expensive prospective study, in which patients and their families were seen both at discharge and a year later, would be available. The final study, begun in 1967 with Jim Birley, John Wing, Judy Clarke, Rita Lang, Margaret Rayfield, and Susan Reid, had been preceded by 2 years devoted to the development of new measures of family life. Although the final prospective study demanded considerable resources, by then the momentum of the program made it relatively easy to justify.

The term "expressed emotion" was comparatively late in emerging. In the accounts of the first study, we simply concluded that it might not always be a good thing for a male schizophrenic patient to return to the close ties of parent or wife. In the second study, we used the term "high emotional involvement"; the more neutral term "expressed emotion" was not formulated until the third. The report of this final study, when published in 1972, was not followed by widespread interest — if this is gauged by the number of other research centers wishing to build on the work. It took yet another study from within the MRC Unit — essentially a replication of the third, by Chris Vaughn and Julian Leff — for this to occur. Before this, I had left the Unit and had turned to the study of depression.

This kind of research is difficult to envisage without close collaboration with others, and I have mentioned so far only some of those involved (others are mentioned below). All have been important, and it would be invidious to try to document their individual contributions. Since talk and exchange of ideas are a constant accompaniment of such research, it would be, in any case, difficult. Therefore, in what follows I do no more than give my partial account of what occurred; something that is perhaps not unreasonable given that I am the only person who links the string of studies between 1956 and 1969. I must, however, record my special debt to Morris Carstairs, who initiated the work with chronic patients, and to Jim Birley with whom I worked particularly closely during the final longitudinal study and the work on life events.

A QUESTION OF CONFIDENCE

When I think of the research, what first comes back to me is the interminable feeling of doubt; on some occasions, I recall, I even entertained thoughts that I had by some kind of subterfuge manufactured the unnervingly clear-cut findings. In 1956 there was little hint in the literature of British psychiatry that the core symptoms of a schizophrenic illness might be importantly influenced by social experience. To their credit, my colleagues were encouraging and scrupulously fair about the evidence I produced, but I cannot recall much enthusiasm. Fortunately, within a few years the psychophysiological work of Peter Venables, whose room at the MRC Unit was next to mine, had shown that there was a positive correlation between physiological arousal level among chronic male schizophrenic patients and social withdrawal (Venables & Wing, 1962), and we discussed how this correlation might be linked to the social material. It was comforting that in the future there might be some coming together. But at this time there was a gulf between the "hard" experimental work of the MRC Unit and its new commitment to "soft" survey research. When I began, all the established workers in the Unit — Neil O'Connor, Jack Tizard, Peter Venables — were involved in experimental work, although Jack Tizard was beginning to have doubts about his allegiance. But, whatever its source, the influence of my uncertainty on what I did was very real. By 1960, for example, a pilot study concerning the role of life events in the onset of florid symptoms had been completed. The results, based on 20 patients, were unambiguous: As I had suspected from earlier unsystematic observations, there was an accumulation of events in the 3 weeks before onset. Yet I delayed embarking on the final study, finally published in 1968, for some 5 years; as I remember, my excuse was that the psychiatrists in the Unit should first develop systematic clinical measures of the illness itself—work that ultimately emerged as the Present State Examination (PSE). It was as though I was asking too much from my colleagues for both sets of results to be taken seriously. I have begun by emphasizing the reality of these early doubts, because in another sense I was confident throughout about the insights, and I think that this paradox takes us to the heart of scientific activity as I have come to understand it. Confidence about ideas can come from many sources; unfortunately, these sources will often conflict, and the result is not necessarily some tidy averaging of the two, but inconsistent beliefs coming to the fore on different occasions and in different settings.

Reasons for my doubt in terms of biography and milieu are clear. When I was approached about joining the MRC Social Psychiatry Unit (then still called the Unit for Research on Occupational Adaptation), I had no ideas at all about schizophrenia, and had to turn to some friends in psychology to find out something about it before I visited the Unit. Since I had studied anthropology, I was not even aware once I joined the Unit of the classic work by Faris and Dunham (1939), or the work on social class and schizophrenia by Hollingshead (1958), which was just beginning to emerge. And yet, despite this almost total ignorance, all of my main insights about the role of social factors in the onset and course of schizophrenia were to come within 2 years of my starting research.

Moreover, I found myself with certain handicaps in rectifying my lack of knowledge. A second dominant memory of those days was my emotional revulsion on reading some of the standard psychiatric accounts of the condition. Was it all so clear-cut? Were the core symptoms and handicaps so clearly linked to underlying endogenous processes? My feelings were so strong that it was several years before I could force myself to finish the account of schizophrenia in Mayer-Gross, Slater, and Roth's (1954) *Clinical Psychiatry*. (It is perhaps of interest that this was before any of the writings of the "antipsychiatrists," which were to cause so much agitation, appeared. I might also add that I never questioned the broad relevance of the diagnostic label of schizophrenia, nor even the presence of an important genetic component, but the interpretations that had been placed upon the diagnostic label.) Given the obvious irrational component to this reaction, as well as my inexperience, I think it understandable that I was unsure about my own ideas. As I have already noted, it did not even seem beyond the bounds of feasibility that the strength of my feelings might in some way have compromised what I had done. But, to make the point again, with this went a steady certainty about the relevance of the findings. It was almost as though the uncertainty and doubt to which I gave expression in my public behavior permitted this deeper conviction to flourish and to play its part in decisions about what research should be done.

THE THREE INQUIRIES

We started the first follow-up inquiry with little preparation. Morris Carstairs had carried out several exploratory interviews with discharged patients and their families. Gillian Topping and I had drawn up a list of questions based on some very general ideas of what might be of interest, and we went to talk to relatives, and sometimes patients, about them. It was very much an initiation by fire. I remember my shock at my second interview with the wife of a paranoid schizophrenic patient. I was quite unprepared for the callousness of his behavior (when his wife developed acute appendicitis, he left her to crawl to the local hospital during the night); the extent of the bizarre delusions that dominated his life at home; and the way in which, despite these delusions, he had been able to hold a job for many years. Among my first impressions were of the extraordinary tolerance of many relatives and the strength of the distress and depression that could arise among them.

Unlike Laing, who also began his work about this time, I did not see myself as having any particular skills in talking to schizophrenic patients. We, of course, spoke with the patients at some length when they lived alone, and often when they lived with others. But our work from the start was aimed at using a relative as the main source of information, and our common experience of finding the patients often uncommunicative reinforced this. In self-defense, I feel I should add that we were certainly not unmoved by our interviews with patients, and some were extremely informative. Nor were we unconscious of the abuse patients could suffer at the hands of hospitals and relatives. Nevertheless, suddenly turning up to ask all kinds of detailed questions about life since discharge (or return to the hospital) is not the best way to relate to schizophrenic patients, and I do not think that any of my ideas about the role of the home atmosphere in outcome came from my conversations with patients. The "inaccessibility" of the schizophrenic patient is, of course, exceptional, even taking into account the achievement of workers such as Laing. I am unclear about the degree to which this taciturnity influenced my general approach to research with schizophrenic patients, but that it had some influence is clear.

Be this as it may, however, the form taken by the whole program of research was undoubtedly decisively influenced by one result from an early set of tabulations of the first study (obtained after considerable labor from our Hollerith machine, which required all subtotals to be counted by hand). This was that schizophrenic patients were more likely to relapse if they returned to live with parents or wives than if they went to live in lodgings or with brothers or sisters. The finding held only for schizophrenic patients (not the 73 of the 229 patients who had other diagnoses, such as "depression," "epilepsy," and "psychoneurosis"); I reproduce a table from our first paper published in *The Lancet* in 1958, which has proved prognostic of much of the work I have done since (see Table 1.1). It deals only with those who had been married at some point and shows that schizophrenic patients apparently thrived when they were "widowed, separated and divorced," and that those with other diagnoses appeared to do better when they returned to live with their wives. ("Failure" was the term used for those returning to the hospital.)

But the core analysis, in the sense of advancing insights into what was going on, involved more than two variables. The next tables reproduce two of them. The patients had all been hospitalized for at least 2 years and the majority for at least 5, and it is therefore unsurprising that a quarter of the patients returned to quite different households from those in which they had been living before they entered the hospital. As it turned out, those who had changed their living group were less likely to return to the hospital after discharge (see Table 1.2). It was particularly interesting that although those who had been "violent" at original admission had a greater chance of return than those who had changed their living group, such "violence" was quite unrelated to readmission among those who had changed their living group (Brown, 1959).

Both results, of course, hint at influences stemming from relationships within the home and not at some working through of an inevitable disease process. (Almost all of these patients had been discharged before the introduction of the major tranquilizing drugs.) Perhaps the most impressive tabulation concerned those returning to live with their mothers (see Table 1.3). Outcome was highly related to whether patients, or their mothers, or both, worked outside the home. Patients had by far the worst outcome when both they *and* their mothers were unemployed. When the mothers worked, patients, even if unemployed, did much better; indeed, outcome in these situations did not

Table 1.1. Marital Status, Diagnoses, and Outcome

Marital State	Schizophrenia		Other Diagnoses	
	Successes	Failures	Successes	Failures
Married	7	7	15	1
Widowed, separated, or divorced	16	2	11	14
Total	23	9	27	15

Note. From "Post Hospital Adjustment of Chronic Mental Patients" by G. W. Brown, G. M. Carstairs, and G. Topping, 1958, *Lancet, ii*, 685–689. Reprinted by permission.

Table 1.2. "Failures" among Patients Who Did and Who Did Not Return to Their Preadmission Living Group by Hospital Discharge Categories

	Failures		Total
	n	%	
All patients			
Change in living group	6	16	38
No change in living group	43	37	116
Total[a]	49	32	154
"Recovered"			
Change in living group	0	0	6
No change in living group	2	13	16
Total	2	9	22
"Relieved"			
Change in living group	2	9	22
No change in living group	25	32	77
Total	27	27	99
"Not improved"			
Change in living group	4	40	10
No change in living group	16	69	23
Total	20	61	33

Note. From "Experiences of Discharged Chronic Schizophrenic Mental Hospital Patients in Various Types of Living Group" by G. W. Brown, 1959, Millbank Memorial Fund Quarterly, 37, 105–131. Reprinted by permission.

[a]Change not known for one patient.

Table 1.3. "Failures" and Amount of Social Contact, as Measured by Mothers' and Patients' Work History, for Discharged Patients Living with Mothers

	Failures		Total
	n	%	
All patients			
Patients working	3	10	29
Patients not working	26	47	55
Total	29	35	84
Patients with working mothers			
Patients working	2	22	9
Patients not working	4	27	35
Total	6	23	44
Patients with nonworking mothers			
Patients working	1	5*	20
Patients not working	22	55*	40
Total	23	38	60

Note. From "Experiences of Discharged Chronic Schizophrenic Mental Hospital Patients in Various Types of Living Group" by G. W. Brown, 1959, Millbank Memorial Fund Quarterly, 37, 105–131. Reprinted by permission.

*$p < .001$.

differ from the outcome in situations where both patients and their mothers were employed. Whether or not a patient was employed could be expected to depend partly on the severity of his current psychiatric state, and these results provided perhaps the most convincing evidence we managed to produce at this point for an environmental effect that held irrespective of this state: Patients apparently did well even if unemployed, as long as their mothers went out to work. (In the next study, this result led to a general prediction about the effect of reducing amount of face-to-face contact in combating the effects of an adverse home atmosphere.)

In terms of the theme of uncertainty I have been developing, at no point in the whole research program did I find any difficulty in formulating quite plausible alternative interpretations. In this particular instance, perhaps mothers were only going out to work when their sons were unemployed and also comparatively well, and that the association between mothers' lack of employment and sons' return to the hospital was merely a selective artifact. Or maybe it was a matter of tolerance of the mothers, rather than actual deterioration in symptomatology. This was the dominant view of American sociologists at the time (see Freeman & Simmons, 1963). My concern with measurement and methodological issues probably dates from such early struggles about alternatives and the need to try to rule them out in future research.

However, it is clear that at this early point of the program we were working with some idea about what might be going on; indeed, worry about alternative interpretations only makes sense on this basis. I can no longer recall the details of this first analysis, but, seen as a whole, it fits well into what Hanson (1958) has called a "retroductive" model of scientific activity. He argues that the two traditionally opposed views of scientific activity (inductive and hypothetico–deductive) are not alternatives, but are in fact compatible. Something is wrong when either is considered alone; in particular, Hanson emphasizes that scientists typically do not start from hypotheses, but from data. Of course, no data is without *some* theory: In this sense, following Whewell, "There is a mask of theory over the whole face of nature" (Medawar, 1969).

In the present instance, the fact that we had bothered to establish both the type of living group a patient had at admission and that to which he returned after discharge does reflect some crude perspective on what might be of relevance, but, as noted earlier in discussing preparedness, it is highly unlike the kind of theory that those with a hypothetico–deductive perspective have in mind. Indeed, we probably only collected information about living groups at discharge because it was the kind of thing that social scientists would be expected to concern themselves with. It did not come from a theory about schizophrenia, but from some dim recognition of what social scientists such as ourselves should be considering. As already implied, a good part of the achievement of this first study was settling on patients' different rate of relapse according to their living groups as something to pursue. Rather than "preparation" in this instance, one might more plausibly cite the reverse — a complete openness and a need to find some key to help us come to terms with the tangle of results steadily emerging from our labors on the Hollerith machine. The fact that the apparent key to this labyrinth brought upon us a good deal of skepticism could not outweigh the excitement and relief at finding a possible way to order the increasing pile of tabulations. And to us it made sense.

I have so far noted Hanson's (1958) emphasis on the importance of data: "The pedestrian process of deducing observation statements from hypotheses comes only after the physicist sees that the hypothesis will at least explain the initial data requiring explanation. It is this creative act that is so often the greater part of his achievement" (pp. 70–71). However, although he insists that the inductionists are largely correct in emphasizing the importance of inferring "laws" from data, he asserts that they were wrong to suggest that these laws are merely a summary of the data. I find Hanson's argument illuminating, because he is not content to suggest that this critical step has to be seen in terms of intuition; he adds that it also has a *logical* component. Although the insight can come as an intuitive flash, it is from the start a very reasonable affair, and this is because it has some logical basis. It appears correct at once; it is an insight in which one feels a good deal of confidence and yet there has as yet been no testing of a hypothesis. The explanation immediately makes sense in terms of what is known about one's own data and that of others. It is for this critical step that he uses Pierce's term "retroduction." He argues that for this to occur, there must first of all be something perplexing about the data — an anomaly. What happens then is that the investigator thinks of a premise or premises that make sense of the anomaly.

In our case, the anomaly was the link between relapse and type of living group. This, in terms of retroductive logic, could be explained if relapsing patients were reacting adversely to close ties, *and* they would be sensitive in this way if, for reasons inextricably linked to their illness, they were particularly susceptible to too much emotional arousal. In more strictly psychological terms, they would be suffering from sensory overload (Antelman & Caggiula, 1980). Given this, the classic findings of Faris and Dunham (1939) made sense if their interpretation is stood on its head. Patients were not developing schizophrenia because of the adverse effects of isolation and life in the inner city; they were more often entering the hospital from such areas of the city because their difficulty in dealing with close emotional ties had earlier led them to withdraw from social contacts to find a way of life that harmonized with their basic defect. About this time, Hare (1956) was demonstrating that something along these lines probably was occurring in Bristol; and Wardle (1960), in an intriguing study at the Maudsley Hospital, showed that schizophrenic patients, once skill or prestige level of job was controlled, tended to have jobs that involved less face-to-face contact with others than patients with other diagnoses.

I have no doubt that something like this retroductive process occurred during the analysis of our data from the first follow-up study; unfortunately, I cannot claim that it came in a flash. Insofar as I am able to recall, the insight came more slowly as I worked through the kind of tabulations I have outlined. The process was already completed by the time I had looked at the effect of change of living group. And by the time I had looked at whether or not mothers and patients were employed, the analysis had reached the stage of testing *derivative* predictions — an activity that Hanson argues is very much of a bread-and-butter nature, although I would add that it is one research workers are likely to see as among their most inventive and rewarding.

Therefore, Hanson (1958, 1971) argues as follows:

1. Some surprising phenomenon *P* is observed.
2. *P* would be explicable as a matter of course if *H* were true.
3. Hence there is reason to believe that *H* is true.

He argues that the second step does not flow from the mere repetition of the first step. What I suspect often occurs is that the crude indicator used in the first step (say, type of living group) is translated into a theoretical concept that makes sense of the anomaly. In the present instance, type of living group relates to relapse because it reflects (albeit rudimentally) emotional atmosphere in the home, and, given the premise that schizophrenic patients are sensitive to emotional arousal, the third step follows. Of course, the second logical step will be influenced by prior experience. I had, for instance, been much impressed by the amount of emotion expressed by *some* relatives and by the apparent need of some patients to withdraw from contact with them, at least in the home. I had also been impressed by certain experiences during the research: For example, the identical twin brother of a patient, at the end of a long interview, totally out of the blue produced a jumble of extraordinary delusions that involved his landlady's pumping gas through his keyhole. These were ideas he had clearly had for a long time, and yet he held a responsible job, had never seen a psychiatrist, and for 2 hours had appeared totally ordinary and unexceptional. He lived alone and led a quiet life. I could not help speculating about the impact of my interview. I had not, however, been impressed by the many formulations in the psychiatric literature about the fundamental role of patients' relationships with parents in the etiology of schizophrenia. There appeared to be far too many exceptions for it to provide a *general* theory about origins of the disorder. However, it seemed likely that such relationships could at times play some role in original onset, and that it might well explain why the families of early-onset patients apparently contain many particularly disturbed members (Brown, 1967).

Some, discussing research from a phenomenological perspective, have argued from a somewhat similar position, but at the same time have emphasized the way in which research workers achieve insight by making sense of *themselves* in the context of the social situations they are studying. The role of researchers as participants is emphasized (e.g., Reason & Rowan, 1981). I believe that I may have been influenced by certain things that had happened in my own family, but I do not believe that this personal involvement has to be present. The whole process can be almost entirely a matter of *logic* in Hanson's (1958, 1971) sense. To take another example, soon after the completion of the first follow-up study, I began to consider the relation among the recent introduction of the major tranquilizing drugs to treat schizophrenic patients, the associated reduction in chances of becoming a chronic patient staying in hospital (i.e., continuously for 2 years), and whether or not a patient had been isolated in the sense of not receiving a visitor in his first 8 weeks in the hospital. Such isolated patients had had in the past a much reduced chance of discharge. Bearing everything in mind, I argued that the introduction of the drugs had played an important role in reducing length of stay, not only by affecting clinical state, but also by making medical and nursing staff more optimistic about the possibility of discharge (Brown, 1959, 1960). This premise led to hypotheses that were confirmed—for example, that the reduction of length of stay in the mid-1950s had involved *only* those who were unvisited in their first 8 weeks in the hospital. (It was for this group that I felt any changes in attitudes could be expected to have most effect.) I find it difficult to relate *any* part of these ideas to personal experience or even first-hand contact with medical and nursing staff, of which I had very little at this time. Nonetheless, I thoroughly agree that investigators do well to try whenever possible to let their own "experience" resonate with the "facts," as long as they maintain some awareness of what they are doing.

I have discussed *retroductive* logic at some length, because I believe it is not only a reasonable summary of what occurred in this instance, but it also helps to explain the confidence I felt in the ideas about the living-group result, despite the fact that I was unsure just what about relationships in the home was important. Given my other reasons for doubt, I think it enough to make sense of the extraordinary mix of confidence and doubt that I experienced at this time and for several years to come. The most sensible next step seemed to be to test some of the ideas by developing a direct measure of family relationships, rather than relying on the crude type of living-group measures used at that time. At the same time, I wanted to do something to combat doubt by trying to rule out two obvious competing interpretations. The first was that there was in fact no direct link between quality of family relationships and outcome; there only appeared to be one because both were linked to a third prior variable that had brought about the correlation between the two. As I have already noted, I had found it distressingly easy to think of plausible alternative explanations to every one of the key findings we had established. I speculated, for example, that those who had changed their living group were less ill, and that this was due to the fact that they had been kept longer in the hospital than necessary because they had no place to which to return. Therefore, severity of past disturbance seemed to be an obvious candidate for such a third variable in the proposed second study; it might well, because of its effect in increasing family tension and increasing chances of relapse, produce a spurious link between home atmosphere and outcome. It would be essential to pay close attention to clinical measures of the patients' condition at the point of discharge. The second competing interpretation was that any measure of family atmosphere that we utilized in the research would be biased by our knowledge, at the time of making the rating, of whether or not patients had relapsed.

We therefore planned a prospective study dominated by methodological concerns: Would the core relationship hold, once these two sources of obvious possible bias had been dealt with? But we still had to develop measures of family atmosphere. One way to proceed would have been to ask the patients about their responses to life at home. However, I have already discussed the difficulty I had experienced in developing a sense of rapport with schizophrenic patients, at least in the setting of a brief research interview that took place at about the time of their discharge. (My skepticism about the nature of such contacts was given some support in the later analysis, when measures of patients' "emotional involvement" at discharge were completely unrelated to chances of later relapse after discharge; see Brown, Monck, Carstairs, & Wing, 1962.) I had been impressed for some time by our apparent ability to pick up very quickly the emotional atmosphere of a family, perhaps within a minute or so of entering a home. We decided to build on this—to see patients and others all together in their homes and to judge the amount and kind of emotion expressed in the interview itself. We now know that it is possible to do this reliably, but at this time the amount of agreement that could be expected between raters was by no means clear. We could find no relevant sociological studies, and those by psychologists had had a somewhat mixed record. Most impressive was the early use of the Fels Parent Behavior Scale, which had been used as long ago as the 1940s to measure some 30 items of parental behavior. It included, for instance, ratings of the parents' relationship to the child in terms of protectiveness, criticism, solicitousness, emotionality, and affectionateness. Correlations between raters observing mothers and children were reasonably high, with most between .60 and .70; for the subscales just listed, they were .39, .74, .72, .57, and .76, respectively (Baldwin, Kalhorn, & Breese, 1949). A key study done at about this time by Hamburg and his colleagues (Hamburg *et al.*, 1958) looked at the reliability of rating expressed anxiety, anger, and depression, and showed that comparisons between the ratings of different judges produced correlations of .78 to .87. We were, however, unaware of this study, and we were only partially encouraged by the levels of interrater reliability that had been reported.

It seemed clear that such judgments were based on ordinary skills used largely unthinkingly in our daily lives. We hoped that by discussing any disagreements during the development of the measures and by using anchoring examples, it would be possible for Elizabeth Monck and me to reach satisfactory levels of agreement. In fact, for the five very general scales recording emotion shown during the interview, we disagreed on only 7 of the 96 ratings we made in the 16 pilot interviews, and on only 3 of these was there a discrepancy between the top and bottom half of the 4-point scales.[1] This high level of agreement was probably due as much to the number of interviews we had carried out together and the extent to which we had talked about the rating scales during their development as to our formal criteria or anchoring examples. (I recall that one of our achievements at the time was obtaining complete agreement in rating the main characters in one of Ibsen's plays.)

Each patient and family were seen together just after discharge, and were characterized by the "emotional involvement" scales. The measures based upon relatives predicted well whether or not a patient's clinical state deteriorated in the follow-up period, but those based upon the patient did not. We also showed, following the insight about mothers' employment, that low amounts of face-to-face contact could be protective for those returning to "highly emotionally involved" homes.

Because of the prospective design, we were able to make a reasonably convincing case that there was a direct causal link of some importance. There was, however, one casualty: Despite their excellent outcome in the earlier study, patients returning to live alone in lodgings had a high rate of relapse. We speculated that this was due to the fact that they stood a greater risk than those living with others of experiencing "life events" that they had fewer resources to deal with. This still seems to me a plausible interpretation, but the matter remained open, as indeed did the complex issue of the relationship of family atmosphere, life events, and relapse. Jim Birley and I have suggested that there was some inkling of a case to be made for an additive effect: Patients coming from a home that we had just characterized as containing long-term "tension" more often experienced such an event in the 3 weeks before onset (Brown & Birley, 1968). Recent work by Leff and his colleagues has in fact carried the problem much further and has suggested that such additive effects will occur when patients are on a maintenance dose of neuroleptic drugs (see Chapter 12). This makes a good deal of sense — without the drugs, patients in a home rated high on expressed emotion will be more liable to break down before an event occurs — but another suggestion we made still re-

---

1. The scales assessed the following: amount of emotion expressed by relative toward patient; hostility shown by relative toward patient; dominant or directive behavior by relative toward patient; emotion expressed by patient toward relative; and hostility expressed by patient toward relative (Brown *et al.*, 1962).

mains to be refuted: that is, that *any* form of emotional arousal, including joy and excitement stemming from obtaining something desired, can trigger a florid attack. From a few instances of such attacks, I am convinced that this suggestion is plausible. Unfortunately, such incidents are rare (probably doubly rare in a population of schizophrenic patients), and it will not be easy to collect a sufficiently large series for the proposition to be properly tested. Until this is done, I will continue to believe that an experience such as falling in love can precipitate a schizophrenic episode in the predisposed. Incidentally, my reaction to the failure of our original result concerning the better outcome of patients returning to lodgings illustrates well the point made by a number of commentators that a likely response to failure to confirm a hypothesis is that the underlying theory will be amended rather than rejected (Lakatos & Musgrave, 1970). Again, an inductive theme emerges. Indeed, after a certain point in a research program, disconfirmation of at least a certain proportion of hypotheses is probably to be welcomed as a way of bringing about new insights and extending the range of theory.

However, at the completion of this second study, I was aware that we had not established what it was about family relationships that was important; nor, for that matter, were my own ideas at all settled about what were the critical features of family life. I suspect that this kind of vagueness is not uncommon. Kaplan (1964) has argued that definition in scientific research tends to be processual, and that its development typically takes a long period of time. Indeed, it is difficult to see how we can have any conviction about what a measure represents until we develop and test a theory about it, and that was certainly not the position in 1962 (Staddon, 1971). Just because something can be measured reliably and a good case can be made for its having a causal impact of some importance, it does not follow that we necessarily will have much idea of how it does so. This would be to confuse causal *model* and *theory*. A causal model merely relates measures in terms of causal links, and, by meeting certain minimal methodological criteria, makes a case that something is going on—that there are probably important causal processes at work, although just what is involved cannot be known unless it is clear what the measures represent theoretically. It is inevitable that model and theory will not keep in step, and progress in science can be said to come from the struggle to close the gap between them.

However, at this point in the research, it did seem clear to me that whatever was at work would need to apply equally to parents of patients and to husbands and wives of patients. For this reason alone, as I have already noted, I was skeptical about the published discussions of the role of family relationships in the etiology of schizophrenia. These dealt only with parents and emphasized enduring, deeply disturbed relationships. It was not that such relationships did not occur and might not at times be of some etiological significance. We had certainly come across a number of them in our visits, and they tended to be interviews that stood out in our memories. Even now they are the ones that most easily come to mind: the father who played the piano on and off during the interview and talked of 7-year cycles influencing both me and his son; another who over the years had shown quite extraordinary devotion to his son, tolerating, for example, great abuse from a youth whom his son had brought home to live with them, because he felt his son needed a friend; a mother who insisted there was absolutely nothing wrong with her son, who habitually dressed up in a weird combination of Christ's garments (he cut his shoes to be sandals) and military paraphernalia, because he could manage to shop locally for her.

But such families were in fact uncommon, and it seemed most unlikely that they could provide a general explanation for what we were observing. In any case, many patients appeared never to have broken down until well after they had left home and married. Although the notion of transference might still rescue the basic theory of parental influence, it seemed important that the occasional presence of *deeply* disturbed or unusual relationships between parents and patients should not be allowed to dominate our thinking. If I had any hunch about what was going on, it was that it often involved something a good deal less fundamental, indeed commonplace. Therefore one way forward would be to develop an instrument capable of recording the range of feelings and emotions to be found in ordinary families. Indeed, the family instrument used to record "expressed emotion" was not developed with the families of schizophrenic patients, and it did not occur to me that there was anything amiss in this.

Soon after the completion of the second study, Michael Rutter joined the MRC Social Psychiatry Unit, planning to study the impact of "neurotic" patients on their children, and we decided to tackle the problem of family measurement in a more fundamental way than we had done hitherto. The developmental work took nearly 2 years, and at one stage eight people were involved. Since a full account of the work has been published, I do not go over the ground again here (Brown & Rutter, 1966; Rutter & Brown, 1966). The key measures were Warmth, Number of Positive Comments, Severity of Criticism, Number of Critical Remarks, Dissatisfaction (eight scales), and Hostility. However, in the end, the families of schizophrenic patients did add something. Once the interview and rating scales had been developed, we tried them out with families of schizophrenic patients, and included parents of patients for the first time. Following our usual procedure, we asked ourselves, following each interview, whether there appeared to be *anything* about the interview that was not reflected in the measures. In response to our conclusions, we added a rating of Emotional Overconcern. This had not been salient enough among the married couples we had used for the main developmental work for us to be able to distinguish it. It was only among parents that overconcern was clear enough for us to feel confident about distinguishing it from such emotions as high warmth.

Our approach was therefore to describe all forms of emotional expression that we sensed in the families we met. We were not bothered if the emotions appeared to be closely linked. We distinguished between critical comments and dissatisfaction, although they clearly often went together: Most critical comments were relevant for rating dissatisfaction, although dissatisfaction could be high without critical comments being involved. We were therefore not bothered about the niceties of discriminant validity (Campbell & Stanley, 1963), and any approach such as factor analysis would also have been quite against the spirit of what we were trying to do. We were using *ourselves* to tell us which forms of emotional expression should be distinguished, and as long as we could make ratings reliably, the only relevant criterion of validity that we recognized was that the measure should be ultimately related to relapse. Thus, although the scales for Critical Comments and Dissatisfaction were highly correlated, the latter turned out to be quite unrelated to outcome, once the number of critical comments was taken into account. It was only the "critical" element in dissatisfaction that was to prove predictive. In this sense the two measures, although highly correlated, have construct validity, and there does not seem to be much doubt that if they had not been distinguished we would have been less effective in predicting outcome. Our approach during this developmental stage was entirely intuitive, and, as I remember, not particularly influenced by what we thought might be ultimately important in predicting relapse among schizophrenic patients. It was enough that the forms of emotional expression could be distinguished.[2]

In this way, we had developed what seemed to be a sensitive series of rating scales to take account of types of emotion centered both on a patient and others in the home. I was happy to wait and see which ones emerged as predictors of outcome. We proceeded inductively; as I now recall, the only thing I felt reasonably confident of was that *something* about family relationships was important. Of course, I had some ideas — for example, I would have been surprised if level of dissatisfaction had proved to be predictive and not critical comments. However, progress at this point did not depend on such insights, and there were certainly a number of things about which I would have had difficulty making a prediction. I like to think that I would have predicted that once criticism and emotional overconcern were controlled, high

2. We were not, however, entirely uninfluenced by the notion of convergent and discriminant validity. We compared results obtained from the interviews held with a single relative with those obtained in a joint interview with patient and relative. But we did this less in a spirit of a test of validity than to prove some continuity with the second study, which had been based entirely on ratings made at joint interviews. As it turned out, although the correlations between ratings made at joint and at single interviews were reasonably high, we were unwilling to gamble on the effectiveness of the single interview, and both types were used in the main research. This in the end proved to be unnecessary, and the joint interview in the event added little or nothing to the predictive power of the ratings based on interviews with relatives seen alone.

warmth would relate to a *better* outcome, but I am by no means sure (Brown, Birley, & Wing, 1972).

PROCESSUAL DEFINITIONS

I have described how I assumed that what was important about family life would emerge as a matter of course as research progressed, and that it was pointless to get too concerned during the development of the measures for the final study with what *might* prove to be significant. It might be called a bootstrap blueprint for research. Not the least of my pleasure in reading about current research is that the approach appears to have been vindicated; we are now that much clearer about what it is about family relationships that is involved. I would also be falsely modest if I did not confess that I am pleased that my hunch that quite "superficial" emotional processes were heavily implicated appears to have been supported, at least in the sense that it appears possible to change substantially the amount of criticism in a good proportion of relatives by a modest amount of intervention. However, the fact that not all were changed and that overinvolvement was uninfluenced by the intervention also underlines the probable role in some families of more complex processes. It is of interest that the only relative whose overinvolvement dissipated with the intervention was that of a wife.

I have therefore emphasized definition as a long-term process. This is commonly misunderstood by those educated to believe that effective science is concerned with explicit hypotheses and fully worked-out theoretical positions. The alternative tradition of interpretative sociology, which emphasizes the importance of dealing with meaning and consciousness and which downplays the whole tradition of hypothesis testing, manages also to convey that things can be made explicit — that effective insights about what is going on will emerge if only the investigators ground themselves sufficiently in social life. I think that I would have found it extremely difficult to proceed if I had believed either position. The aims underlying the emphasis on interpretative sociology in terms of the grounding of observation are entirely laudable and serve as an important corrective to a good deal of unthinking and crude disregard for the problem of meaning, which has characterized much empirical social research. In practice, however, it will often not be possible to make everything explicit in this way; we need to live with uncertainty. Indeed, in the short term at least, we may not even be particularly concerned with truth. My dominant concern throughout much of the work I have described was to convince myself and my colleagues that there were sufficient grounds to justify the next step of the research in terms of cost.

My account of the process of definition can be placed in a larger perspective. In terms of T. S. Kuhn's (1962) influential account of scientific activity in *The Structure of Scientific Revolutions*, I was working without the benefit of a problem solution or paradigm, the basic attribute of what Kuhn has called "normal science." This is enough to explain much of my uncertainty, and the production of the present volume makes clear that the research has entered a phase of normal science. In a recent stimulating commentary on Kuhn's work, Barnes (1982) draws the further conclusion that without such paradigms "there can be no understanding at all of the proper usage of scientific terms" (p. 51) and that "it is the activity of normal science that gives concepts significance, not the inherent significance of concepts that determines the activity" (p. 53). Barnes argues for what he calls a "finitist" account of the use of concepts in scientific research; this account is very close to the processual or step-by-step nature of definition and measurement described by Kaplan (1964), which I have emphasized. Indeed, given in this view that a definition of what we are measuring can never be fully settled, Barnes would argue that "invention" rather than "discovery" would be the appropriate word to use in the title of this chapter. The choice of term nicely reflects different perspectives on measurement, and by retaining "discovery" I have deliberately placed myself at some distance from the extreme relativistic stance of many now writing in the interpretative or hermeneutic perspectives in the social sciences. Nonetheless I have no doubt that our understanding of the measures of expressed emotion will continue to grow, and there is always the possibility that at some point our understanding of them may still change radically.

Let me finally return to the question of confidence. Although the dominant feeling I recall thoroughout the research was that of uncertainty, I never had much doubt that we should continue and that the role of "family atmosphere" should be studied in increasing depth. Doubt lay elsewhere: incredulity that we could really have uncovered such a strong effect; doubt as to whether or not we had sufficient insights into other factors contributing to outcome (say, amount of contact with others in the home) for the effect to emerge clearly in our tabulations; concern whether in our nonexperimental design we had enough grip on possible selective factors, such as basic severity of the disorder, the possible influence of which would need to be ruled out before any finding could then be taken seriously; and, finally, a very personal anxiety that somehow my strong feelings about the then-dominant psychiatric view on schizophrenia had in some way led me to misconstrue and misinterpret what was going on. I believe that we must learn to live with such doubt and not let it cripple our research by looking too soon for certainty — something easily encouraged by fashionable accounts of what is good scientific practice. Although this last, very personal doubt has now largely disappeared, it has been strong enough to bring added pleasure at the replications and extensions of our original findings by other research centers that are reported in this volume.

2

The Camberwell Family Interview

In the preceding chapter, George Brown has provided a stimulating account of the less than straightforward progression to the construction of the expressed emotion (EE) measures. Our task in the next three chapters is to bring these measures to life for the reader by conveying some sense of what EE is and how it is assessed. If we are successful, we also may dispel a few of the myths and misconceptions about the construct that have developed in the years since the British EE results first aroused the interest of the psychiatric community. Clinicians and researchers alike have been eager to learn more about an index of familial attitudes that has been shown to be a powerful predictor of schizophrenic relapse. Yet for many investigators the concept has remained a puzzle: Whatever its predictive value, what EE represents and how it operates are not at all clear. Some think it an esoteric concept, complex and difficult to rate; the lengthy training required of potential raters has reinforced this view. Conversely, others consider it to be irritatingly simplistic, reflecting a narrow and restrictive view of human relationships. We hope to demonstrate that neither of these positions is justified, although one can readily understand how each came to exist.

This chapter features a description of the Camberwell Family Interview (CFI), developed by Brown, Rutter, and their colleagues for the 1972 EE study, as well as the rationale for an abbreviated version of that research instrument. Attention is given also to interviewing procedures and to some of the interviewing techniques used to elicit responses relevant for the rating of EE.

THE INTERVIEW

Brown and Rutter's original decision to use an interview approach as a means of studying the effects of illness on the family and family relationships was by no means an obvious choice. The authors were well aware of the weaknesses of the interview as a research instrument: for example, the heavy reliance upon self-report and the retrospective recall of feelings and behavior;

.

the difficult discriminations required when *modal* behavior is asked for; the tendency to rate on *relative* scales; the failure to allow for independent data sources or other built-in safeguards to protect against obvious sources of contamination. The most obvious alternative to the interview is the direct observation of family interaction in an experimental setting. Brown and Rutter have suggested that this may well be the most useful means of assessing certain variables, such as family communication, that have proved difficult to measure using the interview technique (Rutter & Brown, 1966). But as a primary research tool direct observation has a number of limitations, as noted by Richardson, Dohrenwend, and Klein (1965). It is expensive in terms of time and personnel. It "cannot be used directly to study feelings, attitudes, beliefs, values, or cognitive processes except insofar as these can be inferred from behavior" (Richardson *et al.*, 1965, p. 13). For the observer, there is the additional problem of which aspects of behavior are to be selected out as significant and how to attribute meaning to them. One is left with the observer's subjective impressions of what is happening and its significance for the person studied, rather than the person's own views.

Compared with direct observation, the interview has the advantage of greater flexibility, in that the interviewer through questioning can define, clarify, and expand the statements of the respondent. If the interview can be shown to be both reliable and valid, it is possible to measure a greater range of variables than with other techniques, and therein lies its particular usefulness. Thus, Brown and Rutter reasoned, one could justify the investigation of family activities and relationships using an interview approach if satisfactory levels of reliability and validity could be established for the measures used.

Very good levels of reliability and validity were achieved with the CFI, originally developed for the study of families in which one family member was a psychiatric patient. The aim of its authors was to develop a family interview that would be relatively free of the methodological and conceptual weaknesses that have characterized other family research instruments and have been described by several investigators (e.g., Hirsch & Leff, 1975; Riskin & Faunce, 1972).

A detailed description of the CFI and its development may be found elsewhere (Brown & Rutter, 1966; Rutter & Brown, 1966). Briefly, it is concerned with two kinds of information: One has to do with events and activities, the other with attitudes and feelings. It aims to obtain an account of circumstances in the home in the 3 months preceding the patient's admission, particularly details of the onset and development of the present illness episode and its impact on various aspects of family life, such as the participation of family members in domestic tasks, the frequency of irritability and quarreling, and the amount of contact between the patient and the rest of the family. At the same time, the relative's behavior in the interview situation is being observed, and notice is taken of the feelings expressed about family members, especially about the patient and his or her actions over recent months. Thus direct observation does take place, albeit in an interview setting. All interviews are tape-recorded for later analysis.

The distinguishing methodological feature of the CFI is a distinction between "objective" events and "subjective" feelings about events. It was felt that the confusion of these concepts and/or the treatment of them as a single unitary measure explained the poor results of other researchers. Brown and Rutter maintained that the measurement of events and activities required an altogether different approach from the measurement of attitudes and feelings. Accuracy should be the main concern in the measurement of objective happenings — for example, the frequency of quarreling or how often specific household tasks are done. Therefore questioning about "objective" events was designed to increase the likelihood that the respondent's account was as close an approximation to the truth as possible. It takes the form of a detailed but flexible cross-examination about relatively recent events, with a number of different approaches to the same activity and a cross-checking of contradictions and inconsistencies as they arise. The interviewer tries to get the respondent as involved as possible in order to reduce forgetting and distortion.

The general approach of the CFI differs in a number of respects from that of other scales. First, the emphasis is on a defined recent period of time. The unreliability of retrospective accounts concerning events in the distant past is widely recognized. A 3-month period was believed to be recent enough to lessen inaccuracy, but long enough in time to allow for the occurrence of relatively infrequent happenings. Furthermore, questioning is about actual frequencies (e.g., "How many times did this happen in the week before . . . was admitted to [the] hospital?"), thereby avoiding the use of biasing general phrases such as "often" or "sometimes," which tend to be interpreted in a relative way by the respondent. To quote Rutter and Brown (1966), "Attitudes are much more likely to influence an informant's judgment of whether the spouse 'often' does something than they are to distort his account of who did something on each day during the last week" (p. 26). Of course, it would be wrong to assume that behaviors have a simple modal level of occurrence, as Yarrow (1963) has pointed out. Particularly in such areas as irritability and quarreling, there may be important variations in behavior over a given time period that should not be disregarded. The authors of the CFI have taken this into account by questioning to establish peak frequencies as well as more typical average frequencies of a given event or activity. Finally, the scores used to assess family events and activities are based on frequencies rather than on general ratings.

A very different approach is used with the measurement of feelings and attitudes. The main concern here is to get respondents to express themselves in ways that reflect their inner feelings. The semistructured standardized interview form (Richardson et al., 1965) is characterized by flexibility of phrasing and of questioning sequence, which is believed to be more useful than a fixed questionnaire in probing sensitive topics such as mental illness. Flexibility of questioning is combined with such standard measures as verbal and vocal encouragements on the part of the interviewer (Salzinger & Pisoni, 1960) and the discreet use of both neutral and direct probes. Because it is assumed that a respondent may well have conflicting feelings about the same person, the interviewer is not permitted to point out inconsistencies, as he or she is in questioning about "objective" events. For related reasons, unipolar scales of emotion directed toward a single specified person are used, rather than bipolar scales or more general measures of emotion. For example, a respondent's demonstrated warmth toward a particular person is rated, rather than his or her general warmth as a person. Both self-reports of emotion and spontaneous expressions of feelings are noted, although the emphasis is upon the latter. The actual scales of emotion (described in Chapter 3) are of two types: ratings of observed emotions, such as warmth, hostility, and emotional overinvolvement; and a frequency count of the number of positive or critical remarks the informant makes about a particular person during the interview.

In one of the few successful attempts to assess emotional relationships reliably, Brown and Rutter demonstrated in their pilot work that high levels of interrater reliability (average $r = .85$) can be achieved in the measurement of emotions and counts of emotive remarks, provided that certain precautions are taken. They emphasized the importance of simple, clearly defined scales and the value of intensive and well-planned training of interviewers in maximizing interrater reliability. For example, the main cues to be used in the recognition of emotions were specified, while annotated tape recordings and group discussions helped to establish thresholds for decisions as to the presence and intensity of particular emotions.

In comparing Brown and Rutter's work with earlier attempts to measure emotion (usefully summarized by Davitz, 1964, and Izard, 1971), one is struck by the relative simplicity of the earlier work. In attempting to measure one person's complex attitudes toward another both through self-reported verbal feelings and through vocal and other nonverbal cues, Brown and Rutter were trying to do much more than mere labeling. One measure of their success, and of the validity of the judgments made, is the predictive accuracy of these judgments. In the words of Ekman and Friesen (1968), "The test of the validity of the unit of measurement is the result obtained."

THE CASE FOR A "STREAMLINED" CFI

In 1971, we were sufficiently impressed by the results of the latest of the MRC Social Psychiatry Unit studies concerning the influence of the family on the course of schizophrenia to propose a replication of that study (Brown *et al.*, 1972). In addition to replicating past work, we wished to see whether the factors considered were in any way specific for schizophrenia by studying similar factors in depressive neurotic conditions. The results of all these studies are reported in Section II of this volume. Our intention now, however, is to describe the rationale for and development of an abbreviated version of the CFI, the primary research instrument used in the 1972 study.

In planning our comparatively small-scale replication study, the length of the original CFI schedule increasingly seemed a major obstacle to the assessment of families by a lone interviewer. Although shown to be a reliable and valid instrument, the interview in its original form sometimes took as long as 4 or 5 hours to administer. This could be a taxing exercise for both interviewer and informant, and usually two separate visits were required in order to complete the schedule. Every conceivable aspect of family life was covered. Since the factors most closely associated with symptomatic relapse were not known at the time of the 1972 study, it seemed desirable then to elicit as much information as possible about potentially relevant areas. Also, it seemed likely that it might be necessary to question someone for quite a while, perhaps several hours, before rapport was such that the person would be willing to give an honest account of his or her feelings. This was a most important point, since a primary purpose of the schedule was to provide material from which ratings of emotional response could be made. If however, these same ratings could be made on the basis of a shorter interview, the shorter interview would of course be preferable. The person to be interviewed would be spared an exhausting ordeal, and later investigators interested in the technique for research purposes would not be deterred by its sheer length.

To summarize the main findings of the original study (Brown *et al.*, 1972), it was suggested that the level of the relative's EE at the key interview was the best single predictor of the patient's symptomatic relapse in the 9 months following discharge from the hospital.[1] The single most important measure contributing to the overall index of a relative's EE proved to be the number of critical remarks made about the patient by the relative when the relative was interviewed alone. Hostility and emotional overinvolvement also contributed to the overall index, but hostility appeared to be highly related to criticism, while marked emotional overinvolvement tended to be found only in parents and not in spouses. By itself, it contributed only a small number of cases to the high-EE subgroup. As the number of critical comments was the crucial measure in predicting symptomatic relapse, it seemed desirable to listen to tape-recorded interviews from the original study in order to determine the point in time when, and the area of inquiry in which, critical comments occurred. If the main criticism occurred in the early stages of the interview or during some other specific stage, a carefully abbreviated interview might well be justified.

---

1. The interview with the relative alone, rather than with the patient or with both jointly, produced the significant finding, making it the most important interview for any replication study.

In cases where all critical remarks had been recorded by the interviewer on the rating summary, it was necessary only to listen to each tape and to note at which points individual criticisms occurred and which topics were being covered at the time. Fifteen randomly selected interviews from the 1972 study were listened to in this way, with equal representation of high-, medium-, and low-criticism interviews. Individual time graphs were then plotted (see Figures 2.1 and 2.2).

The results were remarkably consistent. The three sections of the interview that deal with Psychiatric History, Irritability/Quarrelling, and Clinical Symptoms in the 3-month preadmission period accounted for 67% of all critical remarks over the 15 interviews. It is difficult to know whether topic or primacy of questioning was responsible for this finding, since these same three sections were also the first three areas covered in almost every interview. Furthermore, in the first part of the interview, the interviewer would sometimes allow the relative to talk freely about the patient until it seemed possible to begin questioning in a more systematic way. He or she might follow up individual areas of questioning earlier than usual if these were brought up spontaneously by the relative. In any event, the majority of critical comments were produced within the first hour, and there was virtually no relationship between total number of critical comments and length of interview ($r = .08$). Criticism occurred particularly during detailed questioning about the development of the illness and the patient's present clinical condition. What was surprising was that once certain areas were covered, later sections of the interview (with the exception of Household Tasks/Money Matters and, in the case of parental households only, Relationships) produced very little criticism relative to the total amount. Kinship, for example, a lengthy section about which questioning often continued for as long as an hour, accounted for only .5% of all critical remarks over the 15 interviews. The Marital Relationship section, which probes such potentially critical areas as leisure activities and the amount of affection and interest between patient and spouse, contributed only 3% of all critical comments. This is not to say that patients were never criticized for their performance as husbands or wives; they frequently were. The point is that if such criticism occurred at all, it was brought out spontaneously at an early stage in the interview, and not during the direct questioning about the marital relationship.

These results supported the use of a shortened interview in which the areas most likely to produce any criticism were given priority in the sequence of questioning. In practice, only minimal reordering was required. The Household Tasks/Money Matters and Relationship sections now follow the Psychiatric History, Irritability/Quarrelling, and Clinical Symptoms sections. A few additional sections were retained in order to make other required ratings, such as Amount of Face-to-Face Contact and Medication. Once these sections are covered, however, questioning ceases. The present abbreviated version takes from 1 to 2 hours to administer. Length of interview excepted, the administra-

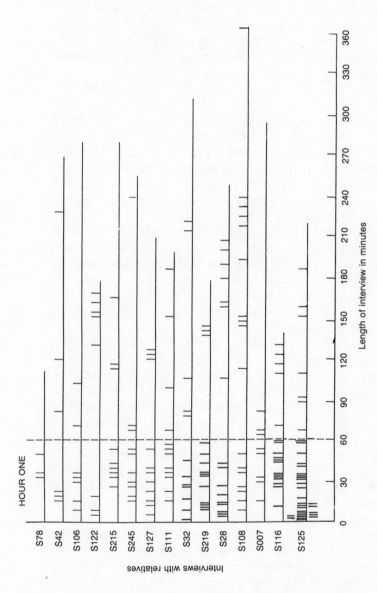

Figure 2.1. The occurrence of critical comments during 15 interviews with key relatives of schizophrenic patients in the Brown, Birley, and Wing (1972) study. Each horizontal line represents the length of an interview with a key relative of a patient, identified by the project case number to the left of the line. The short vertical lines represent individual units of criticism or "critical" comments as defined by Brown *et al.* (1972).

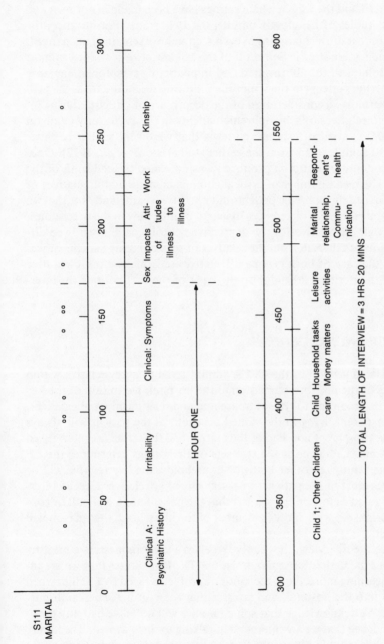

Figure 2.2. The occurrence of critical comments during one of the 15 interviews depicted in Figure 2.1 (enlargement). The upper horizontal line represents the length of the interview with the key relative (spouse) of patient S111. The numbers 0–600 refer to units of time as shown on a Uher 2000 tape recorder. The lower horizontal line indicates the topic areas covered during the interview in order of questioning.

tion of the CFI and the way in which ratings have been made in our own and subsequent studies of EE closely parallel the 1972 study. For instance, the form and content of the questions in each section have remained unchanged.

The findings reported in Section II of this volume provide striking support for the usefulness of the abbreviated CFI in predicting symptomatic relapse in schizophrenic patients in the 9 months following discharge from the hospital. Furthermore, a consideration of the occurrence of criticism during interviews with relatives of schizophrenic patients in the 1976 study (Vaughn & Leff, 1976b) revealed response patterns that were very similar to those shown by the sample of 15 from the earlier study (Brown *et al.*, 1972). Once again, the amount of criticism produced was unrelated to the length of the interview. The mean number of critical comments made by the relatives of the two series of schizophrenic patients did not differ significantly for the two groups, despite the great differences in length of interview in the two studies. Also, although the relatives of the depressive neurotic patients showed different patterns of criticism from the relatives of schizophrenic patients, it was possible in the case of both groups of relatives to achieve a representative measure of their critical attitudes on the basis of the first hour of the interview alone.

INTERVIEWING PROCEDURES

The abbreviated version of the CFI is administered to a key relative within a few weeks of the patient's admission to the hospital. Definition of the key relative varies according to type of household and relationship to the patient. A spouse or parent living in the same household as the patient will always be seen. In a two-parent household, the mother and the father are interviewed separately, and the higher of the two sets of EE ratings determines the EE status of the family. In other kinds of households, the key relative will be whoever sees most of the patient. In cases where key relatives already interviewed and rated as low on EE suggest that the patient has a difficult or conflictual relationship with another member of the household, that person will also be seen.

Prior to the interview, the relative receives a letter requesting a meeting to talk about the patient's recent admission. The letter states that we are interested in learning more about the kinds of problems faced by families when patients go into the hospital, and stresses that the visit is for research purposes only. We acknowledge that some families will not have had any problems, but indicate that we are interested in talking to them as well. The nature of the patient's trouble is not specified; at this stage we cannot assume that the relative is aware of the diagnosis, or indeed even perceives the problem as a psychiatric illness.

Interviews in the British EE studies have almost always taken place in the relatives' own homes. In our experience, relatives are more likely to feel relaxed and comfortable in their own homes, provided that there is sufficient privacy for a confidential interview. But at times it may be necessary or desirable to see the relative in a hospital or clinic setting. For example, families in the Los Angeles replication (see Chapter 7) frequently lived at a great distance from the hospital. While the patients in these families were still in the hospital, it was convenient to schedule the interview on the same day as a prearranged visit by the relative. In cases where the patient had received an early discharge and returned home already, privacy sometimes could be ensured only if the interview was held at the hospital. A final consideration in the Los Angeles study was the nature of the neighborhood. In high-risk areas where the interviewer's safety could not be assured without an "escort" (and there certainly were such areas), interviewers, not surprisingly, preferred to see relatives living in these areas at the clinic. Fortunately, we found no evidence that the quality of the interview varies according to its setting. Where possible, however, a relative's preferences should prevail.

INTERVIEWING TECHNIQUES

The admission period often is a time of crisis for the patient's family; feelings of guilt, bewilderment, anger, and distress are all common. From the moment of meeting, the interviewer is concerned to put the relative at ease. There are no right or wrong answers, the relative is assured; we simply want to have his or her impressions of how the trouble came on and what it was like to be in the home in the time leading up to admission. When they are approached in this way, relatives almost always are prepared to cooperate fully with the questioning process. Most are pleased and surprised that anyone from the hospital should be interested in their views; regrettably, few relatives in our studies had had contact with professionals involved in the patient's treatment prior to the research interview.

The CFI schedule was designed to get the relative talking in an easy and un-self-conscious way about the patient and the illness. Brown and his colleagues believed that if the relative was asked in a neutral fashion about quite specific details of the illness ("Can you describe the last time that behavior occurred? What happened? Who was there? How did each of you react?"), information about feelings would naturally follow. A number of different interviewing techniques help to ensure that this happens. For example, although the interview is standardized, and detailed information concerning a wide range of areas must be gathered during the course of the interview, there is considerable flexibility about the way in which this information is collected. Topics introduced by the relative can be explored immediately with a series of standard questions, while sensitive topics that meet with resistance can be "carried" until a later point in the interview (when the rapport between relative and interviewer is more likely to be established). Given such a flexible format, the interview seems like a conversation rather than an interrogation.

The interviewer may also rephrase questions, using the relative's own words, in certain circumstances. A relative may deny that anything so serious as a "quarrel" took place during the preadmission period, but admit that a "little tiff" might occasionally occur. The interviewer will then ask in some detail about a typical "little tiff" that has occurred recently, to establish whether what the relative dismisses as a "little tiff" does indeed qualify as evidence of quarreling, according to our criteria.

As indicated earlier in the chapter, the interviewer is interested in eliciting two kinds of information from the relative. First, he or she wishes to collect a certain amount of *objective* information about the patient's psychiatric history, symptom behaviors, and role functioning in the months leading up to the present admission. Second, the interviewer seeks information concerning the relative's *subjective* attitudes and feelings toward the patient and the illness. The rules for interviewing vary according to what kind of information is being sought. Thus a relative may be cross-examined on points of fact, but not about inconsistencies of attitude. The EE scales are unipolar; it is assumed that feelings of warmth and concern may coexist with feelings of anger or ambivalence.

Many relatives are open and forthcoming about expressing their feelings and require little in the way of direct "probes" from the interviewer. Occasionally, however, the interviewer will encounter a taciturn or reluctant respondent whose affect is unclear, despite such questions as "How did you react to that?" For such persons a more direct approach may be called for, but there are strict guidelines for additional questions concerning feelings. "Leading" questions are discouraged, and "milking" for EE is positively not allowed. Questions such as "Did that bother you?" or "How did that make you feel?" (with reference to key symptom behaviors) can be asked no more than three or four times in the course of the interview, and the wording of the questions cannot be varied. The rationale for this neutral approach to the elicitation of affect is that it gives a better indication of the natural range of emotional responsiveness in the families under study than does a more leading style of questioning, and hence results in more valid information. Throughout the session, the interviewer tries to maintain a concerned but uncommitted stance — always interested in what the relative has to say, but unwilling to take sides by commenting on reported attitudes or behaviors.

3

The Expressed Emotion Scales

The scales of EE to be described in this chapter represent more than 10 years of developmental work. Many facets of family relationships were investigated by George Brown and his colleagues in the early stages of their research; ratings were made on literally hundreds of scales for the Brown *et al.* (1972) study. Patients' and relatives' attitudes and behaviors were assessed in joint interviews, as well as in individual interviews. Their respective reports concerning the behaviors of other family members also were rated. Only the most salient measures were retained — those that were most reliably measured and that seemed to be important for relapse of schizophrenia. All of these concerned the relatives' responses when interviewed alone.

The scales concern emotion expressed while talking about a *particular* person; criteria such as tone of voice, content of speech, and gesture are used to assess the degree to which emotion is shown.

The measures are of two kinds:

1. *Frequency counts.* Two scales involve a recognition of particular comments ("critical" and "positive") and consist of a count of all such comments occurring at any point in the interview.

2. *Global scales.* While the three scales of Emotional Overinvolvement, Hostility, and Warmth involve recognition of particular kinds of comments, their rating involves more than a simple summation. The rater must make an overall judgment about the degree to which the emotion was shown, taking into account the interview as a whole. However, it should be remembered that since each point is in fact part of a continuum, it is possible to have a range of phenomena included in the same scale point. This is illustrated by case examples in the notes on Emotional Overinvolvement.

Of the five scales to be described, Critical Comments and Emotional Overinvolvement have proved the most important for relapse of schizophrenia. These two scales, together with Hostility (which is rarely found except in association with high criticism), comprise the key components of the index of EE used to predict outcome in the several studies of schizophrenia reported in Section II of this book. Nevertheless, the scales of Warmth and Positive Remarks have not been jettisoned. Because the relationship of the five scales to one another and to the course of an illness may well vary across different cultures and for different diagnostic groups, most EE researchers have continued to rate all of them.

CRITICAL COMMENTS

The EE training manual defines a critical comment as "a statement which, by the manner in which it is expressed, constitutes an unfavourable comment upon the behaviour or personality of the person to whom it refers." (p. 15). Criticisms may be evident in (1) the *content* of the comment alone, but they are principally evident in the pitch, speed, and inflection imparted to the statement by the person making it; that is, by (2) the *vocal aspects of speech*.

Critical Content

Psychiatric patients often behave in odd, unusual, or socially undesirable ways when ill. A relative's mere recognition or description of characteristics of the patient, however unfavorable, is never *in itself* sufficient to define a statement as critical. This type of reporting is common, for example, in response to questions about psychiatric symptoms:

> "Martin has only worked 3 days in his whole life."
>
> "He lies to us quite a bit."
>
> "His problem has been his drinking: He just drinks to excess."

In the absence of a critical tone, these statements would never be rated as critical; they would be considered descriptions only.

A slightly stronger statement would be one in which the relative expresses some dissatisfaction or regret concerning the behavior, or a desire for things to be different, without explicitly blaming the patient. Consider these examples:

> "I wish that he could hold down a job—any job would do."
>
> "I'd rather he didn't lie to us."
>
> "It's such a waste, a wasted life really. He'll be 35 in a few weeks and for the past 10 years he's just existed. It's so sad."
>
> "One of the greatest things lacking is the return of his love. We miss that very much."

Again, one would not rate any of the statements given above as critical unless a critical tone were present. Despite evidence of considerable personal distress on the part of the relative, the dissatisfaction expressed lacks the "critical" element that has proved predictive of relapse. Low-EE relatives frequently describe themselves as "sad," "bewildered," or "hurt," but do not blame the patients for these feelings. As we point out in the next chapter, this particular response style (dissatisfied but not critical) is associated with the view that the patient is suffering from a genuine illness over which he or she has little or no control, and so cannot be held responsible for his or her actions when ill. Remarks are considered to be critical in content under these circumstances:

1. There is a *clear and unambiguous* statement that the relative dislikes, disapproves of, or resents a behavior or characteristic. The dissatisfaction expressed is more intense and emphatic; the relative must use such phrases as "It annoys me," "I got angry," or "I lost my temper." Here are other examples of statements where critical tone would not need to be present in order for a criticism to be rated:

"When I see her sitting all day long, it aggravates me. I figure she's decaying. And I don't like it."

"I said to my son, 'I don't hate you, but I hate some of the things that you do.'"

2. There is a rejecting remark (as defined fully in the notes on Hostility). Rejecting remarks usually involve a pejorative comment about the person as a whole or a statement of frank dislike: for example, "I've washed my hands of her" or "I'd do anything to get away from him." They should always be rated as critical; critical tone need not be present in order for a criticism to be rated.

Vocal Aspects

As we all express ourselves in highly individual ways, no particular vocal characteristics can be held to define statements made by different relatives as invariably critical. Because speech characteristics do differ so much, it is essential to establish the typical vocal styles of criticism for a relative early in the interview.

Relatives who freely express feelings or attitudes present few difficulties in most cases; their critical remarks stand out from the narrative account and can be identified fairly easily. But the more reticent or defensive respondents often display little vocal variation, whether describing distressing events related to the illness or reporting on the more mundane aspects of their everyday lives. With such respondents, the identification of the typical ways of expressing criticism will depend greatly on the skill of the interviewer — on his or her awareness of possibly sensitive topics, and on the use of the probe "How do you feel about it?" early in the interview when a criticism seems likely to

have been made. Once the interviewer feels that the typical ways of expressing criticism have been established, this probe should be used very sparingly
(as we note in Chapter 2) — both to avoid the risk of artificially raising the
rating, and to avoid irritating the respondent.

From the beginning of the interview, close attention is paid to any vocal
variation that occurs, and an attempt is made to relate it to critical comments.
For instance, the interviewer notes in what way tone varies when the relative
makes statements that by their nature are likely to be neutral, positive, or
critical. Some relatives show particular idiosyncrasies when making a critical
comment — nervous laughter, for example, or odd inflections — and these too
are noted. But although the interviewer takes account of idiosyncratic response patterns, it is important (as with all ratings of EE) that no attempt
be made to interpret the "true" meaning of statements made by relatives who
are especially flat in tone.

Whenever a remark is considered to be critical on the basis of vocal
criteria, it is rated regardless of content. Naturally, decisions are easier to
make if the content and the vocal aspects agree. The more positive the content of the remark, the more clear-cut the contrary vocal evidence would need
to be in order to rate a criticism. For example, the statement "He's been just
marvelous" would need very heavy sarcastic inflection before one could be
sure it was critical.

Additional Notes on the Rating of Critical Comments

The rating manual provides a number of additional guidelines to the rating
of Critical Comments (most of which are not described in detail here). For
example, there are clear rules for determining where one critical comment ends
and another begins. A comment is bounded by a new question from the interviewer (other than a clarifying probe such as "How do you feel about
that?") or by a clear change of topic. An extension of a remark about a particular action ("He spent my housekeeping money on drink") to a related
general attribute ("He's no good with money") would count as only one
criticism, even if the relative went on at some length about the characteristic.

In training new raters, most of one's time is spent in teaching them to
discriminate among remarks that reflect dissatisfaction only, "borderline"
remarks that "feel" potentially critical but that one must leave alone because
they fail to meet the minimum criteria for tone or content, and remarks that
do satisfy the criteria. Only the third type of remark is rated; one errs on the
side of caution. Also, even when the rules have been learned, there are other
factors with potential relevance for the rating of criticism that cannot be ig-
nored. For instance, the relative's response style can be very important. Frequent profanity could result in an artificially inflated Critical Comments
score, while one might well underrate a meek respondent who never says more
than "Well, that did annoy me a little bit." Additional considerations are the

context of the remark, and the spontaneity with which a remark is made. The spontaneous comment "That really bothered me!" would be more likely to be rated as critical than the response "Yes, it did" in reply to the direct question "Did that bother you?" In the latter instance, considerable critical tone would have to be present in order for a criticism to be rated. This is generally true of responses to negatively oriented direct probes concerning feelings, whose use is restricted.

HOSTILITY

Hostility is measured on a 4-point global scale: 0 = no hostility; 1 = present as generalization only; 2 = present as rejection only; and 3 = present as generalization and rejection.

Critical comments may vary greatly, both in intensity and in the range of behaviors to which they refer. A highly critical relative is not necessarily hostile; even a large number of critical remarks need not imply dislike or rejection of a patient. Hostility is considered to be present when the patient is attacked for what he or she *is* rather than for what he or she *does*. Negative feeling is generalized in such a way that it is expressed against the person himself or herself rather than against particular behaviors or attributes.

Although hostility probably can be assessed in a variety of ways, we apply a strict definition and use only two criteria: (1) generalization of criticism and (2) rejecting remarks.

Generalization of Criticism

Some respondents tend to take the position that a patient can do no right. Ordinary everyday matters will tend to be described in a critical way, or in a condescending manner, implying that there are just a few things that the person can do satisfactorily. Specific criticisms frequently are extended into general pejorative comments about the person as a whole, as in the following passages:

> "I reason with her for hours. I say, 'It's entirely up to yourself, Mary, you got to help yourself. I can't live your life for you.' But you might as well talk to the wall for all the good it does!"

> "You see, this is the way my wife gets me. I don't know my head from my heels with her. Other people I can weigh up and work out, but my wife I cannot."

> "This weekend I was in buckets of tears, I couldn't help myself, it was just his *presence*. . . . He's a pretty touchy person anyway, he's a right depressive, really. He sounds horrible, the way I'm talking about him, but he isn't the happiest of people . . . even when he's well there's always something."

> "He's not any benefit to himself or any benefit to society or any benefit to the family situation."

In extreme cases, the most neutral of questions may elicit negative comments about the person; virtually every response is unfavorable. All of the following remarks were made by the same relative, the stepfather of a young man in the Los Angeles study. (The interviewer's questions appear in italics.)

What seemed different about Stephen's behavior?
"Everything and anything. In other words, he's the type of person, you don't tell him, he tells you. You don't tell him, he tells you. If he don't get his own way, then shame on you!"

You say that he spent time in a juvenile facility?
"Yeah. This kid is a genuine con artist, believe me. I spent time in the service and I've been around con artists. This kid is a first-class, genuine con artist, bar none."

Did he seem slow doing things?
"Yeah."

Did he always seem that way, or was it something new?
"No, that's been his and his brother's whole life, you know. Take your sweet time. Never agree to do nothing, you know?"

Does he have girlfriends?
"I guess. He tells me he does, I don't know. I don't follow him around, so I don't know."

What do you think?
"Well, he ain't working, he can't support them. I think he's as full of shit as a Christmas turkey, myself."

Just one unambiguous generalization of criticism in the context of a clearly critical attitude is enough for a rating of hostility. The generalizations need not occur throughout the interview. On the other hand, the rating should not be made too readily. When a critical attitude is less clear-cut, more instances of generalizations are required. In the rare cases where generalization occurs in the absence of several other criticisms, hostility is not rated if the interviewer considers that there is no generally critical attitude.

Rejecting Remarks

A rejecting remark is a more direct form of generalized negative feeling, which may involve a statement of frank dislike. Some examples of rejecting remarks are as follows:

"I might do a pile of washing just to get away from him — you get that you can't breathe when you're with someone like that."

"I have to keep *doing* things for her and letting things be for her. . . . I'm not having it, I've really had enough. I just used to sit on the chair, counting numbers, this is how I got, and think to myself, 'Oh, God, hurry up and go out, Rita!'"

"I got tired of it all. So I said to Stephen, 'I'm going to move. I'm going to get the hell out of here. I don't care where *you* go.' So I changed houses. . . . Now he calls every day, wanting something to eat. He told his mother last night that if she didn't feed him he would jump off the bridge and try suicide again. When I saw him I said 'Go ahead and do it, because I'm not going to put up with your garbage,' which I'm not. He's nothing to me, he's not my kid."

"I don't like to have him around, for openers. He's 29 years old and I don't feel that I should be responsible for him for the rest of my life. So I want to get him to the place where he can take care of himself, or get him somewhere where somebody can take care of him, and get him away from my environment — so that I can lead a normal life too."

Although all remarks should be viewed in context, even one such remark is nearly always sufficient evidence for rating hostility.

Recent displays of affection do not cancel out reports of rejecting behavior in the preadmission period. Because all of the EE scales are unipolar, it is possible for an ambivalent respondent to be rated positively on each of two scales that appear to represent incompatible or contradictory attitudes and behaviors. For example, he or she can both show some warmth and be rated as rejecting.

Generalized criticisms and rejecting remarks are the only two criteria used for rating hostility. Frequent criticisms by themselves are not sufficient, and hostility should not be equated with a high score on Critical Comments.

Critical, Hostile, or Both?: Additional Guidelines for Rating

Definitely hostile remarks that either spell out a rejecting attitude ("I'm fed up with him"; "I've given up on a bad job") or are negative comments about pervasive aspects of a person ("She's lazy and neglectful"; "He's a washout, really") are always rated as critical, too. Critical remarks are not necessarily hostile remarks, however. Rather than thinking "Is this a critical remark *or* a hostile remark, or both?", the rater tends to look for a critical attitude first and only then considers whether a particular remark goes beyond criticism as defined. Is the criticism generalized? Is there a rejecting attitude? If the answer to either of these questions is an affirmative one, the statement is rated as evidence for the presence of hostility.

Hostility is similar to Emotional Overinvolvement in that it is a global rating; one takes all the interview evidence into consideration when making a final rating. In addition to critical remarks that also qualify as hostile remarks because of their content, there may be remarks that perhaps are not definite criticisms of specific traits or behavior but that suggest a rejecting attitude. The following remarks by the husband of one patient fall within this category:

"When she said I went to work to avoid her, I didn't do it with that in mind, but I possibly did, because I didn't miss her."

"She's said I've started lying, and I *have* started lying. Half of it is to avoid scenes, and the other half is [that] I just don't care, really."

"I thought, to hell with it — I don't care what happens now."

In the absence of critical tone, none of these remarks qualifies as a critical remark. Nor is any of them a direct expression of hostility, in the sense that "I'm fed up with her" would be. Nevertheless, each suggests a rejecting attitude: The respondent is giving up on the relationship with his wife. These statements of attitude would be taken into account in making a final rating on the Hostility scale.

Context, content, and tone of voice are all important for rating a remark as critical. Of these three criteria, content is the one that determines whether a remark is also hostile. In practice, the interviewer seldom encounters a respondent who is hostile despite a low rating on Critical Comments. As with the other EE scales, one errs on the side of caution, rating hostility as absent when in doubt.

EMOTIONAL OVERINVOLVEMENT

Emotional overinvolvement is measured on a 6-point global scale: 0 = none; 1 = very little; 2 = some; 3 = moderately high; 4 = high; and 5 = marked.

The scale was designed to be used when interviewing parents of a son or daughter aged 18 or over, but it has been applied successfully to other relatives as well.

The assessment of emotional overinvolvement reflects Brown's early conviction that what was going on in families of psychiatric patients was more commonplace than the very extreme responses encountered only rarely. It is assumed that a degree of overconcern is not unusual, particularly in response to a serious illness in the family. Thus a certain amount of worrying about the patient and brooding about possible causes of the trouble is considered to be appropriate and within the normal range of response on the Emotional Overinvolvement scale. While there are interesting parallels between extreme manifestations of overinvolvement and such psychoanalytical phenomena as symbiosis, enmeshment, and infantilization, Brown and his colleagues did not seek to identify an overinvolved "type." Rather, they aimed to describe and rate discrete behaviors and statements of attitude that might, or might not, mirror other family theorists' images of parental overconcern.

This openminded approach to the rating of emotional overinvolvement has been justified by the results of more recent studies by other investigators. These convincingly demonstrated that the behaviors associated with overconcern are not specific to the parents of schizophrenic patients. For example, greater parental overprotection (compared with matched controls) has been reported in studies of patients with neurotic depression (Parker, 1979); anxiety neurosis (Parker, 1981); and psychiatric illness with marked hypochondriacal features, regardless of other psychiatric diagnosis (Baker & Merskey, 1982).

Other diagnoses for which clinical evidence of past parental overinvolvement exists include psychosomatic disorders. According to Minuchin and Fishman (1981), "the characteristics of families where the presenting complaint is a psychosomatic problem include overprotection, enmeshment or over-involvement of family members with each other and an overemphasis on nurturing roles" (p. 60).

Rating Criteria

Emotional overinvolvement can be detected from two sources: (1) reported behavior of the respondent; and (2) behavior of the respondent at the interview.

REPORTED BEHAVIOR

Several kinds of reported behavior by the respondent may indicate over-concern.

Exaggerated Emotional Response. Exaggerated emotional response in the past, such as anxiety directly related to the patient's welfare, is one kind of reported behavior that indicates overconcern. Consider these examples:

> "All I keep saying to myself since my son's been ill — and honestly, in the finish it begins to make you ill yourself — I keep thinking, is it something *I've* done? . . . At the moment we haven't got a clue as to what's wrong with him, so naturally we get frightened. All I think of is his illness now. It's on my mind all the time."

> "I felt terrible — I felt my whole world was shattered. . . . I've spent many a time crying, wondering what went wrong — almost every day."

An exaggerated emotional response can be a reflection of overidentification between relative and patient; when the patient feels badly, so does the relative.

> "Every time I knew my Rita wasn't well, I got a terrible feeling in my stomach. Like a state of depression. My stomach used to revolve round, I had a choking feeling as if I couldn't breathe, and every time I got that feeling she had a setback or something happened."

Self-Sacrificing and Devoted Behavior. Marked concern reflected in unusually self-sacrificing and devoted behavior is another indication of overconcern. Examples include keeping the patient supplied with money even when it is squandered, sacrificing one's own social life in order to devote more time and energy to the patient, or consistently putting the patient's needs ahead of one's own. In extreme cases the relative may appear to live for the patient rather than for himself or herself, and the two may become almost symbiotically dependent on each other. One mother told her second husband that the patient would always come before him and their marriage, because the patient was her own flesh and blood: "So we take him with us everywhere. He even came on our honeymoon."

Extremely Overprotective Behavior. Overprotective behaviors tend to be age-inappropriate ways of dealing with issues of autonomy and independence; they represent attempts by a relative to exert psychological or physical control over the adult offspring. Relevant behaviors range from well-intentioned efforts to act as a buffer between the patient and the outside world ("We got him a job once; we said we'd pay his wages") to highly intrusive attempts to monitor or supervise most areas of the patient's life. Marching into the bathroom after someone to make sure that he or she had taken a shower would be an example of excessively overprotective behavior; so would an insistence that the patient's bedroom door be left open at all times. In extreme instances, there may be a demonstrated reluctance to allow the patient ever to leave home.

BEHAVIOR IN THE INTERVIEW

Overconcern may be shown in the interview by statements of attitude, emotional display, or dramatization.

Statements of Attitude. Statements of attitude may be statements about the impact of the illness on the relative; the relative's attitudes towards the patient's becoming more independent; the extent to which the relative is preoccupied with the patient; or the objectivity (or lack of same) with which the relative views the patient and the illness. Examples include the following:

> "I live in a vacuum. Just getting through the years, in a jail without bars—I find it hard to break out of the isolation. I'd do anything to help him, *anything.*"

> "I miss her, I miss her, I think about her all the time. See, we've always been close, always been together. She seemed to be always 'me and Dad.' She didn't like other people."

> "Andy was always the apple of my eye. I'm very fond of Andy. All I have is Andy, I don't see no faults. I think Andy is a wonderful, wonderful boy. I'm very, very much in love with him, even though this has happened."

Emotional Display. Emotional display, such as one mother's obvious distress and tearfulness when talking about her son, is another demonstration of overconcern that may be seen in the interview.

Dramatization. Overconcern is sometimes displayed by dramatization of trivial incidents or problems, by the tone and tempo of voice, and by the sheer amount of detailed description given. However, dramatization is not necessarily a sign of emotional overinvolvement; it may be merely a style of speech, particularly among certain ethnic groups. To be counted, it must be associated with overconcern about some relatively minor aspect of the patient's behavior or way of life. When this occurs, such dramatization may be taken into account, even though the style of speech is used when describing others in the home. Extravagant praise of the patient might also be found and should be taken into account as dramatization, as well as lack of objectivity.

Allocation of Scores on the Emotional Overinvolvement Scale

As with the other global scales of EE, the rating of Emotional Overinvolvement is decided on the basis of all the interview material. During the interview, the rater notes any nonverbal evidence; later, all relevant verbal material is transcribed from audiotapes. It is common to have evidence both for and against the presence of overinvolvement. For example, a relative may show an intense emotional reaction to the illness, yet may encourage the patient's efforts to recover and become independent. In our experience, evidence of extremely overprotective behavior tends to result in higher ratings, but there are no hard and fast rules for the weighting of particular behaviors. The rater must determine just how *extreme* the relative's attitudes and behaviors are, and rate them accordingly. Although the minority of relatives who merit the highest ratings of 4 and 5 frequently make a striking impression on first meeting, final scores still must be justified in terms of the Emotional Overinvolvement rating criteria and supported by detailed rating notes. Thus the rater cannot rely on the near-intuitive recognition of textbook stereotypes in making final judgments.

In the course of training, raters are exposed to respondents who represent the full range of overinvolved behaviors. They learn to identify the salient elements of overinvolvement and, after discussing all the evidence, attempt to arrive at consensus ratings for each case.

Because it is difficult to gain an idea of the range of possible overinvolved responses from individual statements taken out of context, we now present, for each of the points on the scale, relevant notes for a selection of London and Los Angeles relatives who received that particular score. The following are examples only, however. Each interview is different, and no characteristic response style is associated with a particular scale point.

RATING "NONE" (0)

"None" should be seen as "normal," as the scale is designed to measure emotional overinvolvement. It represents lack of any of the characteristics of overinvolvement.

Case No. C030 (rated 0). Divorced mother of Sandra, aged 35 (third admission for schizophrenia; first onset at 23). Mother and daughter lived alone. No exaggerated emotional response. The mother invariably dealt with the patient's displays of highly disturbed behavior in a calm and rational way (when in one of her "episodes," Sandra was extremely unpredictable, verbally aggressive, and physically violent). No evidence of unusually self-sacrificing, devoted, or overprotective behaviors. The mother had friends and a life of her own. She was prepared to have her daughter return to her after discharge only if Sandra contributed to the household. She encouraged Sandra to develop interests outside the home, even if these conflicted with her own beliefs. For example, when Sandra decided to change religions, the mother said, "If that's what you want to do, you go and do it."

RATINGS "VERY LITTLE" (1) OR "SOME" (2)

Points 1 and 2 represent some presence of emotional overinvolvement, but it should not be present to any significant extent. It may well include behavior within the "normal" range.

Case No. C015 (Rated 1). Stepfather of Mike, aged 32 (first admission for schizophrenia). Patient's mother also in household.

No exaggerated emotional response. Some overconcern shown by an increased preoccupation with the patient's problems. He and his wife had had long discussions about the possible origins of the illness, "trying to analyze if it was something we were doing, so we'd try to avoid the same mistakes." He also said, "I'm doing everything I can to help him solve his problems." Mildly intrusive attempts to elicit the patient's feelings ("The wife and I would try to draw him out, to find out what was bothering him"), but he did not persist in these efforts when Mike refused to comment. Some overconcern with the patient's weight problems and related eating habits. Some self-sacrificing behavior: An entire week's holiday was spent at the hospital with Mike. But none of these reported behaviors were very significant; all seemed understandable and within the normal range of response.

Case No. M019 (Rated 1). Widowed mother of Charles, aged 31 and divorced (third admission for schizophrenia; first onset at 24). Patient's three brothers also in household.

No exaggerated emotional response in the past or at interview, but a certain amount of overconcern as anxiety was present. Relevant comments included "I give a lot of thought to him and I worry over him. He's my only worry, really." Also, "I'm worried all the time when he doesn't eat, and when he sits and secludes himself. I think, well, it's not much of a life for a young man." But there was no evidence of unusually self-sacrificing, devoted, or overprotective behaviors, and the mother was not at all intrusive or interfering. For example, when Charles left his wife for another woman, the mother did not try to discourage the affair (although she did not approve), because

"I knew it was no use where he was concerned. He's a grown man; I've got no say in the matter."

Case No. C018 (Rated 2). Father of William, aged 24 (fourth admission for schizophrenia; first onset at 22). Patient's mother, two younger sisters, and a young female cousin also in household.

Evidence of an exaggerated response included several comments suggesting a symbiotic-like identification with the patient when ill: "When he's feeling bad I have tremendous emotions. The first few times he went to Mental Health I was so overwrought I had stomach cramps and pains, so I was feeling it pretty strongly." (In the past, the patient had complained of stomach pains when in an anxiety-provoking social situation.) Although the father retained his composure throughout the interview, he said at one point, "I'm very emotional now, not speaking as I normally would—just bringing William's trouble up, I'm fraught with emotion about it. My wife and I both sense a deep loss."

There was some evidence of intrusive overconcern in the form of a preoccupation with the patient's diet. When William lived at home, both parents attempted to monitor what he ate and drank, believing that health food and a megavitamin regimen were essential for the patient's recovery. The father maintained that William must agree to follow this regimen if he wished to live at home again after discharge. The father also threatened to cut off William's allowance if he stopped the "program" to which the other family members adhered. This topic dominated the interview and was the source of most of the conflict between the patient and his parents. The mother and father also went into William's room at times to fix it up: "He'd leave it in terrible shape."

There was considerable evidence against a higher rating on Emotional Overinvolvement. No extremely overprotective behavior was reported; William more or less came and went as he pleased. During a period when the patient was living on his own in an apartment, his parents did not see their son for a month, because "he in a sense told us that he wanted his privacy." Father said that he would like to see William working and living independently. "If [he were] healthy I think he could be quite a normal boy. Whatever he'd want to make of himself would be fine with me." Finally, despite his reported emotional reaction to the illness, the father was calm in describing the patient's several suicide attempts; these included jumping off a roof and an attempt to stab himself.

Case No. C009 (Rated 2). Mother of Barry, aged 29 (sixth admission for schizophrenia; first onset at 17). Patient's stepfather and two younger brothers also in household.

Some emotional display as tearfulness during the interview, when expressing a concern about Barry's lack of affection toward her; she feared that he did not like her. She admitted to feeling herself a failure as a mother; she said that she brooded about where things went wrong and how she might have contributed to Barry's problems. But none of her emotional responses were extreme, and there was considerable evidence against the presence of marked overinvolvement. No excessively devoted or self-sacrificing behavior was reported. When the patient spent money extravagantly, the mother refused to cover his expenses or give in to his requests for more money. She was not at all overprotective. When Barry's grandmother (with whom he lived for a period) telephoned to complain about his antisocial and aggressive behavior, the mother would refuse to get involved: "I'd say, 'Phone the police if it gets bad — what do you want me to do about it?'" She and her husband were determined to lead their own lives and insisted on going out alone together at times; on such occasions, they refused Barry's requests to go with them.

RATINGS "MODERATELY HIGH" (3) OR "HIGH" (4)

For a rating of 3 or 4, much clearer evidence of emotional overinvolvement is necessary.

Case No. C008 (Rated 3). Mother of Gary, aged 24 (fifth admission for schizophrenia; first onset at 19). Patient's stepfather, stepbrother, two sisters, and grandfather also in household.

The rating of 3 on Emotional Overinvolvement was made primarily because of the mother's exaggerated emotional response in the past and her emotional behavior at the interview. She broke down and wept when talking about her son and the "horrible" way he would speak to her when he was ill. For example, he would say, "Why don't you break the apron strings — it's all your fault!" and scream and swear at her. She reported that on the day of his most recent admission, she was so emotionally upset that the staff asked her to go home: "I was crying, I couldn't stand it, I just can't take it." She also said, "I'm too close to the picture at this point. I'm just talked out. I've heard it *so* much, I don't know how to approach him anymore." However, there were no examples of excessively self-sacrificing or devoted behavior, and no evidence of overprotectiveness. There was considerable evidence *against* a higher Emotional Overinvolvement rating. For example, she said that she felt she should have sat down and talked more with Gary and find out what was going on in his life, but she had "forty other things going on," so she didn't. She was eager for her son to be away from home and living independently. She was bothered by the idea that Gary might be attached to her in some unnatural way (a recurring theme in interviews with mothers of sons who show no interest in dating). She encouraged him to go out and meet girls, but did not exert undue pressure. Finally, she had an objective view of the illness and encouraged him at an early stage to seek professional help; she was aware that she was not able to deal with his symptoms herself.

Case No. C028 (Rated 3). Father of Nick, aged 23 (seventh admission for schizophrenia; first onset at 19). Patient's mother and two younger brothers also in household.

Overinvolvement mainly present as an exaggerated emotional response in the past. The father spoke of angry verbal outbursts, fistfights with the patient, and his considerable anxiety and distress since the patient became ill: "I went nights without sleep, worrying about him." He said that he was bothered "really bad" by the physical violence: " I didn't sleep for two days. My wife and daughter both worried for me that I'd have a heart attack. I get so upset — something like that really hurts me deeply. I'm a real emotional person."

No other evidence of overinvolvement.

Case No. C024 (Rated 3). Mother of Peter, aged 24 (fourth admission for schizophrenia; first onset at 22). Mother's female "housemate" and the latter's two young children also in household. Patient's father and siblings lived nearby.

The rating of 3 on Emotional Overinvolvement was based on the mother's reports of unusually self-sacrificing and devoted behavior toward the patient when ill. In her willingness to listen to her son and to advise him on his problems for hours on end, on virtually a daily basis, she went beyond what might be considered appropriate caring concern. There was an "enmeshed" quality to the mother–son relationship, which her own descriptions of their interactions illustrate very well. (The interviewer's questions are in italics.)

> "He talked to me a lot — because I was his therapist — the person he shared with more than anybody else. He took me into his process, total. . . . He involves me, ruminates with me, because I allow him to do it. I stay with him. In that way I feel I got taken into his process, I got incorporated into it."
>
> *How frequently?*
> "He would do it constantly. He would do it as much as I would be there with him, because I gave that to him."
>
> *Once or twice a week?*
> "No, it happened daily. All the time I was with him, particularly in the last 4 or 5 months. He would talk to me for hours at a time, worrying and sharing how bad he felt . . . reporting to me every change in mood or feeling from 5-minute to 5-minute period."

Although the mother said that she had mixed feelings about Peter's behavior ("There were times when I would get very worn out and drained"), for much of the time she permitted, if not encouraged, it to happen. "It felt as if he needed to do that with somebody, and nobody else would do that with him." Interestingly, one of the many psychiatrists who had seen the patient offered the opinion that Peter was too dependent and advised the parents to "do what we could to get out of him — stay away from being enmeshed with him." The mother observed, "I did not like that particular message."

There was further evidence of overinvolvement both as reported anxiety and as distress in the interview. The distress was mild; she was tearful at one point in the interview when she said that she would like him to be well and "have some sense of control over his internal life." At the same time, her expressed desire to see him well and independent was evidence against a markedly overprotective attitude. She also encouraged Peter to be self-sufficient around the house and concerned herself very little with his daily routine. She admitted that his admission had made a difference to her daily life: "It's freed me from the time and energy that I put into him — released my inner energy from being concerned and worried, thinking about him so much." Although this too was evidence of overconcern, the revelation that she was able to resume her regular activities and concentrate on other things as long as she knew Peter was being cared for in hospital argued against a higher rating on Emotional Overinvolvement. A more overinvolved relative would be unlikely to be able to "switch off" like this.

Case No. C057 (Rated 4). Father of Nathan, aged 30 (third admission for schizophrenia; first onset at 17). Patient's mother also in household.

The rating on Emotional Overinvolvement was difficult in this case. Because the EE scales are unipolar, it is possible for a relative to be highly critical toward the patient and yet show no or very little overconcern. However, this father's critical attitude was associated with highly intrusive behaviors, which did seem evidence of overinvolvement as well. The father justified these behaviors by repeated references to the patient's "need for supervision" and described him as a very irresponsible young man. However, in view of the patient's age and demonstrated ability to live alone and fend for himself, at least some of the father's actions must be considered as evidence of overprotective overconcern.

The father was intrusive regarding most areas of Nathan's life. When Nathan lived at home, there were repeated attempts to get him to shower, bathe, use deodorant, and dress in ways acceptable to the father and mother. They regularly searched his room for evidence of possible drug use. During a period when Nathan was living on his own in an apartment, both parents would make unannounced visits to "check up on him." On one occasion, they spent 5 hours cleaning the apartment after a wild party; on another occasion, they found a friend of Nathan's in bed in the middle of the day and immediately insisted that the patient come home and live with them again. "He had had strict rules that no one was to go in there with him."

In addition to these overprotective behaviors, the father reported related self-sacrificing behaviors; he seemed to view the latter as undesirable but necessary. For example, the father and mother would not go away on trips together because of Nathan: "He's holding us back." Certain statements of attitude suggested great ambivalence regarding the father's perceived responsibilities and obligations toward his son, as well as his views on Nathan's future autonomy and independence.

"We do feel tied down by him, but he's my kid. I do feel I'm giving up something by him being at home, but I don't hold it against him. After he came home from college, I made up my mind he was going to be a burden for the rest of my life, one way and another."

"He's our boy and our responsibility. We would like to have him leave us and be a man by himself, but if need be I'd personally keep him until the day I die."

Although this father reported no excessive anxiety and was well in control of his emotions in the interview, he definitely seemed excessively preoccupied with the patient. It was a mark of his overinvolvement that he tried to keep such close tabs on the patient, particularly since Nathan was not at all dependent. He did not turn up on his parents' doorstep when things got difficult for him; his father sought him out.

Case No. M064 (Rated 4). Divorced mother of Rita, aged 18 (third admission for schizophrenia; first onset at 14). Mother and daughter lived alone.

The rating of 4 on Emotional Overinvolvement was based primarily on the mother's exaggerated emotional response in the past, and on evidence of dramatization and emotional display in the interview.

Clearly in great distress, the mother wept throughout much of the interview; even when not crying openly, she seemed near tears (she rejected offers to terminate the interview, however). She claimed that she had been made a "nervous wreck" because of the patient's behavior, and that she could no longer cope. For the year preceding the interview she had been afraid of meeting people, and had had to take sick leave from her job. The mother's anxiety and distress culminated in a nearly successful suicide attempt shortly after the patient's most recent admission to the hospital. Upset by a visit to the patient and by the doctor's view that Rita had suffered a "setback," the mother broke down one evening and took an entire bottle of sleeping tablets. "I thought to myself, it's just going to go on and on and on. I just couldn't endure another day of it. I thought, at least when I'm 6 feet under I'll have some peace."

The mother reported that the relationship with her daughter had been turbulent for many years. When Rita was ill or out of sorts she would turn on her mother, who at first would try to keep her feelings in, but who eventually would respond in kind with an explosion of angry words and tears.

As with the father of William (Case No. C018, p. 49), there were reports of terrible physical sensations when the mother thought something might be wrong with the patient. Such feelings may well reflect a near-symbiotic relationship with the patient, an impression reinforced by other evidence. The mother had broken up with her boyfriend of 2 years' standing because of the patient's trouble. In explaining this self-sacrificing behavior, she said, "Doesn't matter who I'm with, with Rita like this it's going to go on forever. It doesn't seem as though I'm going to have any happiness. I want Rita to have hers. . . . I've had my life, anyway."

The mother demonstrated considerable emotional ambivalence toward the patient. Her alternately accepting and rejecting behavior at times suggested a "double-bind" style of response.

"All last week I said I didn't want her home no more, I couldn't cope. But every day last week when I went to see her I was more ill than ever, because I knew that I was all that she had. . . . Sometimes I think I'm going mad, I can't go on any longer, but then I think I've got to have her home, it's not right, 'cause I feel guilty. She should be with me, 'cause I'm all she's got. She's mine, and I do worry about her, and you can't take it away, and it'll never change."

The highest Emotional Overinvolvement rating of 5 was not given, because the mother showed no excessively overprotective behavior. She very much wanted the patient to have a normal life and to be independent, and she actually welcomed her daughter's affair with a young man: "She's a woman now, she's getting on for 19, she's old enough to take care of herself." She disliked the times when Rita became very dependent and followed her everywhere, and recognized that it would be best for Rita to live away from home, if only the patient would consider a hostel or other accommodation (in the past she had refused all such offers).

Case No. M045 (Rated 4). Father of Caroline, aged 17 (first admission for schizophrenia). Father and daughter lived alone.

In this father's words, he and his daughter had "always been close, always been together" since she was a child, and their relationship became even closer after the mother's death when Caroline was 13. "Seemed to be always 'me and Dad.' We were always together; she didn't like other people."

The father's marked concern was expressed in a variety of ways, most notably by his unusually self-sacrificing and devoted behavior. The father and daughter were apart only when he was at work. She objected to his working late shifts, and he frequently took time off to pacify her. "I'd say, all right, I'll have a week off, keep her happy. . . . I do it to please her, you see. I always used to give in." He also gave up a relationship with a woman he was "courting" (and with it, the idea of any further relationships) because of the patient's objections. "She said, 'You're sleeping with her,' and all that. I didn't want to do it, but what could I do? She doesn't like me going with the others, so I don't. I wouldn't make her unhappy."

The father admitted to being upset and worried by the patient's illness and confessed to a near-total preoccupation with her, both before and after her admission to the hospital: "I miss her, I do miss her. I think about her all the time. I worry about her at work, even when she's inside. I shouldn't do, I know, but as I've said, we've always been so close." He also showed a lack of objectivity in his attitude toward the illness. He was convinced that "nothing much is wrong with her that couldn't have been put right years ago if they'd given us a decent place to live. This place is enough to get anyone down."

The highest Emotional Overinvolvement rating of 5 was not given to this father because of the evidence against an excessively overprotective attitude. At several points in the interview, he said that his daughter would be better off with friends and a job and a life of her own, and that he had expressed these feelings to her in the past on a number of occasions. For example, "I thought it would be better for her to mix with young people rather than to stop in here with the old boy. I said to her, 'You're growing up, you want to get out and about, not stop here.' She never said anything, but I just like her to know how I feel. I didn't want to tie her to me." Like other highly overinvolved relatives, he displayed emotional ambivalence toward the prospect of the patient's leaving home and becoming more autonomous. He didn't want to "push her out," and he was hurt when she expressed doubts about being seen with him so much. But on balance it seemed as if he recognized that their "enmeshment" was not in her best interests: "She wants a life of her own. I'd miss her if she weren't here, but that's something I'd have to put up with. . . . Although I'm grateful for her company, I can look after myself."

RATING "MARKED" (5)

The highest rating of 5 is reserved for the most extreme manifestations of emotional overinvolvement; grossly overprotective behavior is given particular weight.

Case No. M022 (Rated 5). Mother of Geraldine, aged 29 (first admission for schizophrenia). Patient's father and brother also in household.

The Emotional Overinvolvement rating was based entirely on the mother's excessively overprotective attitude toward her daughter. The patient was completely dependent on the mother; she had never worked and never had a social life, and the mother said that she preferred it this way. "Geraldine's always been at home with me, and she's always willing to do anything for me. . . . I wouldn't want her to get a job; there's so much for me to do, and she's a help." In response to the question, "Would you like her to have a boyfriend?" the mother replied, "She's not interested in marriage, no. I don't really want her to marry, I would miss her. Anyway, marriages aren't very happy, are they? No, I'm happy to have her home; she would never listen to anybody else if not to me."

Geraldine spent all of her waking hours with her mother, who encouraged the patient's dependency in a variety of ways. She used her complaints of arthritis and migraine as means of controlling the patient, and welcomed Geraldine's antipathy toward her father. The father, who had been treated for paranoid schizophrenia in the past, was accused by both mother and daughter of making sexual advances toward Geraldine, who responded with terrified avoidance and even greater dependency on the mother.

Case No. C049 (Rated 5). Widowed mother of John, aged 25 (first admission for schizophrenia; first onset at 17). Mother and son lived alone.

The highest rating was given to this mother because of her extraordinarily self-sacrificing and devoted behavior, and related overprotectiveness, over many years.

From the age of 17, John had suffered off and on from the symptoms of schizophrenia. For 8 years his mother had thought hospitalization unnecessary; she had become his 24-hour caretaker. She reported, "I did everything for him. He didn't do anything. I didn't expect him to. I've been doing everything for him since he was born. I've taken care of him all the time." She described in great detail all the things she did for the patient. For example, she managed his money: "Anything he needs, I buy it. I know what he wants. He doesn't tell me, I know." Her devoted care of her son consumed nearly all of her time. She said that her relatives understood; her friends didn't expect much from her; and she had no time for men friends. "I've just devoted myself to John."

Case No. C112 (Rated 5). Mother of Lionel, aged 27 (first admission for schizophrenia). Patient's father and two younger brothers also in household.

The mother demonstrated in an extreme form virtually every kind of emotional overinvolvement: an exaggerated emotional response both in the past and at the interview; excessively overprotective, self-sacrificing, and devoted behavior; and dramatization. Although most of the material on which the rating was based concerned incidents from the distant past, the mother's behavior and statements of attitude at the interview supported the impression of deep-rooted and enduring overinvolvement. Had there been evidence of a substantial diminution in her overconcern over time, a lower rating than 5 might have been justified.

At the time of the mother's interview, the patient had not lived at home for several years. While a university student, he became involved with what his mother termed a "hippie cult." Eventually he dropped out of university and made his way to Europe, ostensibly to "find himself." The mother was so horrified by this expression of independence that she vowed to go to Europe herself to find Lionel and bring him back. Since by her own account Lionel showed no signs of psychiatric disturbance during this period, there seemed little justification for her extreme and melodramatic response. When Lionel's father told her to leave their son alone, mother replied "What do you mean, leave him alone? I can't leave him — he wants to go to India, do his own thing. It's absolute rubbish, terrible! I'm going to go over and see what it's all about." She recalled: "I rushed out and saw *Hair*. It was frightening! What was my son supposed to do in between? Die, freeze to death, starve? Well, I was determined he wasn't going to find himself sitting somewhere in a cave until I knew what it was about!" The mother's determination to follow her son led to heated rows with her husband. When he threatened to cut off her housekeeping allowance, saying, "You'll never find him, it's a waste of money," the mother said that she would work her way over if necessary.

In defiance of her husband's advice, the mother then made a number of separate trips to Europe. In her own words, "I walked the streets of France to find my son." These trips occurred over several years and involved considerable financial self-sacrifice, since the father refused to pay for any of them. While in France the mother spent weeks and months following up Lionel's last known addresses, saying to everyone she met, "I want to find the hippie cult." She described in exquisite and dramatic detail all the dreadful places she'd visited: "Such awful places, I was terrified! Rats and mice and God knows what. But I was determined to find him." Eventually she did locate her son. She bribed him with the promise of drugs in order to get him to England and then stole his passport: "His girlfriend wasn't my property, but he apparently was." She imagined that if Lionel were unable to return to the Continent, friends in England could keep an eye on him after her return to America.

Throughout her account of these and subsequent events and her son's later schizophrenic illness, the mother consistently reacted in an overprotective and highly emotional way. She repeatedly used words like "terrible" and "unbelievable" and described herself as in a total state of shock throughout. When at a later date Lionel again turned up "missing," the mother contacted both Interpol and the head of Scotland Yard in her attempts to track him down. Yet during his time in England none of the doctors who were consulted thought him sufficiently ill to warrant hospitalization, and for long periods he managed well enough on his own in communal settings.

WARMTH

Warmth is measured on a 6-point global scale: 0 = no warmth; 1 = very little warmth; 2 = some warmth; 3 = moderate warmth; 4 = moderately high warmth; and 5 = high warmth.

This scale refers only to the warmth expressed in the interview itself about a particular person; the warmth of the respondent's personality is not a consideration.

Criteria Relevant for the Rating of Warmth

TONE OF VOICE

Tone of voice is perhaps the most important criterion on which the rating of Warmth is based. Raters are taught to be alert for enthusiasm shown by a relative when talking about the patient, and also for positive changes in manner and tone when the respondent switches from talking about neutral subjects to talking about the person. Conversely, flatness or coldness of tone is regarded as lack of warmth and is balanced against any evidence of warmth when making the final overall judgment.

Sometimes facial expression and other nonverbal behaviors noted at interview can influence the rating of Warmth. A quiet and withdrawn husband may show little tonal variation, yet may smile frequently when talking about his wife; the changes in expression of another equally taciturn respondent may suggest disgust, disapproval, or lack of interest. Generally, however, the rater relies on verbal and vocal aspects of speech for the assessment of Warmth.

SPONTANEITY

Since the CFI contains very few direct questions about feelings of affection, spontaneous expressions of warmth tend to result in a higher rating. A respondent may go well beyond what is strictly required to answer a question to express positive feelings about the person, as in these examples. (The interviewer's questions are in italics.)

> *Who cooks the meals during the week?*
> "Everybody chips in. Mike, he likes to do a little cooking too — he's come up with quite a few good ideas!"
>
> *How does John get along with people?*
> "He gets along with everybody. In fact, everybody loves him. He's such a gentleman — if you met him you'd find that out. He doesn't approach people, but if they approach him he's a perfect gentleman."

Conversely, the failure to express warmth where opportunities to do so exist would tend to lower the rating. The interviewer would take note of an unenthusiastic reply to, for example, a question routinely asked of spouses: "Are there things that you and your husband/wife enjoy doing together?"

However, a respondent can make few spontaneous expressions of warmth and may still receive a high rating on this scale if there is sufficient alternative evidence.

SYMPATHY, CONCERN, AND EMPATHY

Respondents vary markedly in the degree of sympathy, concern, and empathy they show when talking about the behavior or problems of patients. "Empathy" refers to a respondent's ability to see things from the other person's point of view — to his or her attempts to understand what it might be like to be in that person's shoes. The following responses by relatives all reflect the presence of one or more of these three qualities:

"He wanted to blame somebody for his illness, but he didn't know who to blame—I guess we'd all feel the same."

"She's always been so strong. To be weak and dependent, it must pinch the grain. And she can't understand it."

"A lot of it was that he lost his house, his pride and joy—he'd really fixed it up nice. Then he lost his job. Then he got injured in a cycle accident. Problems just seemed to pile up on his shoulders. . . . I think what he's trying to do now is eliminate anything from the past that he feels has caused his problems. And he wants to do something on his own, rather than for me or his mother to help, which is good. But I've told him, 'Any time you want help, don't be afraid to ask. I'll help you if I can.'"

"I think his time in the hospital has been useful—seeing other patients who also are at a low level. It meant he didn't have to maintain pretensions, it broke down his reserves. . . . I love him as a son and it hurts to see someone you love have this type of problem."

"I couldn't do much about the illness myself, only try and encourage her, reassure her that what's happening to her happens to other people as well . . . that a great many have got over it and won the day. She'd say, 'I've forgotten about the meal.' I used to say, 'Oh, it doesn't matter, we've got all evening.'"

Differences in the extent to which respondents display sympathy, concern, or empathy emerge most sharply in their descriptions of physical or psychiatric symptoms. A detached account would tend to lower the rating of Warmth. For example, the following response was considered to be objective and fair without providing any rateable evidence of warmth toward the patient:

"One can sort of stand back and say, here is someone who is ill, you're not dealing with a normal person, and get irritated. Just handle it as it comes along."

However, it is important to note than any concern expressed should be concern for the well-being of the person, and not anxiety about the effects of any illness or disorder on others. One question in particular from the CFI illustrates this distinction very well: "What has been the most disturbing aspect of [the patient's] trouble for you?" Relatives rated high on Warmth almost always replied in terms of their concern for the ill patient:

"The way people react, and treat him. I don't like him mistreated, because he senses it. It bothers me a lot for his sake, because I know he feels it."

"Trying to imagine the misery he must feel to completely break down—trying to understand how bad you've got to be before you actually feel *so* low. It's terrible. I don't really *know* how he feels, but I can imagine how he might feel— that somebody can feel so completely useless."

In replying to the same question, relatives rated low on Warmth were likely to complain of the effects of the illness on themselves — of the suffering and inconvenience to which they had been subjected — rather than to express any concern for the patient's ordeal.

As a rule, low-EE relatives are more likely than high-EE relatives to show sympathy, concern, and empathy. But there is a subgroup of high-EE relatives — those who are highly overinvolved without being critical — who may possess these qualities in abundance. Statements such as the following are evidence for the presence of both warmth *and* overinvolvement:

> "The doctors have told us it would be better if he didn't live with us. But we decided he would be better off at home. Getting better food — fresh air and sunshine — some of those board and care places aren't what they should be. So that's the reason we had him at home. Lots of people can't live with a schizophrenic person. But we really cared."

INTEREST IN THE PERSON

Enthusiasm for and interest in the person's activities and achievements are also relevant, provided that they are shown in relation to the person as such. It is possible to talk about activities and achievements in a strictly factual way, or in a way intended to reflect well on the respondent rather than on the person. For example, a father might recount his son's accomplishments to suggest what a good parent he has been. In contrast, expressions of enjoyment about mutual activities are particularly good evidence of warmth:

> "Anything we do together we seem to enjoy. We just seem to be pleased with life."

> "Just as long as I've got her company I'm all right."

Factors Not Relevant for the Rating of Warmth

INFERENCES ABOUT "TRUE" WARMTH

The rater should be concerned only with manifest expressions of warmth; speculation about what the respondent "really" feels is to be avoided.

WARMTH OF THE RESPONDENT'S PERSONALITY

The degree of personal rapport between interviewer and respondent should not be allowed to influence the rating. Someone who behaves warmly toward the interviewer will not necessarily show warmth when talking about other family members. The rating should be based only on the warmth expressed about the person who is the subject of the interview.

COMPARISONS WITH WARMTH SHOWN TOWARD OTHERS

It is the amount of warmth shown *toward the person* that should be taken into account, not the difference between that shown toward him or her and that shown toward others (including the interviewer). A mother may favor one of her children more than another and still be rated as high in warmth to both of them.

DEPRESSION OF THE RESPONDENT

Even clinically depressed persons should be considered capable of expressing the whole range of warmth. Our experience is that they may show a great deal of warmth, and that it would be wrong to make allowances or assumptions as to what is possible for a person. The existence of depression in the respondent should neither lower nor elevate the rating, which, as already noted, should be based entirely on the amount of warmth actually expressed about the person during the interview.

CRITICISM OR HOSTILITY

Although the interview as a whole should be considered when rating warmth, the presence or absence of criticism or hostility should not be allowed to contaminate the rating. Frequent criticism is compatible with moderate warmth, and a respondent with ambivalent attitudes may well express rejection of the person at one point in the interview and marked warmth at other points.

STEREOTYPED ENDEARMENTS

Endearments such as "dear" and "darling" are often used in a stereotyped way and should not necessarily be considered evidence of warmth. The rater has to decide for each individual respondent whether the endearments seem to reflect feelings of warmth or not. For example, one husband referred to his wife as "my pet" and "my little girl" throughout the interview, but the terms were used in a patronizing way; the overall impression was of a distinct lack of warmth.

POSITIVE REMARKS

Positive remarks (defined in the next section) are not in themselves evidence of warmth, and should only be considered if they are said warmly. It is possible for a respondent to give a detached account of a person's behavior and personality, and to make a number of positive comments that are fair rather than warm.

Additional Notes on the Rating of Warmth

The nature of warmth is such that ratings cannot be defined mechanically, point by point. The importance of tone of voice for the rating also makes it difficult to provide case examples of respondents who represent the range of possible scores on the warmth scale. However, it is helpful as a general guide to divide ratings into three broad categories:

1. Instances in which there are definite and clear-cut tonal warmth, enthusiasm, and interest in and enjoyment of the person are rated "moderately high warmth" (4) or "high warmth" (5), according to the amount of warmth and enthusiasm expressed.

2. Instances in which there are definite understanding, sympathy, and concern, but only limited warmth of tone, are rated "some warmth" (2) or "moderate warmth" (3). A detached, rather clinical approach with little or no warmth of tone would normally warrant a rating of "some warmth" (2).

3. If there is only a slight amount of understanding, sympathy, or concern, or enthusiasm about or interest in the person, "very little warmth" (1) can be rated. The rating of "no warmth" (0) is reserved for respondents who show a complete absence of the qualities of warmth as defined. There may be either considerable negative evidence (suggesting, for example, a pronounced lack of sympathy) or simply an absence of positive evidence. In the latter instance the respondent will seem flat, apathetic, or indifferent when talking about the person.

POSITIVE REMARKS

A positive remark is a statement that expresses praise, approval, or appreciation of the behavior or personality of the person to whom it refers. As with the Critical Comments rating, a frequency count is used to measure the occurrence of relevant positive remarks during the course of an interview. Similar boundary rules also apply. A positive remark is considered to be a statement made by the respondent that is bounded by a new question by the interviewer (with one or two defined exceptions) or by a clear change of topic. Thus two positive remarks would be rated for the following passage, because of the shift in topic from Household Tasks to Child Care: "She's a very good housekeeper — everything in its place. And she's a wonderful mother, that hasn't changed." An extension of a positive remark about a particular action to a related general attribute (or vice versa) counts as one remark only: for example, "He's very good about helping out with the dishes — in fact, he'll lend a hand with anything you ask him to do."

A positive remark, unlike warmth, is defined primarily by its *content*. The meaning of the remark should express praise, appreciation, or approval without ambiguity. However, since almost any remark can be given a variety of meanings by the tone in which it is spoken, tone of voice is taken into account in determining whether a remark is intended positively or not. Statements that concern physical attributes ("He's a very fast runner") are rated as positive only if approval is clearly signified by the tone of voice. Similarly, an apparently positive remark ("He's an absolute dear") may be said in an ironical tone of voice, which clearly negates the content. It must be stresed, however, that tone may be used only to *clarify* the actual content of a remark. Tone alone can never define a positive remark. The statement "He's so forgetful" may be said with warmth and tenderness, but would not be considered a positive remark.

A positive remark may relate to a single action by the person concerned ("He did that job well") or may be a general comment ("Anything he does, he does well" or "He's a wonderful person"). Statements that express approval explicitly ("I love her" or "I just like being with her—it doesn't matter what we do") would also be considered positive remarks.

Examples of statements that would *not* qualify as positive remarks include the following:

1. Any response that is phrased in the negative, however emphatically or warmly it is said. Thus "He's not bad at doing repairs" is not a positive remark, according to the rating criteria (because of the difficulties in interpretation).

2. Qualified compliments, such as "She's pretty good about that" or "He's fairly careful," because they are insufficiently strong statements.

3. An answer of "Yes" to a question about the existence of positive attributes, unless the respondent goes on to extend the reply. The answer to the direct question "Is she a friendly person?" would only be considered as a positive remark if it were, for example, "Oh yes, very friendly indeed" or "Yes, definitely."

4. Statements made in the past tense that are used to contrast a previously satisfactory state of affairs with an unsatisfactory one in the present. For example, "He was always a good husband—but since the illness came on, he takes no notice."

4

Patterns of Response in High-EE and Low-EE Relatives of Psychiatric Patients

Carefully applied, the techniques developed by Brown and Rutter and incorporated into the CFI appear to reveal a great deal about how one person, the relative, feels about another person, the patient: his or her emotional response to the illness, attitudes toward the patient's behavior, and propensity for reacting to the patient in particular ways. Naturally, the limits of the interview situation impose certain constraints on our interpretations of the data; we cannot presume to understand how a given family functions after conversations of a few hours' duration with one or more of the family members. But we have been reassured by the way in which later observations of families in a therapeutic context have confirmed impressions obtained at interview (see Section III). Evidence from the naturalistic follow-up studies (see Section II) and from psychophysiological experiments (see Section IV) provide further support for our view that differences in interview behaviors reflect genuine differences in patterns of relatives' responses and family functioning in the home. Thus one can use a relative's account to speculate as to what has been happening in the patient's home environment in the months leading up to admission, and to compare and contrast the families assessed.

In 1976, we (Vaughn & Leff, 1976a) published the results of a study investigating the influence of family attitudes on clinical outcome in two groups of psychiatric patients: 37 with a diagnosis of schizophrenia, and 31 with a diagnosis of neurotic depression. For both groups, the EE of a key relative during an interview shortly after the patient's admission to the hospital was the best single predictor of whether or not the patient relapsed with florid symptoms during a 9-month postdischarge follow-up period. These results are presented in detail in Section II.

The quality of the tape-recorded interview material obtained during the 1976 study enabled us to look more closely at the family environments characterized as high or low in EE. The interviews provided considerable information concerning both the quality of the emotional relationships between patients and their relatives, and more general patterns of familial response and interaction, for two very different diagnostic groups. In presenting these additional data now, it must be stressed again that all analyses were based on ratings made at the time of the key interview with each relative, shortly after a patient's admission. Such ratings were made in ignorance of the patient's 9-month clinical outcome.

PATTERNS OF CRITICISM AND THE PREILLNESS RELATIONSHIP

We thought it would be interesting first to consider in greater detail the nature of the critical comments made by relatives during their interviews, and then to relate these findings to more general impressions of the relationships existing within the patients' families as revealed in the relatives' responses to the CFI.

A content analysis of all critical remarks made by 46 relatives of schizophrenic patients and 32 relatives of depressed patients was carried out. For this analysis, a distinction was made between critical remarks concerning symptom behaviors that appeared in the context of the illness episode (e.g., delusional or hallucinatory behaviors, suicide attempts, changes in levels of activity or irritability), and critical remarks about more general, enduring personality traits of the patients. Such distinctions are most easily made when a patient has had a fairly recent acute onset; this was the case for most of the patients in the 1976 study. Relatives of patients with long psychiatric histories may find it difficult to recall a time when the patient seemed "normal" or well; after many years, symptom and nonsymptom behaviors may become inextricably confused. With few exceptions, we felt we were able to make these distinctions satisfactorily.

Common-sense judgments were made for each individual case, based on all information obtained in the interview. This is an important point, because it is impossible to say whether a particular critical remark such as "He's so difficult to get along with" concerns a symptom behavior or a long-standing personality trait, in the absence of additional information about the patient. Did the relative suggest that this patient had always been difficult? Or had he become difficult only in the past few weeks or months? At the end of the interview, the interviewer generally is in a position to decide how such a remark should be categorized.

For each critical remark it was noted (1) whether it concerned a clear symptom behavior or a long-standing personality trait; and (2) what area of dissatisfation was represented. For example, a complaint about the patient's ability to deal with money would be categorized as Dissatisfaction with Finances, in terms of the Dissatisfaction Scales developed by Brown. There may be considerable overlap in the categories, particularly where the Communication, Affection/Warmth/Interest, and Relationship classifications are concerned. The following proportion determined whether the relative's criticisms were predominantly of one type or the other: Remarks about symptom behaviors : Remarks about personality.

Overall Count of Critical Remarks

A few case examples illustrate the different patterns of criticism encountered.

CASE NO. 22-S (MOTHER)

Eight critical remarks, all concerning symptom behaviors. Examples:

> "'You promised you'd go to sleep and wouldn't disturb me!'" (overactivity)
>
> "She'd stand in my way—would not move—it used to get on my nerves!" (underactivity)
>
> "I told her, 'I've got no time to look at faces, I've got better things to do!' It really gets on your nerves." (hallucinations)

CASE NO. 49-S (SISTER)

Three critical remarks, predominantly about symptom behaviors. Two of the three remarks concerned the state of the patient's bedroom when she was ill. The remaining remark concerned a long-standing personality trait: "She won't open up, won't tell you anything—she keeps everything to herself." (critical tone) In this case the interviewer knew (from other information given) that the patient had always been a poor conversationalist; hence the categorization of the last example as a "personality trait" remark. In the absence of additional information, the behavior reported (social withdrawal) could just be part of the illness episode. This example demonstrates the need to take account of the total interview when assessing individual remarks.

CASE NO. 54-S (SON)

Twenty-one critical remarks, all concerning long-standing personality traits. Of these remarks, 13 had to do with dissatisfaction in the areas of Communication and Personal Relationship. Examples:

> "She's very stubborn, my mum, you just can't tell her anything."
>
> "She lies to me, won't play straight, ever. I tell her, 'I just give up on you.'"

The other eight critical comments had to do with Household Tasks. Examples:

> "Unless she wants to do it, she won't *ever* do it."
>
> Descriptions of the patient as "lazy" and "useless": "She's always been like that, for as long as I can remember."

Florid symptom behaviors accounted for less than one-third of all critical remarks by relatives (schizophrenic group, 30%, $n = 113$ of 379; depressed group, 29%, $n = 70$ of 240). This was surprising, in view of the severe behavior disturbance and work impairment shown by many patients in the months preceding their admission to the hospital. However, the majority of critical remarks were about long-standing attributes of a patient that, in a relative's view, predated the illness (schizophrenic group, 70%, $n = 266$ of 379; depressed group, 71%, $n = 170$ of 240). For both diagnostic groups, these remarks tended to center on aspects of the relationship between a patient and a relative with which the relative was markedly dissatisfied. The same grievances, usually having to do with communication or the amount of affection, warmth, and interest shown by the patient, came up again and again. The patient had "always" been "selfish," "spoiled," "snappy and moody," "impossible to get through to."

Our analyses indicated that for both diagnostic groups the major determinant of a relative's *present* response to the patient and his or her illness was the way the patient and the relative got along *before* the current illness episode. If the preillness relationship was a good one, one of two responses to the illness was usual: concerned but noncritical, or critical but with criticism confined to florid symptom behaviors. A critical response depended less on the degree of the patient's disturbance than on the relative's own personality. If a relative was easygoing and tolerant generally, he or she tended to adopt a noncritical stance. If a relative was typically tense or moody when stressed, however, the strain of coping with someone psychiatrically ill could result in feelings of anger, in addition to the more usual feelings of frustration and helplessness. But such feelings invariably were directed at specific symptom behaviors for which the patient was not held responsible.

Where there was a poor relationship between a patient and a relative prior to the onset of the illness episode, critical remarks were almost exclusively about long-standing behaviors. The relatives concerned did not identify these behaviors as manifestations of illness, but considered them to be integral expressions of the patients' personality.

Thus it seemed that the kind of remarks made by a relative about the patient at a crisis point (time of admission) could provide important clues about the way in which patient and relative got along in normal circumstances.

The three very distinct patterns of response revealed by our content analyses of criticism can be vividly illustrated by excerpts from interviews with the spouses of the 13 married schizophrenic patients and 29 married depressed patients in the 1976 study (Vaughn & Leff, 1976a). The focus is on married couples, because only 2 of the 31 depressed patients studied were *not* married and living with a spouse at the time of key admission. When comparing patterns of emotional response and family functioning for different diagnostic groups, it seems desirable to match for types of households, where this is feasible. Nevertheless, the main finding that the content of a relative's criticism reflects the quality of the preillness relationship holds for nonmarital as well as for marital households.

Absence of Criticism

Of the spouses of married schizophrenic patients, 38% ($n = 5$ of 13) made no critical comments when interviewed; the corresponding figure for the depressed group was 24% ($n = 7$ of 29). All except one of these marriages were considered to be at least "good average" relationships prior to the onset of the patients' illness. In each case the spouse was very warm in talking about the patient; indicating that the spouse and patient had always got on well, enjoyed each other's company, shared many interests, and had good communication.

The schizophrenic patients in this subgroup were highly disturbed when ill. But if a marriage had been characterized in the past by mutual understanding and affection, these qualities were reflected in the spouse's response to the ill patient, however great the anxiety or concern might be.

The reactions of one husband (Case No. 41-S) were typical for this subgroup. One's general impression was of a basically happy family whose lives had been subjected to considerable stress and strain as a result of the patient's illness. Tension was marked for at least the last 2 months before admission, when she was deluded and incapacitated. Although there was no overt quarreling, the family was upset by her accusations that they were all against her: "Obviously there was strain, because if every time you move an object you're accused, it must build up. . . . I know it did with me." In his responses to her illness and his many attempts to cope, however, the husband showed considerable understanding of his wife's feelings and actions, and sympathy for her plight. In response to the question, "Was there any nagging or grumbling?", he said:

> "No, not really, I always realized Mary was doing her absolute best all the time. My instant reaction at the time was to feel sorry for her being like this . . . and to rationalize the thing, to try and allay her fears. 'Look at the facts.' I had no feelings at all of anger or irritability with her because of this, only sorrow that she was in a state. We're not fighting any battles."

Although clearly distressed by his wife's illness, he was not at all critical; at no time in the interview did he blame her for anything she said or did when ill.

The spouses of depressed patients, unlike the spouses of schizophrenic patients in this noncritical subgroup, reported negligible tension and strain during the present illness episode. The patient's symptoms were confined to a loss of interest in activities and conversation, tearfulness, generalized worrying, and amorphous feelings of being unable to cope. He or she usually was unable to pinpoint a cause for the depression, but at no time attributed it to anything members of the family had said or done. Within the context of the family, social withdrawal and avoidance were extremely rare. Even when most miserable and least inclined to converse, the patient actively sought and seemed to find comfort in the spouse's company.

The spouse typically responded with sympathy, viewing the illness either as something inexplicable or as due to external stresses or events unrelated to the family. In response to the question, "Has the way you feel about your husband changed at all since the trouble started?", two wives replied as follows:

> "No, I just feel desperately sorry for him and wanted to help him all I could. I realized this couldn't be done at home. I did feel a terrible loss, not being able to do more, but I think this happens. The closer you are to someone . . . it's very difficult."

> "I didn't get irritable with him, because when a person's ill you've got to understand, haven't you? We all accepted that he wasn't well, that's all there was to it. We knew what was wrong with him, the doctor said depression. You couldn't really say to him 'You'll have to snap out of it, luv,' because I've got enough sense to know it's one of those things you don't just snap out of."

Criticism of Symptom Behaviors

When the patient's illness had clearly strained what had been quite a reasonable preillness relationship, some spouses made a number of critical remarks about symptom behaviors (schizophrenic group, 38%, $n = 5$ of 13; depressed group, 28%, $n = 8$ of 29). For example, the wife of one schizophrenic patient, Charles (Case No. 50-S), thought that her husband's delusions were stupid and silly, and she reacted to his talking about them by becoming extremely irritable. In the beginning, when she thought Charles simply was worried by an impending operation, she felt sorry for him, but when the operation was over and he continued to talk in a peculiar way, she became increasingly hostile and intolerant:

> "He was saying the most stupid things — seeing things in the television programs — oh, stupid things!"

> "He'd start off by trying to explain to me what he was seeing and hearing, and I would start off being very calm. Then he'd start being silly, crying, until in the end I lost my temper. I kept saying 'I've got five kids — I don't want six!'"

> "He wouldn't give up trying to explain to me. He'd have these crazy ideas and he'd talk about them over and over again until I would absolutely boil trying to talk him out of it. 'Be sensible!' I just gave up."

All of this woman's critical remarks concerned her husband's symptom behaviors. She described herself as a moody person, easily irritated and inclined to sulk; when Charles became ill, she could no longer rely upon him to provide support. She showed quite a bit of warmth when describing his normal behavior and their relationship when he was well: "I think we've always got on marvelously well together." It seems that her unfavorable comments were directly related to Charles' illness and the distress it had caused her.

The spouses of depressed patients in this subgroup similarly wavered between sympathetic concern and impatient annoyance with the patients' symptoms. When efforts to be attentive and accommodating did little to ameliorate continual worrying and signs of misery, spouses occasionally became quite irritable:

> "She used to ring me up during these panic attacks and I had to keep coming home and picking her up. That put quite a bit of tension on me — it was a very frustrating time. She kept on and on and on about this, and in the end I just said 'Oh, for God's sake, don't keep on — you'll be going like your mother soon!'"

The depressed patients in this subgroup showed somewhat more behavior disturbance when ill than those patients with noncritical spouses. Irritable outbursts were more common, and marked social withdrawal by the patient was quite usual. Social withdrawal in particular tended to make spouses feel tense and on edge:

> "My saying something would help only a minute, then he'd go back into it again. It was beginning to make *me* crack up. . . . He could pass a person by without noticing; he seemed to be in a different world."

> "It was a very delicately balanced edge. You knew if you said the wrong thing she'd be back down again. It got a bit strained, artificial. It got to the stage where you couldn't make any impression on her, or talk to her, or *anything*."

> "He just sits here, he could be a stuffed dummy! He lost confidence in everything. You couldn't be all lovey-dovey to him, he was so — so into himself. I couldn't talk nice to him if I wanted to, because he'd say 'Oh, get out.' He just couldn't be bothered!"

But like the noncritical spouses, these husbands and wives reported mutual consideration and affection under ordinary circumstances, and emphasized how much they wanted to see the patients well and at home again. For example, one husband said, "I've made an exceptional effort to be affectionate to her, to make her see I want her home, that she's what I'm working for."

Criticism of Previous Personality

The third and final pattern of criticism was associated with a poor preillness relationship, characterized by considerable strain and disharmony and by markedly impaired communication. The illness merely exacerbated what had been a highly unsatisfactory situation for many years. Only 23% ($n = 3$ of

13) of marriages of schizophrenic patients fell into this category; 59% of the depressed marriages did so ($n = 17$ of 29; $p = .0347$). Criticism was frequent, spontaneous, and almost always concerned aspects of a patient's personality that the relative believed had always affected relationships with the rest of the family in a negative way:

> "I can't understand her! She knows what she wants and she goes out and gets it, and she don't care how she gets it as long as she gets it! I've always seen it that way, always. She'll only see her point of view; she'll never see any other."

> "She's *always* been irritable, moody, preoccupied—ever since I've known her. She would always twist things round—seemed to take the opposite view for its own sake. Never a happy person, really."

> "He's *always* been awkward, my husband! Very irritable, very difficult to get on with."

> "I've always thought her different, highly strung. When I first met her, I used to be amazed at the extremes she would go to in the event of a row or argument. . . . She's always been like that. It's developed and got worse and you just get plain fed up with it all, being defensive all the time."

> "He's always been a moody man. He expects the best of *everyone*—a perfectionist, really! I couldn't say the pattern of his behavior has altered a great deal; he's been like this for such a long time."

In cases such as these, where the preillness relationships had been very disturbed, the spouses' response to the patients' illness was invariably unsympathetic: The spouses tended to doubt its legitimacy. For example, the relatives of one schizophrenic patient (Case No. 33-S) were all convinced (according to her husband) that she was claiming to hear voices just for an effect, as a way of manipulating them. (The interviewer's question is in italics.)

> "It didn't cut no ice with me—I took no notice of it. It's very hard, you can't get to the bottom of it. You don't know what her object is, you don't know what she's aiming at, but certainly there's nothing really mentally wrong."
> *Did you feel she was acting?*
> "I should say 50% of it was. Any of our crowd will go in [to the] hospital, see her, and say 'There's nothing wrong with her! She's always been like that!'"

In these high-EE marriages of depressed or schizophrenic patients, an atmosphere of marked tension and strain was present long before the patients showed signs of mental illness, so that the illness itself hardly altered the family relationships.

The particular problems reported by spouses of depressed persons in this subgroup must be noted. Such a spouse was likely to say that the patient's "ill" self seemed just an exaggeration of his or her "normal" self; symptom behaviors and long-standing personality traits were difficult to distinguish from each other. Thus, where there was a poor preillness relationship with a critical spouse, the depressed patient almost always was described as chronically insecure and lacking in self-esteem. Frequently the patient's childhood or some traumatic early experience was thought to be responsible. In many cases, the patient had an extremely bleak view of self, the immediate environment, and the future—in the terms of Beck (1967), a "negative cognitive set"—which had colored the person's perceptions and affected attitudes and behavior for as long as the spouse could remember. Complaints of feeling unwanted, friendless, and misunderstood were common. Whatever the origins of these feelings, they were noticeably less prevalent in patients in the "good preillness relationship" subgroups.

These marital relationships were among the most disturbed of any assessed in the depressed *or* schizophrenic groups. Spouses repeatedly spoke of inconsistencies of attitude and behavior that made for an intolerable atmosphere when the depressed patient was in a "mood." The amount of tension and strain generated at these times was far greater than the disturbance caused by any of the schizophrenic patients, even when the schizophrenics were most ill. The depressed patient might be taciturn and secretive at one moment and in a temper the next; frequent fluctuations between rejecting withdrawal and tearful dependency were not uncommon. This was most often the pattern when the patient was a man, as several wives noted:

> "Anything would trigger a row, I don't care how even-tempered you were—he'd keep on and on at you. If you tried to pacify him you're wrong—he'll tell you not to ignore him. And then if you answered him, he'd say, 'You shouldn't answer me.' And then again, if you said, 'Oh, dry up, don't keep on,' you're in the wrong as well. . . . I once said to him, 'Joe, don't you think it's best we go our own ways?' just to see what he'd say. And he burst out crying, 'I don't want to leave.' And yet six nights a week he'd be taking all the cases out of the cellar packing them all up: 'I'm going.' "

> "He used to have a habit of throwing me out. I got a black leather bag upstairs . . . I used to have everything in there. As soon as he used to say anything I used to put on my coat, and I was glad to go! He used to say 'Don't come back' and bolt the door. And I never did come back—until he came for me. Other times he'd wake me up, crying, 'You're going to leave me!' I said, 'Where can I go at four o'clock in the morning? Go to sleep!' "

> "He'd say, 'Don't you get me any dinner,' and then at the end of the week he'd turn round and say 'You've not cooked dinner all week!' And I said to him, 'Well, you told me you didn't want it.' Nothing was right! You couldn't do anything right—whatever you did, whatever you said."

PATTERNS OF CRITICISM AND SOCIAL CONTENT

Within the total group of married depressed patients, a critical response by a spouse was linked both to a poor preillness relationship ($p < .005$) and to low face-to-face contact between patient and family (i.e., less than 35 hours per week; exact $p = .017$), resulting in an association between a poor marital relationship and minimal contact ($p < .005$). No such interactions were found within the schizophrenic marital group. For married schizophrenic patients, the most common pattern of interaction, irrespective of spouses' EE, was high face-to-face contact and no social withdrawal; the illness did not alter this.

Where there was low face-to-face contact between a depressed patient and the rest of the family, the reasons for the low contact differed according to the sex of the patient. Within this subgroup of poor preillness relationships, male patients were significantly more likely than female patients to show signs of marked withdrawal when ill (exact $p = .002$). In order to avoid the family (and there were signs of deliberate avoidance), male patients would retreat into a room alone, work overtime, or simply stay away from the house for long periods of time. Their wives felt shut out, rejected, and frustrated by the husbands' refusal to communicate; in time, they also tended to withdraw, verbally and physically. But despite their highly critical attitudes (and, in several cases, repeated instances of ill treatment by the patients in the past), these wives were notable for their continuing concern for their ill husbands and their attempts to make allowances for the patients' hurtful and often inexplicable behavior:

> "We very seldom hold a conversation . . . never have . . . I like chatting, but I've got so that he's steeled me not to speak. When the telly's on I often feel like saying something—I've done that and he's turned it off, saying 'I'm listening to that and you're chatting—I can't listen to that and you!' So I've trained myself not to make any comment. I think it all dates back to his childhood, being brought up in a children's home and having no mother—that's insecurity all the way through, I think. I think that's more or less why I [have] felt sorry and done what I could."

In response to the question, "Do you ever think of leaving him?", one wife said:

> "No, not really. I still think a lot of him; I must do, to stand this. I don't think there's many who could. I don't know how I've kept myself together. If it wasn't I thought so much of him, I'd just tell him to get out. But I've told him, 'I'm here, I'll stand by you, come what may.'"

Of the 10 female patients with a poor marital relationship, only one showed signs of withdrawal when depressed. Low face-to-face contact, when it occurred, was always due to the husband's avoidance of the patient. In several cases, the patients' feelings of insecurity and related jealousy led to intense and sometimes violent arguments, which the husbands tried to avoid by staying out until all hours:

> "She would keep on and on and on . . . until I lost my temper, or ran out of the front door to escape. She was crying when I left her, but it's happened so many times I just didn't use to bother her. I just thought to hell with it, and away I went. I just wanted to put it all behind me, I'd had enough."

"I get in a temper, a subdued temper, when she's like this. What do I do? Go to the pub. 'Give me a Scotch, Jack!' I'll accept what I am, you know, but I think if things went more smoothly emotionally for me, I wouldn't turn to alcohol for my pleasures."

In the remaining cases of depression in this subgroup, the marital relationships were characterized by extreme apathy, few shared activities, and little or no positive communication. For many years the husbands had led lives independent of the patients and expressed no desire to reestablish contact. Unlike the wives of depressed men, all of the husbands in the poor preillness relationship subgroup seemed lacking in sympathy or concern for the patients; most of them appeared to have remarkably little interest in their ill wives' feelings. If in the past there had been active attempts to improve a difficult situation, these efforts had long since ceased. They were impatient with such symptom behaviors as worrying and "crying over the least little thing," and were inclined to ignore them completely. Comments such as "I never say nothing to that woman—I never say nothing!" and "I wouldn't take much notice of her—I'm past worrying about that sort of thing" were common.

STUDIES OF THE ASSOCIATION BETWEEN RELATIVES' EXPRESSED EMOTION AND RELAPSE OF PSYCHIATRIC ILLNESS

5

Early Studies of Schizophrenia

THE 1962 STUDY

As described in the introduction and Chapter 1 of this volume, a follow-up study of discharged schizophrenic patients suggested that some aspect of the relationship between patients and their relatives might be influencing their prognosis. The next step was to devise measures of this relationship, particularly emotional aspects, on which it was decided to focus. Five scales were developed to assess the following: the amount of emotion shown by the relative toward the patient; hostility shown by the relative toward the patient; the degree of dominance exerted by the relative; the amount of emotion shown by the patient toward the relative; and the amount of hostility expressed by the patient toward the relative. It can be seen that the first two scales are mirror images of the last two, while the dominance scale subsumes both relatives' and patients' behavior; that is, a relative could be dominant over a patient, or vice versa. It is worth emphasizing that while hostility was isolated as a specific named emotion, the other categories of emotion were lumped together under the generic term "expressed emotion." This lack of specificity is evidence of the early stage of development that the assessment had reached at this point.

The study that incorporated these measures was confined to male schizophrenic patients (Brown *et al.*, 1962). Discharges of all schizophrenic men aged 20–49 from eight psychiatric hospitals in London were monitored over a 12-month period. Exclusions comprised those hospitalized for less than 1 month, non-English-speaking patients, non-Europeans, and those going to an address outside London or to a hostel. A total of 128 men made up the final sample.

Each patient's condition was assessed a day or two before he left the hospital, using two sets of scales: one relating to mental state, and the other relating to socially embarrassing behavior on the ward during the previous week. If he planned to live in lodgings or alone, no further contact was made until a year later or at any readmission to a hospital. If he intended to return to relatives, the "key" relative was identified. This was defined as the most closely related female relative, usually the wife or mother. The patient and the key relative were interviewed 2 weeks after discharge. Finally, the members of the household were interviewed on readmission of the patient or at the end of the follow-up year. In this final interview, the patient's behavior was assessed for any deterioration since the initial interview. A time budget was constructed of the patient's daily activities during a typical week to determine how much time he actually spent with his relatives.

The ratings of emotional relationships not only were made on the basis of the content of the respondent's speech, but also took account of nonverbal means of communication, such as tone of voice and gesture. Only behavior that took place during the interview was assessed. Two independent interviewers achieved over 90% interrater reliability on the ratings. Common sense dictates that the judgments to be made involved a major element of subjectivity. It is reassuring, then, that a perfectly satisfactory level of interrater reliability was reached. This was a good augur for the feasibility of this approach to the measurement of emotional relationships, and a spur to the development of more sophisticated scales. On the basis of these ratings, a distinction was made between "high-involvement" homes and "low-involvement" homes.

At the final interview, 55% of patients were assessed as having deteriorated in behavior since their discharge. Behavioral deterioration was seen in 76% of patients returning to high-emotional-involvement homes, in contrast with 28% of those returning to low-emotional-involvement homes, a significant difference. This difference persisted when readmission to hospital was used as an alternative criterion of outcome, with rates of 58% and 21% respectively.

There was a significant relationship between severity of symptoms on discharge and subsequent deterioration in behavior. This association raised the distinct possibility that high involvement on the part of relatives might be an understandable reaction to receiving a severely disturbed patient into the home. Deterioration of behavior in high-involvement homes might then be a direct consequence of a disturbed mental state at discharge, rather than a reaction to the relatives' emotional attitudes. This interpretation trivializes any associations found between the emotions expressed by relatives about patients and the course of the patients' disorders. It casts a long shadow over all subsequent naturalistic studies, which can only be effectively dispelled by the experimental work described in Section III of this volume.

There are other, less compelling ways of countering this objection, one of which was employed by Brown and his colleagues. They excluded patients with severe symptoms or markedly embarrassing behavior as rated on discharge, and found that the difference in behavioral deterioration between patients in the different kinds of homes still persisted. The association between living in high-emotional-involvement homes and deterioration in behavior also held good whether a patient returned to parents, wife, or more distant kin.

Another interesting finding emerged from the material generated by the time budget. The behavior of patients who were moderately or severely disturbed in mental state at discharge and who returned to high-emotional-involvement homes deteriorated less frequently when they spent less time with the key relative.

Almost all the important themes that are recapitulated in subsequent studies are clearly stated for the first time in this pioneering work. The association between relatives' emotional attitudes and deterioration in the patients' schizophrenic illness; its apparent independence of the severity of the patients' disturbance; the seemingly protective effect of social distance from the involved relative — all these are repeated in each replication. The only major issue untouched in this early study is the role of prophylactic medication, and this almost certainly reflects the era in which the work was conducted. As we point out later, the methods of assessment of patients and relatives became considerably more focused and increasingly sophisticated. The study population was diversified to encompass women as well as men, male relatives as well as female, and patients with diagnoses other than schizophrenia. Nevertheless, these methodological advances in no way eroded the stability of the original findings, which stand firm as a landmark in this field of research.

REFINEMENTS IN ASSESSMENT TECHNIQUES: THE 1972 STUDY

The next step was to refine the techniques of measurement, many of which were developed especially for the first study. The development of the CFI and the indices of EE has been extensively described in Section I. Between the first and the second study by Brown and his colleagues, a standardized assessment of the patient's psychiatric state had been developed, the Present State Examination (PSE); a computer program, Catego, was also developed to process the data generated and to provide a clinical classification (Wing, Cooper, & Sartorius, 1974). The PSE has become an internationally recognized instrument and is not described here.

Many measures of a patient's behavior before admission were included in the assessment procedures. Particularly important were measures of the following: work impairment, which took into account the performance of domestic activities by housewives; disturbed behavior in the 12 months before admission or at about the time of admission; and social withdrawal, with account being taken of social contacts inside and outside the home.

Relapse of schizophrenia was taken as the criterion of clinical outcome of the patients, and was categorized in two ways. Type I relapse was defined as a change from a normal or nonschizophrenic state to a state of schizophrenia. In practice, this meant the development of schizophrenic symptoms as classified by the Catego program in a patient who had been free of them at discharge. The average length of stay of schizophrenic patients in hospitals in the United Kingdom is over 2 months, with the result that most of them have been stabilized on medication and are free of psychotic symptoms by the time of discharge. For those with persisting psychotic symptoms at discharge, relapse was defined as a marked exacerbation of these, and was classified as Type II. The decision that a Type II relapse has occurred obviously involves a more difficult judgment than that regarding a Type I relapse. Essentially, the former is a quantitative assessment, while the latter is a qualitative one.

In order to assess relatives' EE, two kinds of interviews were held: one with the relative alone, and another jointly with the relative and patient. It was found that the relative tended to express less emotion in the joint interview, presumably because he or she felt inhibited in front of the patient. Consequently, the joint interview ratings added a mere 3 relatives to the 42 who were assigned to a high-EE group on the basis of the interview with the relative alone. The criteria for the high-EE group comprised a score of 7 or more on Critical Comments, any positive rating on Hostility, and/or a score of 4 or 5 on the Emotional Overinvolvement scale.

Patients qualified for the second study (reported in Brown *et al.*, 1972) if they were aged 18 to 64, were born in the United Kingdom, and lived with relatives at an address in the London borough of Camberwell. Individuals who were beginning a new period of outpatient or inpatient care at any one of the five hospitals serving the area were screened. Those possibly suffering from schizophrenia were interviewed with the PSE; if a diagnosis of schizophrenia was made on the basis of the interview data, they were included in the study. A total of 68 patients entered the study through this route. A further 33 patients were obtained from Bexley Hospital, a large psychiatric institution in South London, with the additional screening criterion that they were within 5 years of their first admission. Thus the whole sample comprised 101 patients, of whom 59 were experiencing their first episode of schizophrenia.

The CFI was carried out at relatives' homes by a research sociologist while the patients were still hospitalized. It usually took two separate visits to each informant to complete and lasted a minimum of 3 hours in all. If a patient lived with both parents, the parents were interviewed separately by different workers.

Both the assessment of a patient's psychiatric state and the family interviews were repeated at the follow-up, 9 months after discharge. However, if the patient was readmitted during this period, the family and the patient were reassessed at that time. Brown and his colleagues (Brown *et al.*, 1972) found that by the 9-month follow-up there had been a general reduction in criticism; 14% of relatives made seven or more criticisms, compared with 30% at the initial assessment. Overinvolvement, however, showed less of a tendency to diminish over time.

By the 9-month follow-up, 35 of the 101 patients had relapsed. However, only 29 of them were readmitted, whereas 3 other patients who were readmitted did not satisfy the criteria for relapse. These findings emphasize the importance of applying standardized criteria of relapse, rather than relying on rehospitalization as an indication of poor clinical outcome. Of the 35 relapses, 23 were Type I and 12 were Type II.

How did the individual components of EE relate to relapse? The number of critical comments was found to be related to the relapse rate. The Critical Comments scale was dichotomized at the point that produced the greatest difference in relapse rates — namely, between scores of 6 and 7. When more than one relative was interviewed, the higher rating was used to characterize the home environment. Where the relative made six or fewer critical comments at the initial interview, 26% of patients relapsed, compared with 57% of those whose relatives made seven or more criticisms. It is worth recording that at the time of the key admission, 29 out of 90 relatives (32%) made no criticisms, while 27 made seven or more (30%).

Hostility was also related to relapse of schizophrenia. If any hostility was expressed by relatives initially, 50% of the patients relapsed. In the absence of hostility, only 32% relapsed. The figures for emotional overinvolvement are rather similar, with 36% of patients in low-overinvolvement homes relapsing, compared with 62% in homes with a high degree of overinvolvement (4 or 5 on a 6-point scale).

Warmth bore a complex relationship to relapse. At the lower end of the scale, patients tended to relapse because relatives rated as low in warmth were likely to be highly critical. At the upper end of the scale, the relapse rate was also high, because marked warmth tended to be associated with overinvolvement. However, if the relatives showed considerable warmth unalloyed with criticism or overinvolvement, the patients did very well; only 9% in this group relapsed over the follow-up period.

The joint interview afforded an opportunity to rate EE in the patients, but this was not generally very high; only 10% of patients were markedly critical of the relatives in the household, for example. Furthermore, the patients' EE bore no relationship to the outcome of their illness.

In order to simplify the analysis, the components of EE that were related to relapse were combined into a single index of EE, and relatives were assigned to either a high-EE or a low-EE group. The great majority of high-EE relatives (80%) joined this group on account of excessive criticism. Another 16% entered this category on the basis of overinvolvement alone. Only 4% expressed hostility in the absence of considerable criticism or overinvolvement. The use of this combined index of EE gives a better prediction of relapse than any individual component. Thus 58% of patients returning to high-EE relatives relapsed, compared with 16% discharged to low-EE homes ($p < .001$).

This significant association replicated the central finding of the earlier study (Brown *et al.*, 1962) and raised the same issue of the possible role of behavioral disturbance in mediating the relationship. Brown and his colleagues (Brown *et al.*, 1972) tackled this problem in a number of ways. First they controlled for the degree of behavioral disturbance and found that the association between EE and relapse was only slightly reduced. Then they controlled for EE, with the result that the association between disturbed behavior and relapse fell initially to zero. Then they looked separately at the patients who had not shown behavioral disturbance prior to the key admission. Of the 11 patients in this category who returned to high-EE relatives, 7 (64%) relapsed, compared with 8 (20%) of the 40 in low-EE homes. This is a highly significant difference ($p < .01$), showing that EE is strongly related to relapse even when there is no disturbed behavior to mediate the relationship. Taken together, these statistical comparisons eliminate the patients' disturbed behavior as an explanation for the association between relatives' EE and relapse of schizophrenia. However, it can always be postulated that some other factor, perhaps one not even measured in these studies, could be acting in the same mediating role.

In addition to relatives' EE, other factors were found to relate to relapse. Men had a much poorer prognosis than women, their relapse rate being double that for women. Marriage seemed to exert a protective effect in both sexes; the relapse rates were lower for the married than the unmarried. The prophylactic value of antipsychotic medication is well established (Hirsch, Gaind, Rohde, Stevens, & Wing, 1973; Hogarty, Goldberg, Schooler, Ulrich, & the Collaborative Study Group, 1974; Hogarty, Schooler, Ulrich, *et al.*, 1979; Leff & Wing, 1971), so that one would expect it to emerge as a protective factor in this study. Two-thirds of the patients took one of the major tranquilizers for a large part of the follow-up period or until relapse. The relapse rate of patients who were off these drugs (45%) was considerably higher than that of patients taking regular medication (26%), but this difference just fails to reach an acceptable level of significance ($\chi^2 = 3.65$). When patients were divided according to their relatives' EE, differential effects of medication appeared. For patients in low-EE homes, relapse rates of patients on and off prophylactic drugs were almost identical (14% and 15%, respectively). By contrast, patients in high-EE homes had a considerably higher relapse rate when off drugs (66%) than on them (46%), although this difference was not significant. Brown *et al.* (1972) interpreted this as indicating that drugs have no effect on patients in low-EE homes and serve mainly to protect patients living with high-EE relatives. As we indicate later, a longer period of follow-up yielded data that necessitate a modification to this supposition.

Another protective factor that was identified in the 1962 study, social distance from the key relative, was also examined in the later study. The time budget of activities during a typical week was constructed in the same way. An arbitrary division was made between patients spending more than 35 hours per week in face-to-face contact with their relatives, and those spending less than this time. Ideally, one would like to be able to estimate the amount of time patients and relatives spend speaking to each other, since it is likely that critical, hostile, and overinvolved attitudes are most clearly expressed during verbal interchanges. Although in this post-Watergate era we are technically able to do this, the ethical issues involved are controversial. Hence an indirect method is used: The amount of time patients and relatives spend in the same room together is assessed. Time spent asleep is excluded. It is a reasonable assumption that the duration of time spent together in the same room, known as face-to-face contact, is closely related to the amount of communication that occurs. If one or both partners are working full-time, it is necessary to spend most evenings and the majority of the weekend together in order to clock up 35 hours of face-to-face contact per week. Therefore, this level represents a considerable amount of social contact.

Brown and his colleagues discovered that the amount of face-to-face contact made no difference to the relapse rate of patients in low-EE homes. However, for patients living with high-EE relatives, low face-to-face contact appeared to confer some degree of protection. The relapse rate was 29% for patients spending less than 35 hours per week in face-to-face contact with high-EE relatives, compared with 79% for those in high contact, a highly significant difference ($p < .01$).

In summary, the second study (Brown *et al.*, 1972), with its more refined and sophisticated techniques, confirmed the findings of the first: the strong association between relatives' EE and relapse of schizophrenia, the independence of this association of patients' disturbed behavior, and the apparently protective effect of reduced social contact with high-EE relatives. In the course of the 1972 study, the crucial elements of EE emerged clearly, and their relative importance was defined. Thus the number of critical comments was found to be the major component of the EE index. Hostility added a little, although closely related to criticism, while overinvolvement was seen to be an independent element. Warmth was dropped from the index because of its complex interrelationships with the other components, which largely explained its relationship to relapse. Consequently, as Brown and his colleagues point out, the term "expressed emotion" has a mainly negative connotation. This is of considerable importance, since this quality of the index is often misunderstood by people unfamiliar with the details of its composition. Thus it is not rare to hear the work misquoted as indicating that relatives of schizophrenics should ideally suppress all their feelings in the presence of patients. As we have seen, this is an incorrect generalization, since if relatives showed considerable warmth in the absence of criticism and overinvolvement, the patients tended to remain well.

Prophylactic antipsychotic medication does not emerge strongly from this study as conferring protection from schizophrenic relapse. The data were suggestive of this effect, but an acceptable level of statistical significance was not reached. It is only in the later studies that the role of maintenance drug treatment becomes clearly defined.

In their paper, Brown *et al.* (1972) raised the issue of whether the factors they had been considering were in any way specific for schizophrenia. They wrote: "We have the impression that the relatives of other kinds of handicapped individuals might also tend to develop such relationships (high EE), though whether the tendency would be as strong as with schizophrenia deserves investigation" (p. 255). A concern with this question was the motivating force behind the next British study of EE.

6

Expressed Emotion in Families of Patients Suffering from Schizophrenia and from Depressive Neurosis

EXTENSION OF THE FINDINGS TO DEPRESSION:
THE 1976 STUDY

The next study to be completed (Vaughn & Leff, 1976a) was both a replication and an extension of the work reviewed in Chapter 5. We were unconnected with the earlier studies, and we undertook the replication in a critical frame of mind. The extension was devised to determine whether the family factors identified as predictive of the course of schizophrenia were in any way specific for this condition. A sample of depressed neurotic inpatients was chosen for comparison purposes. Inpatients were selected so that relatives of both diagnostic groups would be reacting to the same experience of having a family member admitted to a psychiatric hospital. The sample of depressives was confined to those without delusions or hallucinations, in order to ensure that there was no diagnostic overlap with the sample of patients diagnosed as suffering from schizophrenia.

The techniques of behavioral, psychiatric, and family assessment were identical to those used in the earlier study (Brown *et al.*, 1972), with one exception: The abbreviated version of the CFI was employed. The reason for this modification and the way in which it was achieved are fully covered in Chapter 2.

The patients who formed the study population were collected from admissions to three jointly administered hospitals in southeast London. The case records were screened to include those aged 17 to 64 whose native language was English and who were living with relatives at the time of admission. Any person with a suspected organic brain condition was excluded. All patients whose records suggested a diagnosis of either schizophrenia or neurotic depression were interviewed with the PSE. The data generated were processed by the Catego program, and if the diagnosis was confirmed, the patient was included in the study.

Using these criteria, we initially selected 43 schizophrenic patients and 32 depressed neurotic patients. However, the relatives of five schizophrenics and one depressed patient refused to participate. One depressed patient died of physical causes during the follow-up period, while one schizophrenic patient left home shortly after discharge from the hospital. The remaining 37 schizophrenic and 30 depressed patients comprised the final follow-up groups, and represented 86% and 94% of the original sample, respectively.

The schizophrenic sample was heterogeneous with respect to their living groups: 17 came from parental homes, 13 came from marital homes, and 7 were residing with other kin. By contrast, the depressed patients were almost exclusively from marital homes: 28 out of the 30 lived with their spouses. This difference reflects the low marriage rate of schizophrenic patients and is not related to patients' ages since the mean ages of the schizophrenic (33.1) and depressive (38.6) samples did not differ significantly. The disparity in living groups between the two samples placed barriers in the way of making certain comparisons, as we indicate later.

As in the earlier study, the husband or wife of a married patient was always seen for an assessment of EE. In cases where a single patient lived with both parents, the mother and father were interviewed on separate occasions. The interview with the relative alone at the time of the key admission was considered to be definitive for predicting relapse, since this was the finding of the earlier study. Family interviews were not repeated at follow-up or readmission, nor were they given to the patient alone. For similar reasons, the joint interviews with patients and relatives were omitted.

All but 2 of the 67 patients who formed the follow-up sample were personally reinterviewed by Leff. The two exceptions, both of whom had moved out of the area, were reassessed through hospital case records and personal correspondence. The psychiatrist had no knowledge of the EE status of the relatives until all the follow-up interviews were completed. In addition to repeating the PSE at follow-up or at the time of a possible relapse, the psychiatrist took a detailed history of drug treatment during the months since discharge, checking with outpatient records where possible. Strict criteria for compliance with drug regimens were set up: If drugs were discontinued or taken irregularly for more than 1 month of the 9-month follow-up period, a person was considered to be off regular medication. This assessment depended entirely on patients' verbal reports, but Leff and Wing (1971) have shown that these are reasonably accurate as long as the relevant questions are asked sympathetically.

As in the Brown *et al.* (1972) study, relapse of schizophrenia was classified as follows: Type I was the reappearance of schizophrenic symptoms in a patient free of them at discharge, and Type II was the marked exacerbation of persistent schizophrenic symptoms. Relapse of depression was more difficult to determine. In every case assessed as suffering a relapse, there had been a period of freedom from depressive symptoms between discharge and follow-up. Thus these relapses were analogous to Type I relapses in schizophrenia. Of the 16 patients who were judged to have relapsed, 14 had significant symptoms of depression as rated on the PSE at the time of follow-up. The other 2 patients were well at the 9-month follow-up, but reported an episode of depression persisting for 2 weeks or more between discharge and the final month covered by the PSE.

We abbreviated the CFI on the grounds that the majority of critical comments were made in the first hour (see Chapter 2). We were therefore concerned to know whether, by modifying it in this way, we had lost any of the power of the interview to elicit EE. In fact, the mean Critical Comments score for the relatives of schizophrenics in our study, 8.2, did not differ significantly from the corresponding figure for the Brown *et al.* (1972) study, 7.9. Hence our anxieties on this point were allayed. The next step was to compare parents with spouses, and we found that they produced means of 7.0 and 11.9, respectively (a nonsignificant difference). It should be noted that since spouses are not genetically related to the patients, this observation rules out the possibility that critical attitudes of relatives are an expression of an inherited liability to schizophrenia.

Having established that spouses of schizophrenics were at least as critical as parents, we could go on to compare them with the relatives of depressed neurotic patients, who were almost exclusively spouses. The average Critical Comments score for this group was 7.2, indicating that they were just as critical as the relatives of schizophrenic patients. Thus critical attitudes in relatives are certainly not specific to the families of schizophrenics.

What about the other components of the EE index? Hostility was expressed by a minority of relatives of both diagnostic groups, but in no case was it found in the absence of a high degree of criticism; therefore, it was not useful in assigning relatives to high- or low-EE categories. In the Brown *et al.* (1972) study, hostility was found in the absence of excessive criticism or overinvolvement in 4% of relatives. In our own study (Vaughn & Leff, 1976a), this negligible role had shrunk to nothing.

Emotional overinvolvement was considered to be present if a relative scored 4 or 5 on the appropriate scale. No spouse of a schizophrenic patient in our study scored this high. However, one spouse of a depressed patient scored 5 on the scale, showing that overinvolvement could develop in spouses, even though it was rare. This observation was confirmed in subsequent studies, in which we encountered the occasional spouse of a schizophrenic who showed overinvolvement.

Among the parents of our schizophrenic patients, 6 (24%) of the 25 exhibited overinvolvement. Of these 6, 5 were mothers; this suggests that overinvolvement tends to develop within the mothering role, although not exclusively. One of the components of overinvolvement is overprotectiveness, which can be seen as a normal mothering function protracted into a period of the child's life when it is no longer appropriate. Mothering is usually provided by mothers, but can of course be taken over, at least partially, by fathers. Several of the early theorists concerned with the etiology of schizophrenia postulated a crucial role for mothers. T. Lidz (1967) suggested that in the families of schizophrenics, mothers have pathologically intense relationships with their sons, while fathers develop these relationships with their daughters. In our small sample we found no evidence for this, since the schizophrenic offspring of the five overinvolved mothers comprised three sons and two daughters.

As stated above, hostility was found to be unnecessary in assigning relatives of schizophrenics to high- or low-EE groups. The main basis for this assignment was the number of critical comments expressed. Initially we used a Critical Comments score of 7 or more as the criterion of high EE, as in the Brown *et al.* (1972) study. Relatives who were not this high on Critical Comments but who scored 4 or 5 on Emotional Overinvolvement were also categorized as high in EE. Of the 37 relatives of schizophrenics, 18 – that is, just under half – were included in the high-EE group. In the 9 months following discharge, exactly half the patients returning to high-EE homes relapsed, compared with only 12% of those living with low-EE relatives, a significant difference (*p* < .02). These figures are remarkably close to those in the Brown *et al.* (1972) study, as can be seen from Table 6.1, in which the findings from the first three naturalistic studies are compared.

Thus we successfully replicated the main finding of the study on which ours was most closely modeled. Although we used the same criteria to distinguish high- from low-EE relatives that were established in the 1972 study, we were concerned at the arbitrary nature of the cutoff points on each scale. Consequently, for the Critical Comments scale, we experimented with different cutoff points in an attempt to maximize the difference in relapse rates between high-EE and low-EE groups. We found that the best separation was achieved with a cutoff score of 6 on Critical Comments rather than 7. Using

Table 6.1. Emotional Attitudes of Relatives and Relapse of Schizophrenia in Three British Studies

	Relapse Rate (%)	
Study	High Involvement or EE[a]	Low Involvement or EE[a]
Brown, Monck, Carstairs, & Wing (1962)	76**	28**
Brown, Birley, & Wing (1972)	58**	16**
Vaughn & Leff (1976a)	50*	12*

[a]"Involvement" for Brown *et al.* (1962); "EE" for the later studies.
*p < .02.
**p < .001.

this lower criterion, the relapse rates for high- and low-EE groups were 48%
and 6%, respectively, a difference of considerable significance (exact $p =$
.007). The same procedure could not be applied to the Emotional Overinvolvement scores, as the number of relatives concerned was too small. However,
as our experience with this measure increased in subsequent studies, we
became convinced that relatives scoring 3 on Emotional Overinvolvement
should be classified as high in EE.

Having replicated the association between relatives' EE and schizophrenic
relapse, we next examined the other factors that had been identified as important in the earlier studies. As in the Brown *et al.* (1972) study, the amount
of face-to-face contact influenced the relationship between relatives' EE and
relapse. It was only when the patients were in high face-to-face contact with
relatives that the relapse rate in high-EE homes was significantly higher than
in low-EE homes. Patients in low contact with high-EE relatives had a relapse
rate that did not differ from that of patients in low-EE homes. These data
are presented in Table 6.2.

As in the 1972 study, we examined the role of prophylactic medication.
Of the 37 schizophrenic patients, 21 complied with a regular drug regimen,
according to our strict criterion. As can be seen from Table 6.3, maintenance
on neuroleptic drugs conferred a significant advantage on patients who took
them regularly ($p = .023$). However, this advantage is entirely explained by
the protective effect of drugs on patients living with high-EE relatives. For
those in low-EE homes, the relapse rate was very low, whether they took medication or not.

The implication of this finding would be that schizophrenic patients living
in low-EE homes were not in need of maintenance on drugs, at least in the
short term. This would have an exceedingly important effect on management
if implemented, since half the patients in our sample lived with low-EE
relatives. However, we were hesitant about the validity of this conclusion,
since a 9-month follow-up is a relatively short period of time over which to
observe the course of schizophrenia. Consequently, we mounted a 2-year
follow-up of the patients in our sample, which we present in detail later (Leff
& Vaughn, 1981). However, we interpolate one finding at this point, because
of its relevance to the issue of maintenance drug therapy.

Of the 26 patients who remained well at the 9-month follow-up, 25 were
successfully followed up 2 years after discharge. Of these, 15 were living in
low-EE homes; 9 of these were on regular medication, and 6 were on no drugs
according to our criterion. None of the 9 patients on prophylactic medication relapsed over the 2 years, whereas half of those off drugs experienced
a return of schizophrenic symptoms. Although the numbers concerned are
small, this difference in relapse rates is significant ($p = .044$). This finding suggests that maintenance on neuroleptic drugs does exert a significant prophylactic effect on patients in low-EE homes, but that it requires a longer period

Table 6.2. Relatives' EE, Face-to-Face Contact, and Relapse of Schizophrenia

	Relapse Rate (%)	
Amount of Face-to-Face Contact	High EE	Low EE
Less than 35 hours per week	29	14
More than 35 hours per week	57*	0*

*$p = .006$.

of follow-up to demonstrate this than in the case of patients in high-EE homes. The probable reason for this is that prophylactic medication protects patients in low-EE homes from the impact of independent life events, and that it takes a relatively long time for this effect to become apparent because of the infrequency of such events. The data on which this suggestion is based are presented in detail in Chapter 12.

It is necessary to question why a clear advantage for prophylactic medication emerged from our study, but not from the Brown *et al.* (1972) study. The explanation may lie in the strict criterion we applied to compliance with a prescribed regimen. Another factor may be that by the time we mounted our study, maintenance drugs were being used more selectively for the particular patients who were more likely to benefit from them.

Having found that prophylactic drugs and low face-to-face contact each appeared to confer protection against the pathogenic effect of high-EE relatives, we were intrigued as to whether these factors might be additive. Our own sample was too small to allow us to perform the necessary analysis, but because our design and method were so similar to the 1972 study, we felt that it was justifiable to pool the two sets of data. We did this, and we analyzed the material as shown in Figure 6.1.

Table 6.3. Relatives' EE, Use of Maintenance Drugs, and Relapse of Schizophrenia

Relatives' EE	No Regular Use of Drugs			Regular Use of Drugs		
	No Relapse	Relapse	% Relapse	No Relapse	Relapse	% Relapse
High	2	7	78*	9	3	25*
Low	6	1	14	9	0	0
Total	8	8	50**	18	3	14**

*$p = .024$.
**$p = .023$.

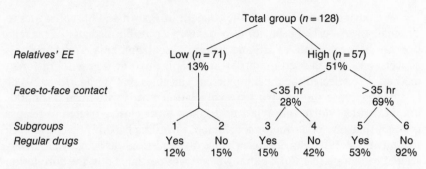

Figure 6.1. Nine-month relapse rates of schizophrenic patients from the Brown, Birley, and Wing (1972) and Vaughn and Leff (1976a) studies.

The relapse rates of the six subgroups depicted in Figure 6.1 provide information about the possible additive effects of the two protective factors (low face-to-face contact and regular maintenance on drugs). Subgroup 6 consisted of patients living in high-EE homes who had neither protective factor operating. They had a very poor outcome: Virtually every member of this subgroup relapsed in the course of 9 months. Patients in Subgroup 3 also lived in high-EE homes, but had both protective factors present. Their outcome was substantially and significantly ($p < .001$) better than that of Subgroup 6; in fact, it was no worse than that of patients in low-EE homes (Subgroups 1 and 2). High-EE patients with one protective factor operating, be it low face-to-face contact (Subgroup 4) or maintenance on drugs (Subgroup 5), had a relapse rate intermediate between the two extremes. These findings suggest that either low face-to-face contact or regular maintenance on drugs gives a measure of protection against the dangers of living in a high-EE home. When they occur together, there is an additive effect, and virtually complete protection is achieved. There is a snag in this interpretation, and that is that patients may select themselves for the various subgroups; that is, they could play a major part in determining their intensity of contact with relatives and their degree of compliance with drug regimens. This issue is explored further in Chapter 9.

It is worth noting that patients in Subgroup 5, who were all regularly taking neuroleptic drugs, nevertheless had a high relapse rate, 53%. This is consonant with the finding from trials of maintenance with neuroleptic drugs that even when schizophrenic patients are known to be taking their medication, there is still a substantial relapse rate (Hogarty *et al.*, 1974; Johnson, 1976; Leff & Wing, 1971). It suggests that the stress incurred in a high-EE home can break through the protective barrier afforded by neuroleptic drugs (see Chapter 12).

We have already discussed the concern of Brown and his colleagues to eliminate the disturbed behavior of patients as a possible mediator of the relationship between relatives' EE and relapse of schizophrenia. We shared this concern and also tackled the problem statistically, but we used a different method. We selected the most important variables that we had found to be related to relapse and constructed a correlation matrix with them. From this matrix, it was evident that relatives' EE was more closely related to relapse ($r = .45$) than any other factor considered, including lack of preventive drug treatment ($r = .39$). Behavior disturbance on admission was actually negatively related to relapse ($r = .20$), so that when it was partialed out, the correlation between EE and relapse actually increased ($r = .52$). This is conclusive evidence that for schizophrenic patients the relationship between relatives' EE and relapse holds good, independently of behavior disturbances.

The findings set out above led us to conclude that we had replicated almost exactly the main results of the Brown *et al.* (1972) study. The only divergence was that we demonstrated a stronger protective effect for maintenance on neuroleptic drugs. Having verified the attainment of one of our two principal aims, we then turned to the other: to investigate the specificity of these findings for schizophrenia. This, of course, led us to a consideration of the data for the depressed neurotic patients.

As we have already recounted, the relatives of the depressed patients were just as critical as those of the schizophrenic patients. The main difference between the two groups of relatives in respect to EE was the virtual absence of overinvolvement among the depressive sample, and this was probably due to the scarcity of parents. The next task was to examine the relationship between relatives' criticism and relapse of depression. We first used the cutoff score of 7 on the Critical Comments scale, but this did not discriminate the patients who did well from those who did badly. The relapse rates in the high- and low-EE groups were 60% and 50% respectively. Since this was unknown territory and there was no reason to expect that the same relationships would hold for the depressive as for the schizophrenic patients, we felt it was justifiable to experiment with different cutoff points. Further analyses revealed that a much lower cutoff score of 2 on Critical Comments gave the best separation in terms of relapse rates, as shown in Table 6.4.

The other two components of EE, hostility and overinvolvement, did not add to the ability of critical comments to distinguish between good and poor outcome of depression. However, we must be cautious in generalizing from this observation, as only a single relative of a depressed patient exhibited overinvolvement. It was decided to call the assessment of relatives' emotional attitudes for this group a "criticism index," in order to distinguish it from the differently constituted EE index used for the relatives of schizophrenic patients. It appears from our data that depressed neurotic patients are even more

Table 6.4. Relatives' Critical Comments and Relapse of Depression

Relatives' Critical Comments Scores	No Relapse	Relapse	% Relapse
2+	7	14	67*
0–1	7	2	22*

*$p = .032$.

vulnerable to the effects of relatives' criticism than are the schizophrenic patients. Almost any degree of criticism expressed by a relative was linked with a high relapse rate of depression.

We questioned whether this relationship was mediated by the patients' disturbed behavior, and found that disturbed behavior bore a negligible relationship to relapse. We constructed a correlation matrix in the same way as we had done with the schizophrenic material, and found that when behavior disturbance was partialed out, there was still a significant correlation between criticism and relapse.

We examined the two factors that had been identified as protecting schizophrenic patients from relapse—face-to-face contact and prophylactic medication. However, only 6 of the 30 depressed patients were on preventive medication at follow-up; this number was too small to make an analysis worthwhile. We found that the amount of face-to-face contact between patients and relatives did not relate to relapse patterns. However, this feature was associated with the relatives' criticism index. Depressed patients whose relatives made two or more critical remarks had significantly less contact with family members than did patients whose relatives were uncritical ($p = .024$).

We cannot comment on the role of prophylactic medication in high-criticism households of depressive patients, but we can assert that face-to-face contact plays quite a different role in depression from the role it plays in schizophrenia. Whereas low face-to-face contact appears to protect schizophrenic patients in high-EE homes, it has no such function for depressives. Instead, there is an association between low face-to-face contact and critical relatives that has no bearing on relapse. We interpret this as an indication of a poor relationship between a patient and a relative that predates the illness. We consider it likely that low contact and high criticism are both indicators of a poor marriage (virtually all these relatives were spouses) and that the poor quality of the marriage predicts relapse of depression (see Chapter 4).

This conclusion echoes the findings of Brown and Harris (1978), who identified one of the vulnerability factors rendering women susceptible to depression as lack of an intimate relationship, usually with a sexual partner. We believe that our measure of criticism in spouses is tapping another aspect of nonconfiding relationships. It remains to be demonstrated that an unsatisfactory marital relationship is indeed a *causal* factor in depression.

We have shown that relatives of depressed neurotic patients can be just as critical as relatives of schizophrenic patients are, and that there is a significant link between relatives' criticism and relapse of depression. This strongly suggests that psychiatric patients other than schizophrenics are affected by the quality of their emotional relationships with key relatives. However, depressed patients appear to be even more sensitive to criticism than schizophrenic patients. Also, the protective factors that are so important for outcome of schizophrenic patients living with high-EE relatives do not relate to relapse patterns in depressive neurosis.

PREMORBID PERSONALITY, RELATIVES' RESPONSE, AND RELAPSE: THE ISSUE OF VULNERABILITY

The content analysis of critical comments made in the 1976 study (see Chapter 4) revealed an association between a patient's previous personality and a relative's emotional response, suggesting that in at least a proportion of cases the relatives were responding to abnormality in the patients. When relatives were highly critical, the data show that they were reacting to features in the patients that antedated the initial illness episode; the majority of critical remarks concerned long-standing personality traits rather than illness-related behaviors. It would seem that a two-way process is involved. Not only do certain environments put the endangered personality at risk, but, in Manfred Bleuler's words, "discordances of personality elicit discordances of the human environment" (Bleuler, 1968).

Brown *et al.* (1972) established that the response of a relative to a patient is specific, not general. In cases where there is, for example, a poor premorbid personality, the relative's reaction to the patient may be entirely understandable. How can one be sure that the link between relative's EE and patients' symptomatic relapse is not due to another intervening variable thought to be associated with a poor prognosis, such as a poor premorbid personality?

The results of the studies reported in Part II of this volume are notable for their clarification of the ways in which different variables interact to influence the outcome of any given patient. The literature on schizophrenia suggests that clinical variables and aspects of a patient's psychiatric history are not linked in any obvious way to the course of an individual patient's illness. The EE results suggest why this is so for patients living with relatives. Patients showing few of the clinical signs associated with a poor prognosis are likely to remain well, whether they return to a high-EE or low-EE home. This finding is consistent with findings of other studies, in which such criteria as an acute onset are associated with a good prognosis or remission in schizophrenia, and it helps to explain the low rates of relapse for married patients in the 1972 and 1976 studies. Among schizophrenic patients, many researchers have found significant links among likelihood of marriage, being of a normal temperament (Ødegaard, 1946, 1953; Stevens, 1969), and functioning at a higher level of work and social performance (Brown, Bone, Dalison, & Wing, 1966; Creer & Wing, 1974; Freeman & Simmons, 1963). Evidence from the analyses described in Chapter 4 supports the view that schizophrenic patients who are married are likely to be characterized by good premorbid personalities. Patients living with spouses rated low on EE tended to have close, mutually supportive marital relationships when well; in their patterns of communication, they seemed no different from persons in a "normal" population. Even those married patients involved in difficult, conflictual relationships at least had demonstrated an ability to sustain some kind of relationship for a prolonged period of time.

Our data suggest that where the clinical indicators are unfavorable, however, the quality of the postdischarge environment is highly important for a patient's clinical outcome. Thus an emotionally more neutral setting, such as a low-EE home, exerts the greatest protective influence on those patients who are constitutionally the most vulnerable. Over a 9-month followup period, patients with poor premorbid personalities who return to low-EE relatives almost always stay well; those who return to high-EE relatives usually relapse. The particular vulnerability of unmarried schizophrenic men once again has been highlighted by the analysis of differential patterns of parental response. Although schizophrenic sons and daughters are equally likely to be found in high-EE homes, the sons are significantly more likely than the daughters to return to homes featuring parental conflict ($p < .05$), according to three different EE studies. At the same time, schizophrenic sons are less likely than schizophrenic daughters to be protected by the combined effects of maintenance with neuroleptic drugs and reduced contact with relatives, both of which can modify the effects of an excessively stimulating environment. These findings explain, at least in part, their greater chances of developing a chronic or relapsing condition after an initial attack of schizophrenia.

Few depressed patients described as chronically insecure or lacking in self-confidence were living with supportive or sympathetic spouses. However, where this *was* the case, the patients were well at follow-up. Thus in both clinical groups, it was the most vulnerable patients — those with poor premorbid personalities or other characteristics traditionally associated with a poor outcome — who derived most benefit from a benign home environment.

RESULTS OF THE 2-YEAR FOLLOW-UP OF SCHIZOPHRENIC PATIENTS

A 9-month follow-up period was originally chosen for our replication, as this was the time span built into the earlier studies of Brown and his colleagues. However, we considered it necessary to take a longer view of outcome, and hence we followed up the schizophrenic patients in our study for a total of 2 years (Leff & Vaughn, 1981). An attempt was made to trace all patients who had not experienced a relapse by the 9-month follow-up. There were 26 of these out of the original cohort of 37, and information was sought on whether the patients had subsequently suffered a relapse of schizophrenia and whether they had taken regular neuroleptic medication. Both of these were defined as in the 9-month follow-up. Of the 25 patients successfully followed up 2 years after discharge, 11 lived with relatives originally assessed as high-EE, and 14 lived with low-EE relatives. The data on prophylactic medication have already been presented (pp. 89–90).

Over the 2-year period following discharge, 3 (20%) of the 15 low-EE patients had relapsed, compared with 8 (62%) of the 21 high-EE patients, a highly significant difference ($p = .015$). It was evident that patients from low-EE homes continued to relapse at a low rate over the whole 2-year period. The relapse rate of high-EE patients slowed down considerably after the first 9 months, but was still almost double that for the low-EE group over the remainder of the follow-up period.

This result indicates that the association between relatives' EE and relapse persists over a considerable period of time. It supports our assumption that the relatives' attitudes toward the patients as elicited by the CFI are representative of enduring relationships over time.

7

Relatives' Expressed Emotion and Schizophrenia: The Los Angeles Replication

RATIONALE FOR AND DESCRIPTION OF THE REPLICATION

The consistent and unequivocal results of the British EE studies reported in Chapters 5 and 6 have clear implications for the management and rehabilitation of schizophrenic patients. The progressive refinement of research methods and verification of results by repeated studies over long periods are impressive, strengthening the case for the results obtained. Yet all of the early EE studies relied on patient samples from a small corner of southeast England; the issue of the cultural specificity of EE remained open. It seemed conceivable that cultural or ethnic variations in the amount and impact of EE might result in different baseline levels for families of non-British background; a particular relationship between EE and symptomatic relapse could not be assumed. Until the cross-cultural relevance of the concept had been established, clinicians might be understandably reluctant to initiate EE-based intervention programs. This was the rationale for the first international replication of the British research, a study that began in Los Angeles in 1977.

The primary aim of the California study was to replicate the studies of Brown *et al.* (1972) and Vaughn and Leff (1976a), concerning the influence of family and social factors on the course of schizophrenia, with a sample of California patients. The standardized interviewing techniques developed in London were used. A similar prospective 9-month follow-up design featured independent assessments of past behavior, present emotional response of relatives, and subsequent relapse or no relapse. While the cross-sectional nature of the study precluded the testing of etiological hypotheses, the California investigators did expect to find an association between a high degree of EE in the relative(s) and a florid relapse of symptoms, independent of other factors such as length of history, type of symptom, or severity of illness at admission.

The participation of the psychologist from the 1976 EE study (Christine Vaughn) and of two British-trained psychiatrists (Ian Falloon and Simon Jones) provided research continuity and helped to ensure the comparability of the social and psychiatric assessments in the two cultures. All efforts were made to replicate accurately the procedures followed in the original British studies. Nevertheless, several modifications of methods and procedures were required over the course of the study because of unanticipated differences between the London and Los Angeles centers. These included differences in the patient populations, in the research settings, in the duration of hospitalization, and in systems of aftercare. The more important modifications are noted in the course of this account of the Los Angeles study; the study is described more fully elsewhere (Vaughn, Snyder, Freeman, Jones, Fallon, & Liberman, in press).

The majority of the patients who participated in the study were drawn from the acute admission units of Camarillo State Hospital; the remaining patients were identified sequentially in a similar way by regular screening procedures at three other inpatient facilities. Sampling criteria specified that patients should be between 17 and 50 years of age; should have been hospitalized within 1 month prior to the initial interview; should be Caucasian in ethnic origin; and should meet the specific diagnostic criteria for schizophrenia as defined in the PSE. The British criteria for inclusion were modified in two respects only. First, the preadmission residency requirements were lowered from 3 months of continuous residency with relatives to 1 month out of the preceding 3 months. A pattern among some unmarried California patients was to return to the family home at intervals after short periods of living on their own or in supervised board and care facilities. Rather than exclude such patients from the study for failing to meet the strict residency requirements of the British studies, the preadmission criteria were altered. Second, street drug abuse did not serve as grounds for immediate exclusion from the study. Because of the large numbers of California patients concerned, cases were excluded only where a primary diagnosis of schizophrenia was in doubt because of recent drug abuse by the patient.

A total of 69 patients who met the criteria described above were selected for participation in the California study. According to the Catego classification system, the majority of the patients (65) were classified as having "schizophrenic psychoses," Class S; the other 4 patients were classed as having "paranoid psychoses," Class P. In addition to the PSE (administered within 2 weeks of admission), eligible patients were assessed with the Psychiatric Assessment Scale (PAS) (Krawiecka, Goldberg, & Vaughn, 1977) and a Psychiatric and Social History Questionnaire. The current mental status interviews (PSE and PAS) were repeated at hospital discharge, except in those rare instances where a patient left the hospital within 1 week of admission. The psychiatric assessors carried out reliability checks at regular intervals during the screening process and throughout the study by co-rating videotaped interviews.

Within days of a patient's initial psychiatric assessment, and after the signing of consent forms, the abbreviated version of the CFI was administered to the key relative(s) exactly as in the study conducted by Vaughn and Leff (see Chapter 6). The interview itself is described at length in Chapter 2. The American interviewers were trained over several months in the use of the CFI and the EE rating scales, using audiotaped interviews from the British studies. High levels of interrater reliability with the original ratings were achieved (minimum Pearson $r = .80$). As with the psychiatric assessments, randomly selected family interviews were co-rated throughout the study to ensure that standards of reliability remained acceptable.

As in the British studies, the spouse of a married patient was always seen. In cases where an unmarried patient lived with both parents, an attempt was made to interview the mother and the father on separate occasions. This proved possible for 36 of the 41 intact two-parent families in the study. In the remaining 5 families, only one parent was seen (in each case, the parent interviewed was high on EE). Ratings of emotional response were made on all the scales employed in the Vaughn and Leff study, with emphasis on the three that formed the components of the overall index of relatives' EE in the British research: Critical Comments, Hostility, and Emotional Overinvolvement (see Chapter 3). As in the earlier studies, the higher of two sets of parental EE scores was used to determine the family's placement in either the high-EE or the low-EE subgroup.

MODIFICATIONS OF PROCEDURES AND CRITERIA

Because the British follow-up procedures and relapse criteria had to be modified in certain important aspects for the California study, we describe them here in some detail. A pilot study revealed a number of system-related differences: For example, California patients were less likely than British patients to be discharged symptom-free or to receive regular aftercare. In view of these differences, it was thought necessary to monitor patients more closely after discharge, and to both extend and tighten the British relapse criteria.

As in the British studies, all patients were followed regularly for a period of 9 months after discharge from the hospital, or for a shorter period if an unequivocal relapse occurred. The progress of each patient was monitored after discharge by the research secretary, who made monthly telephone calls to a key relative. The detailed list of specific information obtained at each call was shared with Dr. Simon Jones. He used both this information and information provided in his own subsequent phone calls to the family to determine whether a change in clinical status seemed likely. He visited the patient and carried out a follow-up evaluation in the following circumstances:

1. When the patient had been readmitted to a psychiatric facility, due to an increase in psychiatric symptoms.

2. When the relative reported a significant worsening of schizophrenic symptoms of at least 1 week's duration.

3. When acting-out behavior or publicly expressed delusions or hallucinations resulted in a significant social disturbance or family crisis (e.g., contact with police).

4. When worsening of symptoms resulted in an unscheduled emergency visit to a mental health clinic, psychiatrist, or physician.

5. When such deterioration had occurred in the level of the patient's functioning that either the patient moved to a more supportive environment (e.g., from own apartment to a parents' home) or friends or relatives felt that they had to increase significantly the level of support they provided for the patient.

6. When symptoms increased to the point at which a significant increase in the patient's medication was required.

The follow-up evaluation included the administration of the PSE interview; completion of the PAS; a detailed recording of medication prescribed to the patient and adherence to the advice for the follow-up period; and an estimate of the hours spent by the patient with family members per week, using questions from the Time Budget section of the CFI. Details concerning medication and patterns of contact were checked with the key relative(s). If the patient was judged by the psychiatrist to have relapsed, there were no further follow-up assessments. Patients judged not to have relapsed, and all other patients, were reassessed 9 months after discharge from the hospital.

Attempts to group patients into the British categories of "relapse" and "no relapse" initially proved problematic. As described in earlier chapters, the British investigators distinguished between two types of "relapse." Type I involved a change from a "normal" or nonschizophrenic state to a state of schizophrenia (as defined by Catego), while Type II featured a marked exacerbation of persistent schizophrenic symptoms. In the California study, it was fairly easy to determine whether a Type I relapse had occurred in a patient who was discharged from the hospital symptom-free. It was more difficult, however, to make a determination of a Type II relapse for the large number of patients who had experienced schizophrenic symptoms (such as hallucinations) at the time of their discharge and throughout the follow-up period.

The approach adopted to assess relapse was a further refinement of the British clinical relapse criteria. Judgments of whether a patient's symptoms were significantly worse were made by comparing the PAS data on the severity of characteristic schizophrenic symptoms: namely, (1) hallucinations, (2) delusions, and (3) incoherent speech. Unlike the PSE, the PAS was designed primarily to reflect changes in severity of schizophrenic symptoms. The three symptoms are each rated independently on a scale of 0–4, with each scale point operationally defined. (In the California study, minimum interrater reliability of .85 was consistently achieved.) Threshold criteria for point increases on these three scales of the PAS were set as a means of defining "relapse" in patients whose symptoms had worsened at follow-up. The PAS and PSE ratings, together with clinical data obtained over the postdischarge follow-up period, were then used to develop six categories of outcome. Expressed in terms of the exacerbation–relapse/improvement–remission continua, the six categories of outcome were as follows:

Status at Discharge	*Status at Follow-Up*
A. Remission	Relapse
B. Persisting symptoms	Exacerbation
C. Remission	Remission
D. Persisting symptoms	Improved
E. Persisting symptoms	Remission
F. High persisting symptoms	Unchanged high persisting symptoms

The categories of outcome above were sorted further into the three categories that follow: exacerbation–relapse (A, B), "relapse"; improvement–remission (C, D, E), "no relapse"; and unchanged (F) "not rateable." Final decisions on types of outcome were made blindly by two psychiatrists who had not administered the mental status exams. The interrater agreement on defining a case in the "no relapse," "relapse," and "not rateable" categories was 92%. As in the British studies, assessors were unaware of the relative's EE at the time of a patient's reassessment.

RESULTS

Before presenting the main results of the California study, it is necessary to say a few words about the characteristics of the patients themselves. In a number of respects, the California sample of 69 differed markedly from the more balanced samples in the two British studies. For example, nearly three-quarters (72%) of the Los Angeles patients were young unmarried males; the corresponding British proportion (combined $n = 138$) was only 29%. Nine in every 10 of the Los Angeles patients were living in parental households at the time of key admission; the British samples were more heterogenous with respect to their living groups. Various clinical indicators also suggested that the California patients were psychiatrically a more chronic group, compared with their British counterparts. Thus they were less likely to be first admission patients (17% vs. 54%) and, despite their relative youth (mean age = 25.6 years), more likely to have had three or more previous admissions (55% vs. 16%). They showed significantly more work impairment and behavioral disturbance in the months preceding admission, according to various indices of social and clinical functioning.

In view of the greater "chronicity" of the California sample, perhaps it is not surprising that these patients were significantly more likely than the British patients to have a poor clinical outcome at the 9-month follow up. As indicated in Table 7.1, only 43% of the 69 patients had "no relapse" status at follow-up; the corresponding proportion in the two British studies was 66% ($x^2 = 10.22$, $p < .001$). The 15 patients in Group F (22% of the total sample) were particularly notable for their high persisting symptoms both at discharge and follow-up, a pattern that did not appear in the British studies. The relationship between clinical condition at discharge and at follow-up was not significant. Neither was there a significant relationship between rehospitalization and symptomatic relapse: 46% of the 24 "relapsed" patients and 37% of the 30 patients in the "no relapse" group were readmitted to the hospital in the course of follow-up. None of the patients in the latter group had suffered a recurrence or exacerbation of schizophrenic symptoms. They were readmitted for other reasons, such as treatment of depression, management of social disturbance, and relief of family burden.

What about relatives' emotional responses? The most striking of the several differences between the Los Angeles and London subjects concerned the patterning of relatives' EE in the two cultures. In the British studies, a bare majority (52%) of the families assessed were rated low on EE; that is, the key relatives made five or fewer critical comments, scored 3 or lower on the 6-point Emotional Overinvolvement scale, and showed no evidence of hostility toward the patients at interview. In the California study, only one-third of the families were rated low on EE when the same criteria were applied (23 of 69; $x^2 = 6.58$, $p < .02$). As shown in the histogram in Chapter 11 (p. 179), the distribution of criticism across the two cultures was quite different. London relatives were significantly more likely (32% vs. 4%) to make no critical comments at all when talking about patients. But the mean Critical Comments scores were similar (7.50 for London vs. 6.86 for Los Angeles;

Table 7.1. Outcome at 9-Month Follow-Up of 69 Schizophrenic Patients

Outcome Group	Discharge Status	Follow-Up Status	n	Outcome Category	Percentage of Total n
A.	Remission	Relapse	17	Relapse	35%
B.	Persisting symptoms	Exacerbation	7		
C.	Remission	Remission	17		
D.	Persisting symptoms	Improved	6	No relapse	43%
E.	Persisting symptoms	Remission	7		
F.	High persisting symptoms	High persisting symptoms	15	Unchanged	22%

n.s.), because the London relatives were more extreme in their patterns of response. Ratings of hostility were significantly more common for the California relatives (28% vs. 18%; $p < .05$). In contrast, there were no cross-cultural differences in the distribution of emotional overinvolvement. Instances of extreme self-sacrifice, overprotectiveness, or overconcern occurred infrequently in both cultures: Only 21% of British parents and 15% of California parents were considered to be markedly overinvolved (i.e., scored 4 or 5 on the 6-point scale). A further 12% and 15%, respectively, scored 3 (moderately high) on the scale. However, in both London and Los Angeles, mothers scored significantly higher on the scale than did fathers (London, $\chi^2 = 8.10$, $p < .002$; Los Angeles, $\chi^2 = 10.42$, $p < .001$).

In devising an overall index of relatives' EE, the best separation in terms of relapse rates was obtained using the same cutoff points employed in the 1976 British schizophrenia study (Vaughn & Leff, 1976a) to allocate families to a high-EE subgroup: a score of 6 on Critical Comments, or Emotional Overinvolvement scores of 4 or 5. Using these thresholds, the clinical outcome data were analyzed in a variety of ways, all of which produced similar results.

The California investigators first considered the relationship between the index of relatives' EE and symptomatic relapse by replicating the main analyses of the British studies. The 15 "unchanged" patients with high persisting symptoms were excluded from these analyses. Relapse figures for the remaining 54 schizophrenic patients from high-EE and low-EE homes are summarized in Table 7.2 (top portion). This group included 11 patients who lived both at home and in board and care facilities during follow-up, and 7 patients who did not live at home at all (although all were in regular contact with relatives). If one restricts the analysis to the core replication group of 36 who, like the British patients, lived at home continuously after discharge, the relapse figures are as given in the bottom portion of Table 7.2. For both groups there is a significant association between high EE and relapse ($n = 54$, $p = .015$; $n = 36$, $p = .009$). The proportions of patients relapsing in the high-EE and low-EE groups in both analyses are remarkably similar to the equivalent figures for the 1972 and 1976 British EE studies (compared in Table 6.1). As one might predict, the association between relatives' EE and relapse is strongest among patients who remained at home for all of the follow-up period. The data for patients who lived away for at least part of this time suggest that high-EE patients are more likely to remain well if they are not at home continuously, while the reverse is true for patients from low-EE homes. The relapse rates for the 11 high-EE and 7 low-EE patients in this subgroup were 45% and 29%, respectively (not a significant difference).

A second set of analyses, not carried out in the British studies, examined the varying strengths of the associations between different indicators of EE (including raw EE scores) and different measures of clinical outcome for the

Table 7.2. Relationship of Relatives' EE to Relapse in the 9 Months after Discharge

EE of Relatives	No Relapse	Relapse	Relapse %
Total Sample (*n* = 54)			
High (6 + Critical Comments and/or marked Emotional Overinvolvement)	16	20	56%*
Low (0–5 Critical Comments; no marked Emotional Overinvolvement)	15	3	17%*
Patients Who Remained at Home during Follow-Up (*n* = 36)			
High (6 + Critical Comments and/or marked Emotional Overinvolvement)	10	15	60%**
Low (0–5 Critical Comments; no marked Emotional Overinvolvement)	10	1	9%**

*Yates corrected $\chi^2 = 5.92$; $df = 1$, $p = .015$.
**$p = .005$ (Fisher's exact test).

total sample of 69. These results are summarized in the correlation matrix depicted in Table 7.3. The alternate indicators of EE were as follows:

1. The overall high–low index (EE status) employed in the relapse–no-relapse analyses.

2. Key relatives' highest scores on Critical Comments, Emotional Overinvolvement, and Hostility.

3. Mothers' and fathers' individual scores on these same EE scales. Mothers were coded as EE1 and fathers as EE2.

The different measures of clinical outcome included a PSE-derived "total schizophrenic symptom" score at follow-up, or relapse if earlier (PSE 3); a PAS "total symptoms" score at the same point in time (PAS 3); and an overall measure of clinical outcome in which "relapsed" and "high persisting symptoms" patients were combined into a single "poor outcome" category (OUTCOME 2).

As revealed in the matrix, dichotomized EE status (high vs. low) was as highly correlated with outcome as any of the raw EE scores. But all raw scores on Emotional Overinvolvement showed statistically significant correlations with one or more measures of poor outcome. The importance of overinvolvement in these analyses very likely is due to the large proportion of "high persisting symptoms" patients with relatives scoring 3 or higher on the Emotional Overinvolvement scale (73%). The data suggest that a lowering of the Emotional Overinvolvement threshold from 4 to 3 (a convention that has already been adopted in the London intervention program for clinical reasons) may improve the ability of the EE index to predict a variety of poor clinical outcomes. If this is done for the California sample, the proportion of high-EE patients in the "high persisting symptoms" group rises to 93% (from 67%). At the same time, the association between EE and relapse (narrowly defined) remains strong ($p = .017$), which indicates the robustness of the index.

Of the many clinical variables under study, the California investigators were particularly concerned to eliminate severity of illness as a possible explanation of the relationship between EE and relapse. They attempted to do this by examining the correlations between, first, the overall EE index (EE STATUS), and second, the raw EE scores mentioned earlier, and two indices of severity of illness at admission: the patient's "total schizophrenic symptom" scores on the PSE and PAS, respectively (PSE 1 and PAS 1). The results of these analyses are shown in the correlation matrix in Table 7.3. They strongly suggest that EE is not an artifact of patient morbidity. Its association with relapse and with a generally poor clinical outcome cannot be explained by the patients' clinical condition at admission. Only 1 of 20 correlations between the various EE measures and the measures of severity of illness is significant at the .05 level: Mothers' scores on Hostility are correlated with PSE 1. This isolated significant finding could have occurred by chance, given the number of correlations. The matrix also reveals the lack of association between the admission measures of severity of illness and the three measures of outcome used (PSE 3, PAS 3, and OUTCOME 2).

No other clinical variables measured, nor any aspects of psychiatric history assessed, added to the value of the EE index for predicting relapse. This is precisely in accord with the British findings reported in earlier chapters.

Let us now consider the influence of two postdischarge factors, each of which improved the clinical outcome for British patients living in high-EE homes: antipsychotic medication and amount of contact with the family. As reported in Chapters 5 and 6, neither factor was important for British low-EE patients over a 9-month follow-up period; these patients were likely to remain well, whatever the patterns of medication taking or contact with relatives. However, the 2-year follow-up of the patients in the 1976 study did suggest that low-EE patients benefited significantly from prophylactic medication over a longer period of follow-up.

In presenting the California findings concerning the role of medication in the prevention of relapse, it must first be acknowledged that conditions for determining whether or not a patient took medication regularly were less satisfactory than in the two British studies. It was usual for British patients to attend an outpatient clinic regularly after discharge from the hospital. The researchers were able to obtain detailed information concerning changes in medication or in patterns of intake from psychiatric case notes made every 3 or 4 weeks. Any queries concerning these notes or a patient's account at follow-up could be directed to the treating clinician because of the links among

Table 7.3. Correlations for Overall EE and Clinical Measures ($n = 69$)

		1. EE1CRIT	2. EE1EOI	3. EE1HOST	4. EE2CRIT	5. EE2EOI	6. EE2HOST	7. PSE1	8. PSE2	9. PSE3
1.	1.00									
2.	-.03	1.00								
3.	.46*	-.23	1.00							
4.	.11	.04	.01	1.00						
5.	.01	.30*	-.07	.30*	1.00					
6.	.28*	-.06	.29*	.38*	-.14	1.00				
7.	.11	-.14	.25*	.06	-.13	.07	1.00			
8.	-.01	.11	-.10	.02	.07	.001	.17	1.00		
9.	.13	.26*	.11	.14	.36*	.04	.11	.21	1.00	
10.	.53*	.16	.25*	.40*	.18	.39*	.08	-.02	.20	
11.	.52*	.04	.20	.76*	.27*	.38*	.01	.02	.21	
12.	.03	.80*	-.10	.12	.47*	.01	-.09	.12	.33*	
13.	.31*	-.10	.48*	.26*	-.11	.71*	.14	-.05	.14	
14.	.23	.08	.07	.05	.08	.14	.18	.10	.12	
15.	.07	.26*	.03	.02	.12	-.02	.18	.57*	.25*	
16.	.09	.26*	-.02	.16	.27*	.06	.17	-.01	.67*	
17.	-.05	-.11	-.03	-.22	-.36*	-.18	-.05	-.07	-.75*	

Note. For explanation of abbreviations in column heads, see text.

*Significance levels for correlations: r of .24–.31 = p of .05–.01; r of .31–.39 = p of .01–.001; $r > .39 = p < .001$.

the hospital, the outpatient clinic, and the research unit. Because of the quality of aftercare routinely given to their patients, the British researchers were able to be reasonably confident regarding designations of regular and irregular taking of drugs. Their California counterparts were less fortunate. Few patients in the California study received any kind of routine aftercare. Only 36% of the total sample (a lower proportion than in either of the British studies) satisfied the criteria for regular maintenance therapy: use of prescribed dosage of neuroleptics during at least 75% of the 9-month follow-up period, with no period of 6 consecutive weeks off medication. Equal proportions of low-EE and high-EE patients failed to take medication regularly. Lacking regular contact with treating clinicians in most instances, Jones had to rely primarily on detailed questioning of the patients at follow-up, supplemented by information from the monthly phone calls to the families. In the circumstances, he had to be as rigorous as possible in his judgments; if there were any doubts about the regularity of intake, a patient was considered to be off regular medication.

However, although few patients on regular medication received it under optimal conditions, the California relapse rates on and off medication were

Table 7.3. (*continued*)

10. EESTATUS	11. H1CRIT	12. H1EOI	13. H1HOST	14. SUMPAS1	15. SUMPAS2	16. SUMPAS3	17. OUTCOME2
1.00							
.64*	1.00						
.23	.10	1.00					
.45*	.38*	−.13	1.00				
.17	.23	.19	.07	1.00			
−.02	.02	.27*	−.01	.43*	1.00		
.28*	.15	.35*	.11	.24*	.29*	1.00	
−.29*	−.26*	−.21	−.22	−.11	−.12	−.63*	1.00

remarkably consistent with those obtained in the two British studies. Results concerning the relationships among relatives' EE, medication, and relapse are shown in Table 7.4. Paralleling the British results, the 9-month relapse rates for low-EE patients were low, whether or not they took medication regularly. But these figures should not lead one to conclude that low-EE patients have no need of antipsychotic medication. Two additional pieces of evidence argue against such an interpretation. First, the small number of California patients who lived away from low-EE homes during follow-up did not do as well as the at-home group in the absence of regular medication (see Table 7.4, bottom portion). It may be that low-EE patients have an increased risk of relapse when away from a supportive environment, perhaps because of an increase in life events (see Chapter 12); at these times they may benefit from regular medication. Second, it is notable that in the California study, as in the 1976 British study, no low-EE patient who was on regular medication relapsed during follow-up. By contrast, high-EE patients experienced a high rate of relapse on medication, rising to 44% in the at-home group (see Table 7.4, middle portion). For these patients, regular medication seemed to provide only limited protection against relapse, despite an independent and unconfounded effect in the sample as a whole ($\chi^2 = 4.77$; $p = .029$).

The association between amount of face-to-face contact with relatives

Table 7.4. Relationship of Relatives' EE, Medication after Discharge, and Relapse

Medication/EE Status	No Relapse	Relapse	Relapse %
Total Sample ($n = 53$)[a]			
Irregular medication			
High EE	7	15	68*
Low EE	9	3	25*
Total	16	18	53
Regular medication			
High EE	8	5	38
Low EE	6	0	0
Total	14	5	26
Patients Who Remained at Home during Follow-Up ($n = 35$)[a]			
Irregular medication			
High EE	4	11	73**
Low EE	7	1	13**
Total	11	12	52
Regular Medication			
High EE	5	4	44
Low EE	3	0	0
Total	8	4	33
Patients Who Did Not Remain at Home during Follow-Up ($n = 18$)			
Irregular medication			
High EE	3	4	57
Low EE	2	2	50
Total	5	6	56
Regular medication			
High EE	3	1	25
Low EE	3	0	0
Total	6	1	14

Note. No chi-square results for any of the interactions were significant.
[a]Missing data, one patient.
*$p = .019$, Fisher's exact test.
**$p = .008$, Fisher's exact test.

and relapse of patients from high-EE homes was not statistically significant, although the relationship was in the expected direction. Patients who saw their high-EE relatives for more than 35 hours a week had a higher relapse rate (77%) than those who spent less time with family members (46%), but the low contact rate was higher than in either of the corresponding British groups. Low-EE figures, however, again were very similar to equivalent British figures: patterns of contact between low-EE patients and their relatives made no difference to their relapse rates.

The California investigators then considered the additive effects of the three factors (relatives' EE, medication, and amount of face-to-face contact) in a further analysis of the data. Subgroup relapse rates indicated that the best prognosis for high-EE patients occurred when they were protected by *both* regular medication and low contact with relatives. The relapse rates for these patients were 11% in the total sample and 0% in the at-home group. These rates, comparable to those for patients from low-EE homes, were significantly lower than those of high-EE patients for whom neither protective factor was operating (total sample, $p = .025$; at-home group, $p = .028$). This finding may seem familiar, as it exactly replicates the main finding of a similar analysis carried out for 128 patients in the two British studies (see Chapter 6, p. 91.

The California results differed, however, in suggesting that regular medication and reduced contact are interactive, as opposed to additive, in protecting high-EE patients against relapse. In London the high-EE relapse rate was reduced somewhat if at least one of the two protective influences was operating. In Los Angeles this was not the case; the high-EE relapse rate remained high unless both factors were in effect.

This result may possibly be explained by cross-cultural patient differences — in particular, by the greater proportion of unmarried, male, chronic patients in the California sample. As in the British studies, there was a significant relationship between sex and outcome ($p < .05$); the relapse rate for men was more than triple that for women. Furthermore, it was high-EE males who were responsible for the significant association, as the following relapse rates indicate:

- Male: high-EE, 66% (19 of 29); low-EE, 17% (2 of 12); overall, 51%
- Female: high-EE, 14% (1 of 7); low-EE, 17% (1 of 6); overall, 15%

Similar sex differences were revealed in the two British studies. According to evidence from all the EE studies, it is the most vulnerable patients (i.e., those for whom the clinical prognostic indicators are least favorable) who are in greatest need of *maximum* protection. Such protection may be afforded by either (1) an emotionally more neutral, low-EE environment, or (2) the *combined* effects of regular medication and low contact with high-EE relatives. Yet in both centers unmarried male patients from high-EE homes were significantly less likely than their female counterparts to be protected by both factors (California, $p = .004$; London, $p = .006$). Furthermore, parental conflict, shown to be associated with a high rate of relapse for the unmarried patient ($p < .05$, both centers), was more likely to be present in two-parent households when the patient was a son rather than a daughter ($p < .05$, both centers). Together, these findings go some way toward explaining the large difference in relapse rates between men and women in all three EE studies—a difference that is consistent with similar results from many other prognostic studies of schizophrenia. The data suggest that the patients who may be in greatest need of protection from the effects of a stressful environment—unmarried males—are the least likely to be receiving it.

A final variable that interacted with sex and outcome, for the California patients only, was the use of street drugs (excluding marijuana). Of the relapse sample of 54, 44% used such drugs as cocaine, barbiturates, and phencyclidine (PCP) in the year before admission. Patients who reported street drug abuse were significantly more likely to relapse than those who did not ($p < .05$). Drug abusers tended to be male, from high-EE homes, and off regular medication, although none of these trends was statistically significant.

An additional factor of prognostic significance in the British studies was marital status, but too few of the California patients were married and living with spouses at key admission for this analysis to be carried out. For the same reason, it was not possible to test the British claim that EE is not a function of parenting, but cuts across conjugal and other relationships as well; the California sample was too heavily weighted with unmarried male patients living in parental households.

CONCLUSIONS

In summary, three factors each were associated with a high risk of relapse in the California study, as they were in the 1972 and 1976 British studies: lack of regular medication, male sex, and parental conflict (in two-parent households). A fourth variable, street drug abuse, was related to relapse in the California sample only. The independent effects of these factors, which are confounded with one another to an extent, can only be determined with larger and demographically better balanced samples of patients. For each "risk" variable, however, the presence of a low-EE relative is a protective influence, and when the variable is controlled for, the main relationship between EE and relapse remains. Thus likelihood chi-square tests in the California study revealed an unconfounded effect of EE on relapse, independent of medication ($\chi^2 = 9.66$; $p = .0019$).

Allowing for differences in the patient sample, the California attempt at a cross-cultural replication of the British findings concerning the influence of the family on the course of schizophrenia must be considered a success. It represents the third replication of the finding that a high degree of criticism or overinvolvement expressed by a key relative is the best single predictor of the return or exacerbation of positive symptoms during the 9 months following discharge. Once again, this association is independent of all other variables assessed, including severity of illness at admission and clinical condition at discharge. Of course, some other, as yet unidentified, variable may be responsible for or may mediate the relationship between EE and relapse. The confirmation of causal interpretations requires clinical intervention programs (such as those described in Section III), in which attempts to manipulate relatives' EE experimentally or to lower the "emotional temperature" in families' homes produce a change in relapse rates in the expected direction.

The cross-cultural differences in relatives' emotional responses remain to be explained. The differing distributions of high and low EE in London and Los Angeles cannot be explained by the higher levels of impairment and disturbance in the California patients, since the latter bore no relationship to relatives' EE. But whatever the reasons for the different patterns, what is significant is that the high-EE response style, as defined by identical thresholds for Critical Comments and Emotional Overinvolvement, retained its predictive power in a very different culture.

Of all the many cross-cultural comparisons made in the course of the California replication, the most interesting perhaps are the findings concerning the role of medication in the prevention of relapse. Considered together, the medication results for the three EE studies have important implications for the treatment of schizophrenia. Controlled drug trials have also shown a substantial relapse rate on medication, even when compliance has been ensured by long-acting injections (Falloon, Watt, & Shepherd, 1978; Johnson, 1976). Hogarty *et al.* (1979) found that the most important predictor of relapse in patients who received fluphenazine decanoate was the amount of intra-familial stress in the home prior to treatment. The London and Los Angeles EE results also suggest that medication "failures" may well be explained by the emotional atmosphere in the home, in cases where patients live with families. It is notable that no low-EE patient on regular medication relapsed over the course of follow-up in either the California study or the 1976 British study. At the same time, a sizeable proportion of high-EE patients (as many as 44%) relapsed on medication in both cultures. The particular vulnerability of unmarried males in high contact with relatives needs to be explored further; parental conflict was a common feature in these families, when mothers and fathers lived together. But data from both centers suggest that maintenance drug therapy, even when guaranteed, is unlikely by itself to neutralize the effects of such stressful home environments. Pharmacological and social treatments must be prescribed together if these most vulnerable patients are to survive in the community for any length of time after discharge. Clinical support for this view comes from recent successful attempts to reduce relapse rates of high-risk schizophrenic patients through a combination of regular medication, mental health education, and direct family interventions; several of these efforts are described in Section III.

8

Low-EE versus High-EE Relatives: Distinguishing Characteristics

The extensive material we have now accumulated by interviewing relatives of psychiatric patients with the CFI allows us to characterize high-EE and low-EE relatives in terms of a constellation of attitudes and behaviors. Throughout our research, we have been impressed by the way in which differences in levels of EE tend to reflect differences in attitudes toward the illness and related coping techniques. In our experience, these differences hold across cultures and across diagnostic groups. Both in the 1976 London study of schizophrenia and neurotic depression (Vaughn & Leff, 1976a) and in the more recent Los Angeles schizophrenia study (Vaughn et al., in press), we were able to identify a number of characteristics that tend to distinguish relatives who showed high criticism or overinvolvement from those who did not, as judged by their behavior in the interview and reported behavior toward the patients. These characteristics concern (1) a relative's respect for a patient's relationship needs (which may vary from patient to patient); (2) the relative's attitude toward the legitimacy of the illness; (3) the relative's level of expectations for the patient's functioning; and (4) the relative's emotional reaction to the illness. The particular qualities and coping abilities of many low-EE relatives deserve to be noted. The more positive and constructive aspects of the low-EE response style represent behaviors that can be modeled in intervention programs with high-risk (i.e., high-EE) families.

RESPECT FOR THE PATIENT'S RELATIONSHIP NEEDS

Our data support a view prevalent in the literature — namely, that schizophrenic patients and depressed patients have rather different emotional needs where personal relationships are concerned. Many studies have suggested that persons vulnerable to episodes of schizophrenia are susceptible to sensory overload, and that patients will often attempt to reduce face-to-face contact as a means of dealing with their social deficits. Conversely, depressed persons have considerable affectional and supportive needs and tend to rely on others for the maintenance of their self-esteem.

In both the London and Los Angeles studies, low-EE relatives were notable for the way in which they adapted to patients' demands for either greater reassurance and social support, or increased social distance. In general, high-EE relatives showed no such sensitivity. Since high-EE and low-EE patterns of response differed by diagnostic group, we first discuss the varying patterns of interaction reported for schizophrenic patients; we then do the same for the depressed neurotic patients.

According to their relatives, unmarried schizophrenic patients in particular frequently found close relationships difficult, even in households in which there was little or no tension or strain. They seldom confided in relatives and at times seemed uncomfortable even when making casual conversation. Relatives frequently made statements such as "I can't get to know him or what he's thinking," and "He doesn't confide — wouldn't say anything unless you asked him." Relatives showing low EE (i.e., little or no criticism or overinvolvement) were notable for their acceptance of this state of affairs. They were willing to respect the patient's desire for social distance; they did not intrude. Family relationships were described as ordinarily comfortable, but somewhat detached:

> "I'm as close to him as anyone, but we may be in the same room for hours without speaking."

> "He's very comfortable with me — as long as I don't say anything to him, he's all right."

> "You've got to be very, very careful how you approach her. We're very quiet people, keeping ourselves apart, and I think by doing this, we're very good friends."

By contrast, high-EE relatives of schizophrenic patients were normally very intrusive. They repeatedly tried to make contact when the patient was quiet or withdrawn. For example, the mother of a young woman in the Los Angeles study had a habit of waving her hands and snapping her fingers in front of her daughter's face in an attempt to elicit some kind of response from her. High-EE relatives also tended to disregard requests for privacy; they disliked closed bedroom doors and frequently would walk in on the patients unannounced. Attempts to monitor a patient's routine activities (such as bathing and dressing) and offers of unsolicited advice were also common.

By the relatives' own accounts, schizophrenic patients responded to their widely varying behaviors in predictably different ways. Thus, patients seldom avoided relatives who were low-keyed and nonintrusive. Even if disinclined to converse, they tended to stay in the same room and were unlikely to retreat from the relatives' physical presence. But in high-EE households, protective withdrawal was common. Often the link between a stressful stimulus and social withdrawal by a patient seemed quite clear. For example, one young man in the California study spent more and more time by himself, retreating to his room or going for solitary walks, after returning to his mother's conflict-ridden household. During family arguments he ceased to speak at all; he would cower in a corner of the room and put his hands over his ears as if to shut out the noise. He showed none of these behaviors, however, during periods of living with his father in less tense circumstances. Agitated aggression was another common reaction by patients to overstimulation and stress. Relatives frequently acknowledged that any show of intrusiveness provoked a strong outburst from the patients; the relatives were well aware of the impact of their actions, even when unable or unwilling to modify them. All of the following observations were made by high-EE parents. (The interviewer's questions appear in italics.)

Would he ever get excited, agitated?
"That would be if somebody was too much pressing him."

"He likes the quiet, to be talked to softly; he doesn't like it when you try to press him. It makes him very nervous."

Would he ever get irritable?
"Only if you aggravated him."

In what way?
"Well, like if you kept saying, 'For goodness sake!'—yelling at him—'Let's get going! Get on the ball! Get out there and walk!' I used to yell at him once in a while, really get it on, say, 'You know, you're never going to get well.' I realized after a while this didn't do any good. It would make him very angry, very upset. . . . He wouldn't say anything, but he'd get very aggressive because I was aggravating him. He would kick chairs or throw something, to take his frustration out."

"I scream and holler, get it out of my system, then it's over with, but I think that's what my son doesn't like. He doesn't like to hear the screaming and hollering. Being confronted—he doesn't like people to become upset with him. It does no good at all to nag, it just causes more problems—he becomes more irritable.'

Unlike the schizophrenic patients in the London and Los Angeles studies, the majority of depressed patients we studied were described as fearful of loss and rejection and desirous of continual comfort and support; this finding supports the views of Weissman, Klerman, Paykel, Prusoff, and Hansen (1974) and others. This was particularly true of the female patients. As described earlier in this chapter, spouses responded to these demands for reassurance and support in very different ways. Low criticism spouses did all they could to lift the patients' spirits; they were consistently sympathetic and concerned. For example:

What difference has your wife's admission made to you?
"Quite a worry; it's not the same without her. I don't think there's anything I could do about it, not myself, only try and encourage her, reassure her that what's happening to her happens to other people as well."

This response can be contrasted with the reply of a critical spouse to the same question:

"Generally worried, but personally thinking how far behind I've fallen in my accounts. I don't know whether I'm making money or not."

While critical wives of depressed men wavered between displays of concern and annoyance, critical husbands of depressed women almost invariably were unsympathetic and disinclined to provide emotional support:

"She looked like a poor dog that you're going to leave. . . . All the time she'd say, 'I'm not a good wife to you, you'd be better off without me.' I'd say, 'Oh, you're just feeling sorry for yourself.' She's always blaming herself for things that to me don't mean anything."

"'Oh,' I said, 'You get on my nerves. Pull yourself together!' 'It's alright for you,' she'd say, 'You don't worry.' 'It's a damned good job, I don't,' I'd say. 'If I was to worry like you we'd be down a big hole by now!'"

ATTITUDE TOWARD THE LEGITIMACY OF THE ILLNESS

The low-EE view that an illness was genuine, together with respect for a patient's feelings and perceptions when ill, usually evolved in the absence of any professional counseling. The majority of relatives in both the British and California studies reported receiving little or no information from professionals about the disorder, medication and its side effects, and other related issues. Thus their opinions tended to be uninfluenced by the advice of "experts."

For both diagnostic groups, low-EE relatives showed greater empathy and made more of an effort to understand the patients' ordeal. Low-EE relatives of schizophrenic patients sought rational explanations for patients' bizarre behaviors and delusions. For example, the mother of a girl in the California study related an incident in which her daughter had gone to the grocery store one morning with red crayon all over her face.

"I said, 'Sandra, why have you done that?' 'I want to be an Indian,' she said. 'Oh, please take it off,' I said. You see, she loved Indians when she was a little girl. It seemed as if things from her childhood were getting in the way of her being an adult. She would just get all mixed up."

While low-EE relatives were objective enough to recognize that symptom behaviors were signs of illness, they nevertheless accepted that for the *patients* certain peculiar ideas or experiences might be real enough, and so they tended to adopt an attitude of tolerance:

"He had some strange experiences. He told me, 'I saw Christ walking up this hill,' while we were sitting on the porch. He said Christ had on a purple robe and sandals. I just listened to him and said nothing. At the very beginning of the illness I might have thought, 'Well, I've heard of miracles,' but later of course I knew he was ill."

A small number of overinvolved relatives (usually mothers) lacked such objectivity; they accepted reported delusions as facts and became caught up in the patients' psychotic systems. Generally, however, high-EE relatives were intolerant of sick talk, repeatedly engaging in confrontations with patients:

"I'm trying to knock it out of his mind — that he's *not* Jesus Christ. I always tell him, 'That's a bunch of horse shit — don't give it to me!' And that's putting it mildly!"

High-criticism relatives were also convinced that the patients could exercise control over symptom behaviors, given the will to do so:

"He won't do anything about it. I keep telling him, 'You have to cooperate — it's you yourself that can cure yourself.'"

EXPECTATIONS FOR THE PATIENT'S FUNCTIONING

The low-EE view that the illness was legitimate was associated with lowered expectations for the patient's performance both during and after an episode of illness. Low-EE relatives differed markedly from high-EE relatives in their reported ability to tolerate low levels of functioning. Thus one low-EE relative acknowledged that her sister had never been the best of company:

"She won't open up and she won't tell you anything. . . . She keeps everything to herself."

But the atmosphere was a positive one. The two sisters cared for each other, and although the relative gave more to the relationship than she received, her expectations were not high; she respected her sister's eccentricities and demands for privacy:

"I don't worry her about anything, really. I just give her jobs to do that I think she can do, and if she doesn't do them, then I do them."

Another low-EE relative said that, although she was dissatisfied with her daughter's failure to communicate or show much affection or interest, she was seldom irritable, "because I know her makeup and I try to make the best of it."

Would you like things to be done differently?
"Yes, but I realize she has always been that way, I can't demand that of her. So I just leave her alone."

How would you like it to be different?

"I would like her to be closer to us, and discuss more . . . to have more in common to discuss, and to trust us. I would like that, but I can't expect it."

In contrast, high-EE relatives who were critical made few allowances for the illness or for the patients' known deficits. For example, one young man had observed his schizophrenic mother's fluctuating behavior over many years. She did not work and even at her best showed signs of impairment around the house. The key admission episode was characterized by less behavioral disturbance than in the past (no violence, no talk of hearing voices), but there was an increase in underactivity, which her son termed "not making any effort." His attitude toward his ill mother was one of impatience with her low performance and a feeling that she could control her behavior but would not. He had high expectations that remained unfulfilled. He was very critical, sometimes to the point of hostility, although he was not altogether rejecting. He was quite warm when describing her "well" self, but he exerted considerable pressure on her all the time to improve herself; he did not accept her as she was, and constantly drove the point home:

"I'd like to see her up and about, sort of with an eye on the place. As I said to her 'I'm not asking you to get to the moon—everyone has setbacks—but promise me you'll at least try! Show me that you're trying, not just say you are and do nothing!"

EMOTIONAL REACTION TO THE ILLNESS

It may seem tautological to state that relatives who are rated high and low on EE may be distinguished from each other by their emotional reactions. Over the years, however, we have been struck by the exceptionally calm and self-contained responses by low-EE relatives, sometimes in the face of extremely agitated or bizarre behaviors. Only very occasionally did this response style seem inappropriate, overcontrolled, or indicative of some denial mechanism at work. In most cases, these relatives simply seemed concerned without being overly anxious. Many displayed an admirable ability to defuse a crisis; in such circumstances they appeared to have a calming effect not only on the patients (an impression supported by the biological data reported in Section IV), but also on other family members. During interviews, they offered dispassionate and even humorous accounts of their efforts to deal with the patient. One father, whose son suddenly turned on him one night and announced a God-sent mission to kill him, managed to disarm his son through gentle persuasion. He did not contact the hospital until the following morning. He said that while he "felt" for his son when ill, he was not unduly disturbed by his actions:

"It didn't worry me. I thought, 'If he goes for me, I'll put him in his place.' I wasn't too upset, though, as the wife had a breakdown once. . . . I do take things as they come, I suppose."

A cool response in a crisis does not necessarily indicate a lack of emotion. There may well be feelings of considerable distress and dissatisfaction, as in the following example from the California study:

"He could be very violent, unpredictable. Once we were driving down the freeway and he tried to gouge my eyes out . . . he was sitting in the back seat and attacked me from behind. I had a hard time driving, I can tell you! [Laughter] I came out of that one looking a bit of a mess!"

How did you feel?

"Oh, I felt terrible. My biggest problem was in fighting him off. All I did was to defend myself. It wasn't in my nature to hurt him. But I was very depressed. I thought, 'Why does he attack me? Does he hate me so?'"

Sometimes low-EE relatives describe themselves as naturally easygoing, as in the first example above. More commonly there is evidence that low-EE relatives have learned to control their emotions over long years of trying to cope — dealing not only with occasional crises, but also with the everyday problems of living with someone who is vulnerable to episodes of psychiatric illness. In the absence of professional advice, they learn to cope by a process of trial and error, trying different things in an effort to discover what works best:

"I realized that if I got upset, exploded, it was bad for Martin. It had a more calming effect on him if I kept very calm. So I let many things pass. I wouldn't make an issue. I became more permissive in order to survive. . . . You just do the best you can each day. My husband and I are pretty happy-go-lucky. We don't let many things bother us; we try to keep a sense of humor. In any event, we're not the same people we were when we started out."

It is this quality of *flexibility* that, perhaps more than any other feature, distinguishes low-EE relatives from their high-EE counterparts.

COMMENT

It is hoped that the data presented in this chapter have helped to illuminate the concept of EE. It is clear that a high or low rating represents more than a simple expression of positive or negative feeling at a single point in time. The data suggest that the EE rating is a reflection of the quality of the preillness relationship between patient and relative, and of the atmosphere in the home in the months before the patient's admission to the hospital.

The EE studies to date have been concerned with one measure of outcome only: the reappearance or exacerbation of florid symptoms over a 9-month follow-up period. Other measures of outcome, such as presence or severity of secondary impairments or handicaps, were not attempted. There is some evidence that when a low-EE relative of a schizophrenic patient has no expectations for the patient and exerts no pressure to perform, there may actually be an increase in negative symptoms and higher levels of social impairment. Thus a home environment that is benign by one criterion may not be so by another.

Having issued this caveat, we are able to make some tentative statements about the patterns of response that appear to be "toxic" for a patient vulnerable to symptomatic relapse. Although we are not able to document the interpersonal family behaviors that differentiate high-EE and low-EE families, it has been possible to identify certain characteristic response styles that are associated with a good or a poor clinical outcome. For example, we have suggested that a nonintrusive, tolerant approach by relatives is most effective for ensuring that a schizophrenic patient remains well after recovery from a florid episode. Brown (see Chapter 1, pp. 20–21) has postulated that certain environments produce high and sustained levels of arousal in schizophrenic patients, which make the them more likely to become ill again. In our experience, these environments are characterized by discord and/or intrusive attempts on the part of a relative to advise, complain, or merely "get through to" a patient. Whether or not these overtures are well-intentioned, they are likely to be viewed as threatening by persons vulnerable to episodes of schizophrenia, who may require more than the normal amounts of social distance and personal space in order to feel at ease with other people.

It remains for other researchers to explore the meaning of the major EE variables and their manifestations in the natural family context. We welcome attempts to develop measures of direct family interaction that are conceptually linked to the EE construct — for example, the codes for parental affective styles of communication developed by Doane, West, Goldstein, Rodnick, and Jones (1981). Also, as Brown has pointed out elsewhere (1967), there is a need for more systematic studies of coping behavior assessed at more than one point in time. Relatives adjust over the years, altering their levels of expectations in response to social crises and to short-term and long-term changes in the patient. These complex processes of adjustment and the effectiveness of particular behaviors in reducing symptomatology need to be explored in greater detail.

Throughout this research, we have been concerned with the applicability of our findings to clinical interventions with patients and their families. We believe that the value of the information obtained in family studies such as ours depends on the quality of the assessment instrument and the proper training of the persons making the assessment; from this conviction stems our concern that the CFI and related rating scales be used only by persons who have undergone a thorough training in interviewing and rating. At the same time, we realize that a full training in the use of the CFI is not a practical proposition for most therapists.

It is hoped that the analyses of the present data will provide clinicians with some clues for identifying high-risk and low-risk families, so that treatment efforts can be concentrated on the former. For example, we would predict that schizophrenic patients whose relatives are judged by a clinician to be reasonably nonintrusive, tolerant of symptom behaviors, and understanding of the illness are likely to remain well, while those who come from conflictual or intrusive environments are at greatest risk and most in need of protective medication and clinical support.

For *all* patients and their families, mental health education would seem to be a basic imperative. In the 1976 study (Vaughn & Leff, 1976a), only half of the relatives interviewed considered the patients' illness to be a *mental* problem. The majority reported receiving little or no information from professionals about the disorder itself, medication and its side effects, and other related issues. Furthermore, in both London and Los Angeles, highly critical relatives were significantly more likely than other relatives to take an unsympathetic view of the illness — to blame patients for their symptoms and hold them responsible for not exercising control over them. Almost certainly, "administrative" solutions to the problems associated with relapse and readmission are likely to fail unless the persons most directly concerned — the patients and those around them — are involved in the treatment process from the very beginning. Where there are residual disabilities that are unlikely to be overcome by social methods of treatment, the development of more realistic expectations for a patient's performance is desirable.

A final point, also related to present findings, concerns another possible kind of intervention: efforts to change the attitudes of overinvolved or highly critical relatives. The content analysis of relatives' critical comments in the present study (Vaughn & Leff, 1976a) has important implications for any intervention program aimed at preventing relapse of schizophrenia or depression. The fact that two-thirds of all critical remarks made by relatives concerned long-standing personality traits that antedated the illness suggests that it would be unwise to concentrate therapeutic efforts on symptom behaviors alone. Attention to "secondary" and "extrinsic" impairments, particularly characteristics of personality and related social handicaps, is almost certainly necessary.

STUDIES OF INTERVENTION IN FAMILIES OF SCHIZOPHRENIC PATIENTS

9

Intervention in Families of Schizophrenic Patients: The London Study

The significant association betweeen high EE and relapse of schizophrenia has now been repeated in too many studies conducted by different investigators in a variety of settings to be dismissed as a chance finding. The same is true of the lower relapse rates associated with low face-to-face contact with a high-EE relative and with maintenance on neuroleptic drugs. Associations of these kinds, however, can be interpreted in quite different ways. The most obvious interpretation is a causal one — for example, that life with a high-EE relative has a deleterious effect on the course of a schizophrenic illness (see Figure 9.1a). An alternative view is that patients who behave badly at home are more likely to provoke criticism and overinvolvement in their relatives, as well as being more liable to relapse. In this case the association between high EE and relapse is an indirect one, mediated by the intervening variable of patients' bad behavior (see Figure 9.1b).

As we have seen (Chapter 5, p. 82) when patients' disturbed behavior is allowed for, the association between high EE and relapse remains significant. This demonstration does not satisfactorily resolve the problem of interpretation, since any number of other intervening variables can be postulated as mediating the association. No matter how many are eliminated, it can always be argued that factor X, which was not measured, still remains to be investigated. Hence this approach to the problem cannot provide a definitive solution. This can only come from an experimental approach in which the presumed causal factor is manipulated and any changes in the presumed dependent factor are studied. This approach has been utilized many times to investigate the prophylactic effect of maintenance on neuroleptic drugs in schizophrenia; it has firmly established their protective role (Hirsch et al., 1973; Hogarty, Goldberg, & the Collaborative Study Group, 1973; Hogarty et al., 1974; Leff & Wing, 1971). Until recently it has not been applied to the association between high EE and relapse, or to that between high face-to-face contact and relapse.

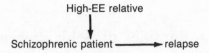

Figure 9.1a. The causal interpretation of the association between high EE in a relative and schizophrenic relapse.

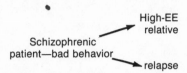

Figure 9.1b. The "intervening variable" interpretation of the association between high EE in a relative and schizophrenic relapse.

DIFFICULTIES IN EVALUATING SOCIAL THERAPIES

The main reason for the delay in carrying out an experimental study of this kind has been the difficulty in designing a scientific evaluation of a social intervention. This problem is not confined to the area under discussion, but affects the whole range of social therapies. The obvious model to turn to is the double-blind, placebo-controlled trial, which has become the standard design for evaluating drug treatments. Unfortunately, there are many ways in which this is inapplicable to the assessment of social treatments. First and foremost, there is no placebo for a social treatment. It is not possible for a therapist to pretend to be treating a patient without actually doing anything. Any contact between a therapist and a patient is potentially therapeutic, even if no words are spoken. This is well recognized by researchers into the efficacy of drugs; the recognition led to the introduction of a placebo into trials to control for the psychological effects of administering a drug, so that the pharmacological effects could be evaluated independently. In the case of social therapies, we do not wish to control for psychological effects, since these are the objects of evaluation. Instead, the aim shifts to the differentiation of specific from nonspecific psychological effects. This confronts the researcher with the problem of devising a nonspecific social treatment.

In the past, researchers have tended to use "supportive treatment" as a control for more specific social therapies, or else have devised a form of therapy that would not be expected to be of much benefit to patients—for example, asking them to record and relate dreams without the therapist's commenting on them. The latter strategy has an advantage over the former in that there is a clear specification of what activity is to take place, whereas "supportive treatment" is so vague that it could contain a multitude of therapeutic elements. Unfortunately there is always the risk that the fabricated therapy, although apparently valueless, might have a specific therapeutic effect.

Another issue raised by the selection of a control treatment is that of who is to be in control of its administration. If a member of the research team gives the control treatment, there is the advantage of being able to determine exactly what goes on in sessions. However, problems arise with maintaining the blindness of the researchers and with the possibility of contamination between the treatments. The therapists giving the specific treatment to the experimental group are usually enthusiastic about it and naturally talk about their apparent successes. Enthusiasm is very contagious and may easily influence the therapists managing the nonspecific treatment to shift their therapy in the direction of the specific treatment, albeit unconsciously.

There is a clear necessity to stipulate what occurs in sessions between patient and therapist if specific therapies are to be distinguished from nonspecific. This has the additional advantage of providing the basis for an increasing standardization of social treatments. In this area, another departure from the drug trial design is forced by the nature of social treatments. In the case of a drug, we can be certain that the same chemical is being given to each patient in the trial, although the dose is often allowed to vary to suit the needs of individuals. With social treatments, there is a need to vary not only the quantity but also the quality of therapy to suit each client. It is nonsensical to standardize the content of a social treatment to such an extent that it cannot be adapted to the varied requirements of individuals. To give an obvious example, a patient living with a spouse is inevitably going to have different treatment needs from one living with parents. The methodological dilemma is how to remain responsive to individual needs for treatment and still retain a grasp on standardization and replicability. The latter aspect must never be lost sight of, since whatever precautions one takes, it is almost impossible to eliminate the therapeutic effect of personal charisma. The only assurance against this factor as an explanation for successful results is the replication of a study by independent workers.

The best answer currently available to the dilemma posed above is to compile a package of social treatments, the individual elements of which are stipulated in as much detail as possible. The preparation of a package of this kind allows for flexible use of individual components, each of which is relatively standardized. The descriptions of treatment elements should be sufficiently detailed to enable other workers to replicate the procedures.

DESCRIPTION OF THE LONDON TRIAL

We have spent some time in examining these methodological issues, so that the reader will appreciate the rationale behind the design of the two trials of social intervention to be described in this part of the book. The first of these (Leff, Kuipers, Berkowitz, Eberlein-Vries, & Sturgeon, 1982) was conducted specifically to test a possible causal relationship between relatives' EE and relapse of schizophrenia. Our strategy was to select a group of patients at highest risk of relapse, namely those in high contact with high-EE relatives (Subgroups 5 and 6, Figure 6.1). For ethical reasons, it is obligatory to prescribe maintenance neuroleptics for these individuals. Wherever possible, long-acting injections of phenothiazines were employed, so that problems with drug compliance would not obscure interpretation of the results. Patients with a diagnosis of schizophrenia, as determined by use of the PSE and the Catego program, were selected for the study if they lived with at least one relative. The patients were picked out from admissions for a first episode or relapse, and their clinical progress in the hospital was monitored. Almost all of them were stabilized on long-acting injections prior to discharge, which occurred an average of 3 months later.

Patients qualifying for the trial because they were in high contact with high-EE relatives were randomly assigned to experimental or control groups. The control group received routine outpatient care, over which the research team had no control. A calculated risk was taken that the control relatives might be offered some form of professional therapeutic help, and the situation was monitored throughout the trial. The experimental group were candidates for a package of social treatments, which was tailored to the needs of each family. The package consisted of three main components: an education program, a relatives' group, and family sessions. The reasons for choosing these particular forms of therapy need to be expounded in some detail.

The therapeutic aims in the experimental group were to reduce relatives' EE and/or face-to-face contact with patients. The latter aim could be brought about most directly by removing a patient from the home. This might be possible in the case of a parental home if suitable sheltered accommodation were available in the community, and if all the people involved agreed to it. It would not be justifiable in the case of a marital relationship, where efforts should rather be directed at providing sheltered occupational facilities for unemployed patients, and at restructuring the use of leisure time. These are all administrative measures that involve no attempt to alter EE directly. In order to achieve that aim, it is advisable to understand the origins of the emotions concerned.

With this in mind, the content of critical remarks made by relatives in the 1976 study (Vaughn & Leff, 1976a) was analyzed. It was discovered that only 30% of these remarks related to the florid symptoms of schizophrenia, such as delusions and hallucinations. The remaining 70% were directed at the negative symptoms, such as apathy, inertia, and lack of affection. The florid symptoms give rise to abnormal behavior, which is readily identifiable as part of an illness. By contrast, the negative symptoms are manifested as the absence of normal behavior (Leff, 1982). As such, they are not obviously the products of illness, and indeed most relatives viewed them as long-standing personality characteristics that were under the patients' voluntary control.

Consequently, they blamed the patients, using such terms as "lazy," "selfish," and "spoiled." In view of these findings, it was considered possible that education about the nature of schizophrenia might modify relatives' critical attitudes. An education program was compiled, with short sections on the diagnosis, symptoms, etiology, course, and management of schizophrenia. These were written in straightforward language, avoiding jargon and technical terms, and were designed to be read out to the relative, each topic occupying 5 to 10 minutes. The education program we used appears as an Appendix to this chapter. Following each exposition, unlimited time was allowed for the relative to ask questions.

Another approach to lowering EE that was adopted was the formation of a relatives' group. The idea behind this was that low-EE relatives had developed a range of coping behaviors that enabled them to deal with the day-to-day problems of living with a schizophrenic patient without becoming excessively critical or overinvolved. It was thought possible that if high-EE relatives were brought together with low-EE relatives in a group, the latter might teach appropriate coping strategies to the former. The task of the professionals in the group would then be to elicit accounts of coping behaviors from the low-EE relatives and aid their adoption by high-EE relatives. Patients were deliberately excluded from the group, as it was felt that otherwise any active symptoms would dominate the discussion and impede the relatives' learning of coping strategies. Another reason for the exclusion of patients was the intention that relatives should use the group to ventilate feelings of anger and hostility, to which we did not wish the patients to be further exposed. All experimental high-EE relatives were invited to join the group, as well as a random selection of low-EE relatives, with the aim of including a higher proportion of the latter.

The third method of attempting to lower EE was family therapy. It was evident that the nature of the group would militate against the discussion of personal issues, such as marital problems, that did not relate directly to coping with the patients. Yet we saw interpersonal relationships as a very important factor in the generation of criticism and overinvolvement directed at the patients. Furthermore, we wished to have an opportunity to hear the patients' reactions to relatives, and for the relatives to be present when these were aired. Therefore we organized family sessions that included each patient and his or her spouse or parents, as well as any siblings who wished to attend. These were invariably held in the patient's home.

In considering our research aims, we recognized that the three kinds of intervention aimed at lowering EE varied considerably in the degree to which we could specify their content. There was no problem with the education program, since it was written down. The relatives' group, being more flexible, was subject to considerable diversity of content, although the overall aims were consistent. Each session was audiotaped, with the participants' consent, to provide a permanent record of what went on. The family sessions were even more difficult to describe in detail. The therapists involved did not hold to one theory of family functioning, nor did they employ the same techniques in each case. In families that were considered able to make use of them, dynamic interpretations were given. In others, symbolic language was judged to be inappropriate, and a more behavioral approach was taken. Each session was discussed among the therapists beforehand, and specific aims were formulated. Sometimes it was necessary to alter the aims as the session progressed. An account of the session was written up immediately afterward as a permanent record.

PROCEDURES IN THE TRIAL

Having described the treatment elements in some detail, we can now recount the trial procedures that the patients and their relatives went through.

The patients were obtained from the inpatient psychiatric wards of three hospitals, the Maudsley Hospital and the South-Western Hospital in south London, and St. Pancras Hospital in north London. All admissions were screened to select patients between the ages of 16 and 65 who lived with at least one relative and were within commuting distance of the hospital. If they appeared from the admission notes to be suffering from a functional psychosis, they were interviewed with the PSE. The data generated were processed by the Catego program, and those patients classified as schizophrenic were included in the trial if in addition they spent more than 35 hours per week in face-to-face contact with at least one relative. Patients satisfying these criteria entered the study, and demographic and historical data were collected with a standardized schedule.

Relatives in high face-to-face contact with the patients were interviewed with the abbreviated CFI and were assigned to high- or low-EE groups on the basis of the ratings made. The cutoff point for Critical Comments was six comments in the course of the interview, as in the previous study (Vaughn & Leff, 1976a). With regard to the Emotional Overinvolvement scale, our opinion of what constituted an excess of this emotion had altered subsequent to the 1976 study. We had encountered a number of relatives, mostly mothers, who could not be scored higher than 3 on this scale of 0–5, yet who seemed to be generating a pathological atmosphere in their homes. After much discussion, we decided to lower the cutoff point on this scale from 4 to 3 for the intervention study. The further procedures and assessments that were applied to the families in the various groups are shown in Figure 9.2.

It will probably help the reader to visualize the conduct of the trial if we describe the progress of experimental high-EE patients through the procedures. Once each patient had passed the preliminary screens, he or she was

Figure 9.2. Flow chart of intervention program.

seen by a research psychiatrist, who administered the PSE and a time budget. The patient remained under the care of the clinical team that was treating his or her acute schizophrenic illness. Meanwhile, the relatives were contacted by a research psychologist, who arranged to carry out the CFI on any relative in high face-to-face contact with the patient. If one or more relatives were rated as high in EE, the family was assigned by a random number table to the experimental or the control group. A total of 24 patients living with high-EE relatives were included in the trial, 12 being assigned to each group. In the case of an experimental family, the consultant psychiatrist responsible for the patient was contacted and informed of our wish to educate the relatives about schizophrenia. The clinicians responsible for both experimental and control patients were asked to prescribe maintenance neuroleptics in the form of long-acting injections if at all possible.

The next step was to arrange a joint interview between each experimental patient and one relative. This was carried out in a studio that allowed us to videotape the patient and relative simultaneously, so that eye contact could be assessed. In addition, psychophysiological measures were made on the patient throughout the interview. For the first 20 minutes or so, the patient was with an interviewer who made conversation on neutral topics. The relative then entered, and the interviewer conducted a semistructured interview on the basis of nine stipulated questions that were designed to elicit criticism and/or overinvolvement. The aim of this part of the interview was to monitor the patient's psychophysiological responses to high-EE comments made by the relative (Sturgeon, Kuipers, Berkowitz, Turpin, & Leff, 1981).

During the first half of the interview, while the patient was alone with the interviewer, a research psychologist saw the relative in order to administer a Knowledge Interview (KI). This instrument requires some explanation. Since the education program was a brief and discrete part of the intervention, it was open to separate evaluation. To achieve this, an interview was constructed to assess the acquisition of the information we were attempting to impart. This interview, the KI, was administered before and after the education program in the experimental group in order to assess its effect. The KI was also given twice to the control group, at the same interval apart but without the intervening education, in order to control for any effect of the simple passage of time. The KI was given to both groups a third time at the 9-month follow-up in order to evaluate the effects of the other interventions on the experimental relatives' knowledge about and attitudes toward schizophrenia. As it was in the nature of a pilot schedule, the KI comprised a series of 21 open-ended questions. This rendered it difficult to score, but prevented premature decisions as to what was important to inquire about. After completing the intervention study, we produced an amended version with more focused questions and a precoded range of answers for each question.

Following the joint interview in the video studio, the education program was given to the experimental high-EE and low-EE relatives. We decided to do this in the relatives' homes, with the expectation that they would be better able to assimilate the information in familiar surroundings and on their own territory than in a clinical setting. At first we gave each of the four topics on a separate occasion, but this seemed to spin out the program unnecessarily, so we condensed two topics into each teaching occasion.

Comparison of the KI responses on the first and second occasions revealed that the education program did have an impact, although it was somewhat limited (Berkowitz, Eberlein-Vries, Kuipers, & Leff, 1984). The greatest change that occurred was an increase in the number of high-EE experimental relatives who knew that the diagnosis was schizophrenia after the program. This may seem facile, since the relatives were told the diagnosis was part of the education, but this is not an area in which common sense holds sway. We learned early in the study that being told the diagnosis is no guarantee of retaining the information. We were surprised by the number of relatives who insisted that they had never been told what was wrong with the patients. This did not seem to us to reflect a good standard of clinical practice, so we approached the clinicians concerned and asked them if they had informed the relatives. In nearly every case, they reported that they had; this left us with two irreconcilable assertions in most instances. The truth became clear to us only when one relative was able to recount her experience of being told the diagnosis by the clinician. She said that as soon as she heard the word "schizophrenia" she went into a state of emotional shock and was unable to take in anything that was said subsequently during the interview. Later, numerous questions came flooding into her mind, but she never had another opportunity to ask them. We presume that the emotional impact of the term "schizophrenia" was so great that in many cases relatives were unable to absorb the information; as a result, they later denied having been told the diagnosis. In our education program, we deliberately proceeded at a leisurely pace, encouraging relatives to spend as much time as they needed to ask questions. We cannot necessarily ascribe their increased knowledge of the diagnosis to this technique, since for most of them it was the second occasion on which they were exposed to the term, and this may have been the crucial factor.

We can be more certain about ascribing the other changes that occurred to the education program, since they were directly related to its content. In particular, the high-EE experimental relatives became less pessimistic about the future. The section of the program on prognosis states that a proportion of patients with a first attack of schizophrenia will remain free of symptoms indefinitely, while the majority will recover from the acute attack but will remain vulnerable to further episodes.

The other information that the high-EE relatives in the experimental group acquired in the program related to management of the illness. They learned the importance of the patients' avoiding stressful situations, and of the relatives' trying to avoid worrying and becoming upset with the patients. These may seem modest gains, but they were the product of a small input of professional time. Furthermore, they provided a sound basis for the changes we were trying to bring about with the other, more time-consuming interventions.

Once the second KI had been administered, the experimental relatives, both high- and low-EE, were invited to attend the group. It was usually at about this time that the patients were discharged from the hospital. The group met every 2 weeks in a large comfortable room in the London Institute of Psychiatry for 1½ hours. Relatives were asked to attend for a minimum of 9 months, but were free to continue thereafter if they wished; a number continued to come for over a year. The group had a maximum of seven members at any one time and included two professionals for most of the study, but only one during the last part of the study. Our intention of outnumbering high-EE relatives with low-EE relatives in the group was never fulfilled. This was because of the difficulty in persuading low-EE relatives to continue attending. They would characteristically say after a few sessions that they did not need the kind of help the group was offering, as they had already satisfactorily solved the type of problems discussed. This was, of course, a confirmation of our method of categorizing relatives by EE level, but it negated our original strategy. Fortunately, by talking to the low-EE relatives, both in the course of the CFI and during sessions of the group, we were able to build up a picture of their coping strategies. Thus the professionals could introduce these into the group as suggested alternatives to the current coping behaviors of the high-EE relatives. This had the effect of promoting greater activity by the professionals in the group than we had first envisaged.

As a result of these experiences, we were able to formulate some general propositions about the contrasting styles of high-EE and low-EE relatives when faced with similar problems. High-EE relatives did not allow patients the reality of their pathological experiences. For example, if a patient reported hearing voices, the relative would say that it was not possible since nobody was there, or would tell the patient that he or she must be mad. By contrast, a low-EE relative would acknowledge the reality of the patient's experience, but would make it clear that he or she did not share it: for example, "I know you are hearing voices, but you must understand that I don't hear them."

Another aspect of high-EE relatives' behavior was its confrontational nature. Faced with a conflict with a patient, a high-EE relative would pursue his or her own course unwaveringly until one or both parties lost their tempers. Low-EE relatives were much more flexible and resourceful. They had often worked out ways of sidestepping conflict or of conciliating the patients, without, however, allowing too great an intrusion on their own lives. For example, one wife would say to her husband, "I know you have to talk to the voices, but please go and do it in the bedroom." A low-EE mother would ask her son to take the dog out for a walk whenever the situation between them became tense.

In general, it seemed that low-EE relatives had more empathy with the patients than high-EE relatives. One method we occasionally used in the group to attempt to increase empathy was role playing. We would instruct a high-EE relative to play the part of the patient he or she lived with, while another relative played the high-EE relative's own part. When high-EE relatives were faced with a reflection of their own attitudes, they could be shocked into an awareness of the need for change.

The group was run on a flexible basis with regard to membership and attendance. Relatives joined and left the group serially as the respective patients entered the study and completed 9 months in the community, although, as already mentioned, some relatives chose to carry on in the group for well over a year. High-EE relatives attended the group an average of 9.1 times over the 9-month follow-up period, with a range of 6–21 attendances. The number of relatives present at each session varied from two to seven, with a mean of four. In addition to the formal contacts of the relatives' group and family therapy sessions, relatives were encouraged to phone members of the team whenever they felt the need. Ten relatives used this method of contact between 2 and 19 times, the mean being 7.5 times.

Family therapy sessions were held in the home for all experimental families. These were almost always conducted by a male research psychiatrist and a female research psychologist, acting as cotherapists. For one married couple, a research psychologist worked with the clinical team's social worker, who wished to gain experience of marital therapy. When the key relative was a spouse, we saw the patient and spouse together. When parents were involved, we saw the patient with both parents if available, and adult siblings living at home were also encouraged to participate. We did not hold to any single theory of family functioning, nor did we have a preferred technique of intervention. We would make dynamic interpretations of individual's behavior or of family relationships if we considered a family capable of making use of them. Otherwise we would help the family work in a behavioral way on problems, breaking them down into small, manageable components. Occasionally we would employ a structural approach, strengthening the parental coalition to allow us to prise the patient away from too close a relationship with one of the parents. If communication was unclear, we would attempt to clarify it by insisting on no more than a single speaker at any one time and by encouraging family members to address each other directly. We would also highlight positive statements that family members made about each other, at the expense of negative ones.

We saw each family for a minimum of 1 and a maximum of 25 sessions, with a mean of 5.6. Only one family was seen more than 10 times. This was a marital couple in which the husband was unable to attend the relatives' group because of the demands of his occupation. We did not record the sessions, but each was discussed afterwards and a detailed account was written up.

During the 9-month trial period, virtually all the patients, both experimental and control, attended outpatient clinics on a regular basis. A note was included in each patient's case record, asking the responsible clinician to contact the research team if there was any suggestion of an impending or actual relapse. In the event, it was possible to see all but one of the patients who suffered a recurrence of symptoms at an early stage in their relapse. A full PSE was performed at the time, and a history of life events was taken for the 3 months prior to relapse.

"Relapse" was defined as a recurrence of schizophrenic symptoms, as detected by the PSE, in patients who had been free of them at discharge (Type I relapse of Brown *et al.*, 1972). For the small proportion of patients who still exhibited schizophrenic symptoms at discharge (two experimental, three control), "relapse" was defined as a marked increase in the number or intensity of symptoms (Type II relapse). As it happened, all the relapses in the study were Type I.

All patients in the trial were followed up at 9 months after discharge. This period of time was chosen to conform with the design of the earlier naturalistic studies of EE. If the patient had not already relapsed, the PSE and a life events history were administered. The relative or relatives were reinterviewed with the CFI, and EE was assessed independently by two raters. When they disagreed, or when the rating was particularly crucial, the recording was sent to Vaughn, who rated it blindly. As part of the CFI, a time budget was completed, and a third KI was given to the relative.

RESULTS

The experimental and control high-EE patients were compared on a number of demographic and historical features. These are displayed in Table 9.1, and it can be seen that only one item distinguished the groups significantly. The duration of unemployment before admission was substantially greater in the experimental group; this would have made our therapeutic task more difficult.

The PSE data were processed by the Catego program to produce a list of 38 syndromes. The experimental and control groups did not differ in the distribution of any of the syndromes. In terms of Catego classes, 11 patients in each group were labeled as having S + (schizophrenia), while the remaining patient in each group was classified as having P + (paranoid psychosis).

Since we had chosen not to take responsibility for the care of the control relatives, it was essential to check on any interventions they might have received from the clinicians looking after the control patients. We found that

Table 9.1. Demographic and Historical Characteristics of Trial Patients

Characteristic	Experimental	Control
Number	12	12
Male/female	6/6	6/6
Living group: Parents	6	6
Spouse/sibling	6	6
Mean age	39	30
Education: CSE[a] or above	4	4
Ever married	6	7
Ever divorced or separated	1	2
Mean number of children	0.8	1.3
Drop from highest level of intensity and duration of relationships with the opposite sex	3	2
Occupation: 3 (nonmanual or above)	6	2
Mean length of unemployment before admission in months	16.5	4.8*
Employed at admission	4	7
Abnormal premorbid personality	8	5
First admission	4	4
Mean number of previous admissions	2.3	1.2
Age at first onset	33	27

[a]CSE = lowest examination obtainable by a school child in the UK.

*$p < .05$.

in eight cases, no therapeutic help was given to these relatives. In two cases the relatives were seen by a psychiatrist to receive treatment for their own overt symptoms; the focus of this treatment was on the relatives' own pathology and not on their attitudes toward the schizophrenic patients. In only two families did the therapeutic assistance have aims similar to those of our own intervention. In one case it took the form of a single family session held in the 9 months after discharge, with the aim of persuading the patient to attend a day hospital. In the second case, the wife of a schizophrenic patient was seen every 2 weeks by a psychiatric social worker, and one family session was held in the 9-month period. The social worker gave the wife some advice on how to handle aspects of her husband's behavior that stemmed from his delusions. It is worth noting that this wife's level of overinvolvement had actually risen by the end of the follow-up period. Thus our gamble of not taking responsibility for the control families paid off, since in only one case did the relative receive professional help of the nature and scale we were offering the experimental families. Furthermore, this help did not effect any of the changes we were aiming at in the experimental group. This meant that any differences in EE and face-to-face contact found between experimental and control relatives at follow-up could confidently be ascribed to our intervention.

How effective was the package of treatments? To answer this question, we need to examine each of the targets in turn. Table 9.2 displays the mean ratings for Critical Comments and Emotional Overinvolvement as they were recorded initially and at the 9-month follow-up assessment.

At the point of entering the study, the experimental and control relatives did not differ significantly in the amount of either criticism or overinvolvement they expressed. This finding endorses the effectiveness of the randomization procedure. At the follow-up, 9 months after the patients' discharge, the mean number of critical comments made by the control relatives had hardly changed. By contrast, among the experimental relatives, there was a dramatic and highly significant fall in criticism to less than half the initial level. The intervention had far less impact on overinvolvement, the mean level of which did fall in the experimental group, but not quite to a significant degree. However, concentrating on the mean obscures the dramatic fall from a score of 4 to 0 that was shown by one relative, the wife of a patient. Obviously this woman's overinvolvement with her husband could not have preceded their meeting 6 years previously, which may have been a key factor in its amenability to our intervention. We gained the impression from the relatives' accounts of their attitudes toward the patients that overinvolvement often began very early in the patients' lives, sometimes at birth. For example, one mother saw the elder of her two sons as being the vulnerable one in childhood; she allowed

Table 9.2. Experimental and Control Relatives' Ratings for Critical Comments and Emotional Overinvolvement, Initially and at 9-Month Follow-Up

Group	Number Scoring at or above Cutoff Point[a]	Mean Score	
		Initially	At 9-Month Follow-Up
Critical Comments			
Experimental	12	16.7	6.5**
Control	8	12.0	10.7
Emotional Overinvolvement			
Experimental	5	4.0	2.4*
Control	6	4.0	3.7

Note. Except where noted, all interactions were nonsignificant.

[a]For Critical Comments, a score of 6 or more; for Emotional Overinvolvement, a score of 3 or more.

*$t = 2.4$, n.s.

**$t = 3.7$, $p < .005$.

him to sleep in her bed, from which his brother was excluded. He continued sleeping in his mother's bed until the age of 15, and developed schizophrenia 6 years later. Another mother became overinvolved with her daughter when it became evident that she was failing to grow at a normal rate. She was discovered to have Turner syndrome (XO constitution) and never attained a normal height. Her dwarfism provoked her mother into overinvolvement in her childhood, and she fell ill with schizophrenia when aged 20.

Of course, these anecdotal accounts are not hard evidence, but they do suggest that overinvolved attitudes toward the patients begin much earlier in their lives than is the case for criticism. This may explain why critical attitudes proved to be more malleable than overinvolvement. The issue of whether these attitudes preceded the first onset of schizophrenia is taken up again in a later chapter.

The reductions in both mean Critical Comments and Emotional Overinvolvement scores in the experimental families contributed toward an alteration in EE classification from high to low in a number of relatives. Out of the 13 experimental relatives rated as high in EE initially, 7 had become low in EE by the follow-up interview. As two of these relatives were the parents of one patient, this represents six families in which a reduction from high to low EE occurred. Among the control relatives, two individuals changed from high to low on Critical Comments, one of them being a spouse and the other a sister, the only sibling of a patient in the study population. As neither relative had received any therapeutic help from professionals, we must regard these alterations in attitude as spontaneous. No control relative dropped from high to low on Emotional Overinvolvement during the course of the study, whereas one moved in the reverse direction.

The other target of our intervention was face-to-face contact. At follow-up, this had fallen below 35 hours per week in six experimental relatives, two being the parents of one patient. One patient achieved this reduction by obtaining a full-time job, and another did so by attending a day hospital, while the remaining three made alterations in the way they spent their leisure time. Low contact was found at follow-up in three control families; this was not significantly different from the proportion in experimental families. However, the way in which this was achieved in two of these families differed from that in the experimental group: One control patient's husband left her during the follow-up period, while another patient began sequestering himself in his room whenever he was at home.

It will be remembered that our initial postulate was that *either* altering EE from high to low *or* reducing contact below 35 hours per week would lead to a significantly lower relapse rate. This premise was derived from the data displayed in Figure 6.1. Hence one or the other of these achievements would indicate a successful intervention. The changes that occurred in EE and face-to-face contact are shown in Table 9.3. It can be seen that there was an overlap

Table 9.3. EE and Face-to-Face Contact at
Follow-Up in Experimental Group

Patient Number	Relative	EE	Face-to-Face Contact
1	Mother	Low	Low
1	Father	Low	Low
7	Husband	Low	High
13	Wife	High	High
30	Wife	Low	Low
31	Wife	High	Low
40	Wife	Low	High
41	Mother	Low	High
45	Husband	High	Low
49	Mother	High	Low
53	Mother	High	High
55	Mother	High	High
61	Mother	Low	High

Note. Change from high to low: 7 in EE, 6 in
face-to-face contact.

in the achievement of the two aims in some families, with the result that one or both targets were met in 9 out of the 12 families. Hence our intervention was successful in 75% of the experimental families.

Did these alterations in the family environment have any effect on the course of the patients' condition? The relapse rates of the various groups are displayed in Table 9.4. The relapse rate in the control group was significantly higher than that in the whole experimental group; hence our social intervention produced a significant reduction in the relapse rate of schizophrenia. Some light is thrown on the specificity of the intervention by comparing the relapse rate in the control group with that of the patients in whose families we achieved one or both of the aims of social intervention. In fact, in these

Table 9.4. Relapse Rates over 9 Months in High-EE Families

Group	Relapse Rate
A. High control	6/12 (50%)
B. High experimental	1/12 (8%)
C. High experimental with change to low EE and/or face-to-face contact	0/8 (0%)

Note. A vs. B, exact $p = .032$; A vs. C, exact $p = .017$.

nine families, not a single patient relapsed — a difference from the relapse rate in the control group of even greater significance (exact $p = .017$). This suggests that it was indeed the achievement of the aims of our intervention that reduced the patients' relapse rate, rather than some nonspecific effect of our contact with the families.

There is some support for this interpretation in the findings of Hogarty *et al.* (1974, 1979). In two separate controlled studies, social therapies were also added to maintenance on neuroleptic drugs to treat schizophrenic patients. In the first study, the social therapy was a combination of intensive social casework and vocational rehabilitation counseling, while in the second it comprised intensive individual and family social casework. In neither study did the social intervention significantly reduce the relapse rate when added to maintenance on drugs. There is no doubt that a great deal of professional attention was lavished on the patients and their relatives in these two studies without producing the desired effect. Our interpretation of these disappointing results is that the quantity of care given to the families is less important than its focus. The therapeutic effort needs to be directed at those specific aspects of family relationships that have been shown convincingly to be linked with relapse of schizophrenia. That is what we see as the strength of the new generation of studies, which includes those described in this part of the book.

CASE EXAMPLES

To conclude this account of our intervention study, we describe in detail our therapeutic efforts with three families — two successes and a failure. We hope that this will leave the reader with a better idea of how we actually set about achieving the aims of our intervention.

Case 1

The patient, John, was a man aged 23, living with his mother, his stepfather, and a younger brother. The mother had turned her first husband out of the house because of his drinking when her two sons were very young. She had brought them up by herself for many years. She had viewed the patient as the more vulnerable of the two boys, since he had developed a severe chest infection in his early childhood. He had slept in her bed until the age of 15 years, when she sent him off to America for a holiday.

At about this time she became involved with her second husband and remarried; however, the marriage was not very happy. She was a very dominating woman and stated quite clearly that if it came to a choice between her son John and her husband, she would have no hesitation in getting rid of her second husband, as she had her first.

The EE ratings revealed that the mother had a score of 11 on Critical Comments and 3 on Emotional Overinvolvement, placing her firmly in the high-EE group. The stepfather scored 9 on Critical Comments, but showed no overinvolvement.

Our initial assessment of the family was that the poor marital relationship led the mother to turn to John for her emotional satisfaction, thus maintaining an overinvolved relationship that had a long history. The stepfather felt excluded from the mother–son coalition and was consequently very critical of John. The situation was compounded by the fact that John's illness was dominated by negative symptoms, such as lying in bed all morning and letting his hair grow long. The stepfather had been a professional soldier, so both kinds of behavior infuriated him. Both parents had great difficulty in recognizing that John was ill, and it was about a year before he was brought for treatment.

Our prime aim was to extract John from the family in order that he could develop a measure of independence, but also to prevent his illness from dominating the scene and overshadowing the marital problem. The clinical team responsible for his care agreed with this objective and arranged for him to be placed in a hostel on his discharge from the hospital.

The first stage in working with the family was to administer the education program. This had a surprisingly great effect on the stepfather, who rapidly accepted the fact that John was ill; he became much less critical, as illustrated by the following quote from the relatives' group:

"He's slipped right back into laying in bed in the mornings, and I've had to sort of be a bit firm again and chase him up in the mornings. But I'm doing it in a bit more polite manner, because I realize that it's not all his fault probably. He can't help it. But, before, I thought that he could and he was playing up, and so I took stronger measures of getting him out of bed. But now I don't."

This modification of the stepfather's attitude was very gratifying, but we became somewhat alarmed that he was swinging over into overinvolvement. Fortunately, though, he was a sensible man who realized the potential dangers of this response and articulated them clearly.

"Really, I have to ease up sometimes because I'm starting to think for him. And that's bad, I realize that. I've got to control myself for thinking for him, because he'll be putting me in the same category as his mother, which is wrong because one of us has got to sort of keep away from him, so he can see the difference, or find out the difference eventually."

The education program had far less impact on the mother, who, during the first few relatives' group meetings, repeatedly asked questions about the illness that had been answered in the program. Her style of communication was to interrupt other relatives and steer the conversation back to her particular worries. Although other members of the group tried to reassure her or voiced disagreement, it did not have much effect. The therapists gently but firmly pointed out what she was doing on several occasions, and after four or five group meetings she successfully modified her behavior. Other relatives in the group put pressure on her to be firmer with John and allow him more independence. Toward the end of the 9-month period of attendance, she showed some signs of responding to this.

John actually moved straight from the hospital into a hostel, so that our family sessions in the home did not include him, although his brother sometimes attended. In these sessions we focused on the mother's inability to let John go, and on the tension in the marital relationship. We attempted to reinforce the stepfather's position as an authority who knew when to be firm without being punitive. Over the course of several family sessions, we considered the marital relationship improved.

Unfortunately, John was not happy living in the hostel and discharged himself after 3 months. Plans were made for him to go to another hostel very close to his home, but these never came to fruition, largely because of parental opposition. However, John did attend a day hospital following his discharge from inpatient care and rarely missed a day. As a result, his face-to-face contact with both parents had dropped below 35 hours per week at follow-up. When the CFI was repeated, the mother made only one critical remark, and her Emotional Overinvolvement score had dropped slightly to 2. The stepfather's Critical Comments score was only 2, so that we had been successful in reducing EE from high to low in both parents and also in reducing face-to-face contact from high to low. John was maintained on long-acting injections of fluphenazine and had no recurrence of schizophrenia, either at the 9-month follow-up or at a more extended follow-up 2 years after discharge.

Case 40

The patient, a married man aged 56, was admitted for the 10th time with a psychotic illness. In the past, his diagnosis had varied among schizophrenia, mania, and schizoaffective psychosis. On this occasion he had first-rank symptoms as well as grandiose delusions, and was diagnosed by the Catego program as having S +, or nuclear schizophrenia.

His wife had been a social worker and had given up her job on marrying him 6 years previously. It was evident that she had decided to dedicate her life to keeping him well, and this was reflected in an Emotional Overinvolvement score of 4. In addition to being overprotective, she also showed a degree of symbiosis, in that she insisted on sharing all her husband's experiences. When he retired to bed at 9.00 P.M. because the medication made him sleepy, she would accompany him because she did not want to watch television without him. She was also mildly critical of him, with a Critical Comments score of 3.

The relapse of his illness was a devastating blow to her, as she took it to mean that she had failed in her role of professional caregiver. She developed a combination of anxiety and helplessness, which she managed to convey to the clinical team looking after him. The ability of families to transfer their emotional conflicts to the professional team is sometimes quite striking. This can readily disrupt the working of the team if it goes unheeded (Berkowitz & Leff, 1984).

We administered the education program to the wife, and then decided that our main aim was to explore the patient's need to abdicate responsibility to his wife and her need to take it on. We hoped that she would eventually return to full-time work. We held a family session shortly after his discharge from the hospital, in which these themes were introduced. The patient recounted an episode during World War II in which he had made a mistake in an important task he was given. It was clear to us that he attached excessive blame to himself for the failure, and was consequently reluctant to take on responsibility, even for himself. On the other hand, his wife was determined to show that she could cope with anything without weakening. We stimulated an open discussion about these attitudes and the strains they placed on the couple.

The wife attended the relatives' group regularly, and the theme of her need to overprotect her husband came up repeatedly in more general discussions. The other relatives encouraged her to return to work, and eventually she took on a full-time job. She found the job quite demanding and difficult, and came home after the first day in some trepidation as to how her husband had coped without her help. She found that he had done all the housework and the shopping and had everything ready for her return. She was so relieved that she burst into tears, and he was able to comfort her.

The balance of their relationship continued to shift toward equality. The patient became increasingly competent and eventually took over the management of their finances. He also took a 10-week training course, but was unable to find a suitable job, so continued doing their domestic chores in an efficient way. The wife was able to be open about her inability to cope with all the demands she met at work and to accept comfort from her husband.

By the 9-month follow-up, the wife's overinvolvement had totally disappeared, and she made one critical comment. The husband and wife were in high contact, but as the wife was now low in EE, this was not in any way dangerous to the patient. He was maintained on regular medication and remained well throughout the 9 months. He was still free of symptoms at a follow-up 2 years after his discharge.

Case 53

Some details about this patient have already been given on p. 137. She was discovered to have Turner syndrome in early childhood and developed schizophrenia at age 20. At the time of key admission, she was aged 25 and was living with her mother and the mother's boyfriend.

At the initial CFI, the mother was found to be highly overinvolved (her Emotional Overinvolvement score was 5), and also excessively critical (her Critical Comments score was 15). We hoped to involve her in the relatives' group, but she failed to attend until her daughter had already been out of the hospital for 2 months. At this point we conducted a session in their home and began to discuss the patient's need to depend on her mother and the mother's reciprocal need to protect the patient. It emerged over the course of several of these sessions that the mother had lost her own parents very early in her life and had been brought up in an orphanage. There she had taken on the responsibility of looking after other motherless children. We felt that she had effectively denied her need to be mothered, and instead had acted toward other needy children in the way she really wanted to be treated herself. She volunteered the statement that she had never missed her own mother until she found herself to be pregnant for the first time.

Unfortunately, before we really had time to explore these issues further or to engage the mother in the group, the family went on a holiday in a caravan (mobile home). This threw the patient and the two adults together in very close proximity and resulted in almost continuous face-to-face contact. Within a day or two, the patient relapsed and had to be readmitted to the hospital.

We continued to work with the family after the patient's discharge, but we found the mother very resistant to change. Whenever we were on the verge of extracting the patient from the home, the mother would step in and put a stop to the process. She seemed to be driven by her guilt over having "damaged" the patient, leaving her stunted in growth and unable to develop into a woman.

At the 9-month follow-up, the mother's Emotional Overinvolvement score had dropped slightly to 3, but she remained highly critical, with a Critical Comments score of 14.

APPENDIX: EDUCATION PROGRAM

1. Diagnosis

We are meeting to talk to you about your relative who is in hospital at the moment. We would like to have four of these meetings. In them we will first give you some information and then you can ask questions.

The four meetings will cover the diagnosis made by the doctors, what the illness is like, what normally happens during it, some possible causes, treatments that are given, and finally what you yourselves can do to help.

Today we will try to describe what it is that has happened to your relative, and what it is called.

In the past you may have found that your relative is not his usual self; that he does not talk to you like he used to, that he may prefer to spend time alone or that he sees and hears things which you cannot. You may also have found that if you try to talk to him about it, you cannot persuade him that these things are not true.

You have probably asked yourselves, what is the matter with him? Is it serious? What happens now? You may have found out some of the answers already, but you may not know how they apply to a member of your own family. We hope to answer these sorts of questions today and in the next three meetings.

The things that may have worried you are the signs of a well recognized illness. We now know quite a lot about it. For example, we know that sometimes the patient can hear and see things which are not there. His thinking can get muddled so that it is difficult to talk to him and he doesn't always seem to listen to what you say. This can mean that he loses touch with what is really happening around him, and then things he says or does can look odd or unusual. Also, his feelings may change, they may become more intense so that he appears very miserable or very excited, or they may diminish so that he loses interest or shows less affection.

Patients who have these sorts of experiences suffer from a form of what is called schizophrenia. Schizophrenia is an illness. It affects people in different ways. The difficulty is that the sort of experiences it gives rise to seem completely real to the people suffering from it but are hard to explain. For instance, someone who hears voices may talk back to them because he thinks they are voices of people who are actually there. Someone who seems to be very cold may not be able to be friendly because his feelings have been swamped by the illness. Someone who is very awkward or does not want to do ordinary things like the rest of the family, may be like that because the illness has made him completely wrapped up in himself, and he does not realize or care that he is upsetting others.

Because the patient cannot usually explain what is happening in his mind, it is not always easy for other people, even those who live with him like yourselves, to realize that many of the odd or upsetting things he does are *caused* by the illness. It is especially hard because it is a mental and not a physical illness, so there are no outward signs of anything being wrong. For example, it is much easier to understand why someone with rheumatism can't do so much around the house, or perhaps can't get to work, than is to understand why someone with schizophrenia may not be able to do those things.

Schizophrenia is not a rare illness. One out of every hundred people will probably suffer from it during his lifetime.

It can affect anyone. It is an illness that starts mainly in young people in their twenties, when most people are getting married or moving out of home. Both men and women can suffer from it, although it tends to start some years earlier in men. Schizophrenia also occurs all over the world, it is not something that just affects people in Britain.

2. Symptomatology

Now we would like to go into more detail about the sort of things that can happen to someone who has schizophrenia. Certain things happen to almost every patient at some stage of the illness.

Disturbances of thinking are very common. You may have noticed that sometimes your relative says things to you which you don't expect, or don't understand. It doesn't seem to make sense; or perhaps he talks a lot but loses the thread of what he is saying. This kind of thing can make communication between you very difficult.

What happens is that the patient has lost his ability to think clearly and to keep his thoughts in order. Thoughts become jumbled, so they don't always make sense. Sometimes it seems as though there are too many thoughts, and the patient feels he can only get rid of them by sharing them with someone, so he may talk endlessly although you may find it hard to follow his meaning. On the other hand, he may suddenly stop talking, because his mind seems to be 'blank.' All this can be very frightening, and the patient himself often can't understand what has happened to his thoughts. When this happens, he may spend a lot of time worrying about it and trying to work out what is going on. For instance, he might think that the neighbors are to blame for what is happening, or that you yourselves are being unfriendly towards him. He cannot be persuaded that this is not true however often you tell him, or try to argue him out of it. To him, all these things are real and he will be convinced by them. This means that the illness changes his whole world and he loses touch with what is really happening to him.

Another thing that often happens is that the patient's imagination plays tricks on him. As a result he hears, and sometimes sees things which are not there. He may hear noises or voices. Sometimes he understands what he hears; at other times he can make no sense of it at all. He may hear voices talking to him or about him, and he may say he knows where they are coming from, for example, the wardrobe, the television, or from a part of his own head. These voices can say unpleasant things, and the patient often talks or shouts back at them, even when other people are present. Occasionally, they may tell him to do things, like opening the front door at night, or to stay awake. He sometimes feels he must obey these voices, and this can become very distressing for him.

Schizophrenia can also affect feelings. The patient loses his ability to feel the right emotion at the right time, so that he may laugh about bad news, or may cry when everyone else is laughing. You may have noticed that he doesn't seem to care for you as he did before, or to show his love for you in the same way. There may be fewer and fewer times when you can really talk to each other, and you may sometimes wonder whether he still feels anything for you at all. He can't help all this, because his usual feelings have been swamped by the illness and he has become very wrapped up in himself. There may be times when he threatens to smash things or to harm someone he is fond of; this is because he is not always in control of how he feels, but is usually quite unaware of the effect this can have on other people. More often, though, he is shy and withdrawn rather than threatening, and may be easily upset, particularly if you become irritated by the things he does.

From time to time he may realise how much he has changed, and how different his life has become. This can make him miserable or desperate, and say that life is not worth living. Occasionally, he may become very excitable and overactive, and say he has no problems at all.

Something else commonly affected by schizophrenia is the amount of energy the patient has, and his willingness to do things. What usually happens is that the patient prefers to be by himself. He may sit in his own room for hours on end listening or talking to his voices, or pacing up and down. He may hurry through meals, hardly noticing what he eats, and then go back to his room. At times he may refuse to eat at all with the family. This happens because he finds he can no longer feel at ease with other people — he feels awkward and unable to do or say the right thing. He may even actively avoid other people's company, whereas before he seemed to enjoy it. Some patients feel that people in the streets stare at them and avoid going out.

Often, the patient sleeps a lot of the time and may refuse to get up in the mornings. He may be asleep and awake at completely different times from the rest of the family, and this can make it very hard for him to keep a job.

A big problem is when he shows little interest in anything and has no idea what to do with himself. His mind may seem to be a complete blank, or he may pester you to do things to keep him occupied. His lack of energy causes him to take a long time over such things as housework or his job. This can be very hard to live with.

Finally, many arguments can arise over his personal cleanliness, again due to his lack of interest and energy. He may neglect to comb his hair, refuse to bathe himself, or [fail to] clean his teeth. He may dress unusually or refuse to change his clothes.

Sometimes, being careless about some things, he becomes unusually fussy about others; he may insist that his room is kept in a certain way, or that you do not disturb his possessions.

These then, are some of the general ways in which schizophrenia can affect people, but as we said before, each individual will be affected in a somewhat different way.

3. Etiology and Course

Last time we talked about the sorts of things that can happen to someone with schizophrenia. Today we would like to tell you what is known about why the illness appears, the likelihood of further attacks and how it might affect the future.

We know that *inheritance* plays some part in the development of schizophrenia but by no means explains fully why the illness appears in a particular person. Just because schizophrenia occurs in one person in a family, it does not necessarily mean that other family members will develop it. Often there are no other relatives at all who have such attacks. Neither does it mean that a schizophrenic patient should not have children because they will be affected. All we do know is that there is an *increased risk of schizophrenia for children with a schizophrenic parent*; one out of ten children of a schizophrenic patient will develop it in later life.

There are other factors, which seem to influence the occurrence of schizophrenia. Research work has been done on many of these factors but at present we can hold no single cause responsible for schizophrenia; there seem to be a number of different contributory factors. We would like to look in some detail at one of these causes which may be important for you as members of the same family.

A lot has been written about the influence of the family on schizophrenia. We have no evidence that a *family's influence* on a child can *cause* schizophrenia. But, once the illness has appeared the family can play an important part in helping the patient to stay well. Other features help to decide whether the patient will do well, such as his *personality*. However, we will concentrate mainly on the part played by the family and will discuss this in more detail next time.

Also, we know that *the more things a patient has to cope with* in his life the more likely he is to have an attack. Increased stress can affect anyone badly, but schizophrenic patients seem to be particularly sensitive to it. Changes and conflicts in their lives can also bring on further attacks. We will talk about that next time as well.

Well then, what happens to someone who has had schizophrenia? It is important to stress that most people will get better with treatment. They will think more clearly and then the 'odd' ideas will go away. Unfortunately, recovery is not always complete, some patients being left with difficulties, but the overall response to treatment is good.

Some people only have one attack of schizophrenia; they recover from this and never have another. Others, luckily only a small number, do not respond to treatment at all. However, most patients although they recover from the attack are likely to have other attacks. These may occur within weeks of recovery, or may happen years later. During further attacks new kinds of odd behavior can appear, but often the same pattern will repeat itself.

In between attacks you may notice that your relative is not the same as he was before. For instance he may continue to take a long time to get things done. He may say very little when with other people. He loses interest in things and may be content to sit all day doing nothing. This can lead to difficulties in getting or keeping a job and he may remain unemployed for long periods.

If the person affected is a housewife, the family often finds that she cannot manage to do all the housework she used to. Chores remain undone and the house gets neglected. This means that the family has to rally round and do more.

Finally, even when well, your relative may not be as involved in the family as before. He may stay aloof from family events and seem much less affected by them.

These sort of things are not done to annoy you. They are partly the result of the medication, partly due to the illness itself, and partly due to the person's own attempts to avoid becoming upset and ill again.

We will say more about this in the final meeting, next week.

4. Treatment

Today we would like to talk about the treatment of schizophrenia.

You may have noticed that your relative has been given tablets while in hospital. These play an important part in the treatment of schizophrenia. They help to stop the voices in the patient's head, they make him less anxious and restless and help him to think more clearly. They protect him against stresses coming from his own experiences and his everyday life.

If drug treatment is started the effects cannot always be seen straight away. It may take days or even weeks before he improves. Even so the tablets have to be taken regularly. They are not like aspirins which you just take when a headache comes on. Some patients are not given tablets but are put on injections. These have the same effect as tablets but can be given less often. This is because one injection lasts for quite a long time. It is often more convenient for patients to have their drug treatment in this way, but again it is important that they have injections regularly.

Once a medicine has been found helpful, it has to be taken for a long time, even when the patient feels better. A lot of people find it very hard to stay on their drugs when they feel well, because it seems pointless. Unfortunately schizophrenia does not usually just go away. Like many diabetics, who have to take a daily injection even when feeling well, schizophrenic patients often have to stay on drugs to prevent further attacks and to remain well.

In the same way that there is no sudden improvement when patients start drug treatment, there is no sudden change if they stop it. When a patient has not taken his tablets or if he has missed his injections, a relapse does not occur immediately. It can take months, until symptoms reappear depending on the amount of changes and conflicts the patient has to cope with.

Drug treatment is not the only thing that helps. The atmosphere in the home and the way daily problems are tackled are equally important.

This is because people suffering from schizophrenia are very sensitive to things happening around them. They are much more easily upset than other people by the ups and downs of daily life. Changes in routine can make them feel unsettled and things like moving into a new house or having to face an examination can bring about another attack. When such events can't be avoided it is a good idea to tell the patient well in advance if any changes are expected to enable him to prepare himself.

Life with a schizophrenic person can be extremely difficult. He may behave oddly, talk to himself, spend all day lying in bed and take hours to get things done. This can make you angry and you find you lose your temper. Or you may feel intensely worried and find that you are always wondering where he is and what he will do next. The inevitable questions arise, what happens in the future if things go on like this, how am I going to cope, and you get anxious and upset.

It is not surprising if you find yourself reacting like this. Unfortunately it is not helpful for the patient and can make things worse. This is because he is easily upset himself, as we have said, and is unable to take being criticised or fussed over.

The best thing for you to do in this situation is firstly, not to spend so much time with him so that you don't get on each other's nerves. It is important that the patient leads as independent a life as possible. It helps him to gain confidence and to begin to look after himself again. Sometimes the hospital will arrange for him to spend his day at a day centre or help him get a job. Sometimes, if the patient lives with his parents, it is a good idea for him to leave home and live in a hostel. It may be difficult to accept, but the patient actually does better if he lives a life of his own as much as he can.

Secondly, if you *have* to be together a lot of the time, the best thing to do is not to shout or criticise or get too involved. This is the hardest part as it means that you feel you are not caring enough, or worry that your relative will think you are not interested in him. However, in the long run it is better for both of you; he will find things easier if you are less involved with him, and you will find you are feeling less strain.

Most families with a schizophrenic relative have to solve similar problems. The purpose of these talks is just to give you information, to let you know what you can expect and what you can do to help. We will now be arranging group meetings with other families in your position and if you talk to the people there you may find they have ideas that you can use, and that they find your suggestions helpful.

10

Behavioral Family Therapy: A Problem-Solving Approach to Family Coping

IAN R. H. FALLOON
*University of Southern California
and Buckingham Community Health Service*

INTRODUCTION

The behavioral family therapy approach that has developed over the past decade represents a clear departure from the focus on psychopathology as a result of "abnormal" family interaction patterns, which has figured prominently in psychodynamic and nonbehavioral family theories of mental illness. Instead of proposing that the family has a detrimental effect on a member who is suffering from a mental illness, this approach proposes that the family is the basic unit of health, and that it is a crucial determinant in the recovery and rehabilitation of mentally ill family members. For this reason, the behavioral family therapy approach seeks first to evaluate the healthy elements of family communication in solving everyday problems, before teaching problem-solving family interaction strategies that may lead to even better results in the future. Minimal attention is accorded to patently ineffective problem-solving communications. The aim is to build upon preexisting family strengths, rather than to focus on manifest weaknesses. It is assumed that at all times every family member is doing his or her utmost to cope with the stressors that he or she perceives. Family members' ability to achieve the ideal solution to any problem may be limited by a broad range of personal and environmental constraints. But it is assumed that they will endeavor to fashion the most effective response from all the resources within their grasp. This paradigm of effective problem-solving interaction in families fundamentally alters not only the way in which we assess family functioning, but also the manner in which we formulate our therapeutic interventions.

ASSESSMENT OF FAMILY PROBLEM-SOLVING EFFECTIVENESS

The early studies of family problem-solving effectiveness focused almost exclusively on the ineffective communication of cognitive and emotive messages in the family that may have contributed to the development of schizophrenia

150

in one or more family members. The "double-bind" interaction was the most widely cited version of postulated etiological factors (Bateson *et al.*, 1956). Others included the marital "schism" and "skew" of T. Lidz (T. Lidz, Cornelison, Fleck, & Terry, 1957), the "pseudomutuality" of Wynne (Wynne, Ryckoff, Day, & Hirsch, 1958), and the "interpersonal perceptual distortion" of Laing (Laing, 1967). While the serious methodological limitations of the studies that attempted to validate these theories prevented any clear conclusions about etiological factors, they did suggest a relationship between problem-solving functioning and adequacy of social functioning. The specific communication patterns that were considered pathogenic occurred with a low frequency in family problem-solving interactions, whereas a high frequency of effective problem-solving behavior was often observed.

A series of studies conducted by Wynne and Singer focused on carefully analyzing the communication process in families with schizophrenic and normal offspring. They found that parents of schizophrenics consistently showed deficits in sharing a joint attentional focus when compared to other groups. Parents of schizophrenics spoke in vague, fragmented, tangential ways. They used words idiosyncratically, lacked commitment to ideas presented, and had difficulty achieving closure on a topic area (Singer, 1968; Singer & Wynne, 1963, 1965, 1966; Wynne, Singer, Bartko, & Toohey, 1977). These transactional communication difficulties clearly interfere with effective problem solving.

The EE studies that have been described in the earlier parts of this volume examined the emotional responses of family members to episodes of florid schizophrenia in the index patient prior to his admission to hospital (Vaughn & Leff, 1976a). In these studies it was concluded that negative attitudes expressed about the patient were the *best* predictors of future exacerbations of schizophrenia. Although the authors found a positive correlation between positive statements and warmth expressed toward the index patient and the absence of relapse, this was only true when critical remarks and emotional overinvolvement were low (Brown *et al.*, 1972).

In a more recent analysis of the coping behavior of family members in handling a florid schizophrenia episode, Vaughn (1977) found that in families where relapses were less frequent, the family members tended to solve their problems in a calm, objective, and often highly creative manner. They tended to conceptualize the patient's bizarre behavior as an understandable response to a serious illness, and to avoid excessive personal criticism. This healthy problem-solving behavior has considerable relevance to the clinician, but has received much less attention than the less common, highly emotional, and ineffective responses of high-EE family members. Berkowitz and Leff (Berkowitz *et al.*, 1981) attempted to take advantage of the effective problem-solving skills of the low-EE relatives by having them discuss and model their skills with high-EE relatives in a biweekly group session.

The EE studies have been concerned exclusively with the problem of relapse of the index patient, and with his or her return to a hospital. The prevention of symptom relapse is a laudable goal for a clinical program, but only one of several to be considered in the successful management of a major illness. From a behaviorist's point of view, the crucial outcome variables must include not only the health and well-being of the index patient, but that of his or her family and community contacts. Health is not merely the absence of florid symptoms; it involves competent functioning in society. While negative emotional attitudes and communication difficulties may best predict the clinical course of vulnerable family members, positive aspects of family interaction may prove better predictors of competence in community functioning. Merely lowering the emotional tension of family members may serve to improve the florid symptoms of schizophrenia, while enhancing the social deficits.

The natural support system for promoting social role behavior is the family. Encouragement, role modeling, rehearsal, and supportive feedback are provided by the healthy family in training social competence in its members. This learning environment is further supported by the special knowledge of the capacity of each family member to deal with stressors — knowledge that enables families to pace progress toward goals in a manner that modulates stress and avoids overstimulating a vulnerable family member. Support for this natural rehabilitation capacity of the family can be provided through an emphasis on this aspect of family functioning.

In addition to supporting its members as they develop social competence, the family also provides a buffer against extrafamilial life events. There is evidence to suggest that episodes of florid schizophrenia are triggered by life events (Brown & Birley, 1968; Leff, Hirsch, Gaind, Rohde, & Stevens, 1973). In low-EE families, these appear the most common source of stress-precipitated exacerbations (Leff & Vaughn, 1981). Effective problem solving may allow the family to seek strategies to cope with stressful events and to avoid the unwanted consequences of this source of stress.

The behavioral family therapy approach that we have developed was designed to enhance the effective problem-solving functions of the family system. It is not specific to the treatment of families with members who have schizophrenia, but can be employed in any family where deficits in this important area can be pinpointed.

BEHAVIORAL ANALYSIS OF THE FAMILY SYSTEM

The initial step in behavioral family therapy involves an assessment of the strengths and weaknesses of the family system, with particular reference to the manner in which they handle the problems of everyday living together, as well as major life crises. The former include the attainment of the personal goals of individual family members.

The first step is to interview family members individually to establish their unique assets and deficits, their goals, their contributions to the family, and the assistance they obtain from the family. Their feelings and attitudes toward other family members are explored in relation to specific functional issues. The CFI provides a useful adjunct to this individual analysis, although in its shortened form (Vaughn & Leff, 1976b), it focuses mainly on relationships with the family member with schizophrenia and on his or her behavioral disturbance. The specific goals and problem issues are listed for each individual, and the manner in which family problem solving reportedly addresses these precisely defined issues is noted.

The second step involves an assessment of the interrelationships between the various goals and problems of individual family members. The relevance of individual goals and problems to the family as a whole is determined wherever possible. For example, a son may want to spend more time away from the house, but his mother, fearing loneliness, may discourage him in his efforts to socialize outside the home. In another family, the mother may want to engage in more activities outside the home herself and may eagerly support her son's attempts to socialize. This assessment of the function of problems in the family system is called "functional analysis." The many individual problems can be broken down into fewer family problems, and a clearer view of potential solutions can be obtained.

The third step in behavioral analysis involves observation of the family's attempts to resolve a problem. While reports from family members may provide some information on the problem-solving behavior of the family, such information is seldom objective, and often focuses on the deficiencies of the process rather than its strengths. Several methods have been employed to obtain naturalistic observation of family problem-solving behavior. Undoubtedly the most objective of these methods is to observe the family members interacting in their home environment. The availability of resources usually limits the use of this approach. However, the value of home visits in the assessment of family functioning is considerable, and at least one home visit should be attempted wherever possible. In the absence of observations in the natural habitat, clinic-based analogues of family problem-solving discussions have been developed. These involve choosing a problem situation and having the family attempt to resolve the issue within a timed interval (e.g., 10 minutes). A wide range of situations have been chosen as stimuli for such problem-solving discussions. These have included highly relevant "hot issues" for each particular family, or less relevant tasks such as planning a vacation, or even agreeing on perceptions of a Rorschach card (Singer, 1968). The family problem-solving behaviors are coded by reliably trained raters for both effective and nonconstructive components.

Finally, with interview and observational data collected, the behavioral family therapist is in a position to formulate a unique treatment plan to correct the major problem-solving deficits of each family. Wherever feasible, the strengths of the family serve to support the treatment program. But the baseline behavioral analysis is merely the initial phase of assessment; throughout the course of treatment, assessment continues, and strategies are modified as new information is gathered. This ongoing behavioral analysis continues to be based upon careful observation of family problem-solving functions.

THE TREATMENT PROGRAM

The behavioral analysis constitutes the vital first step in treatment as the specific functional deficits of the family are pinpointed. The subsequent intervention is then comparatively straightforward. Most families who are living with a member who has had schizophrenia have deficits in their communication and problem-solving behavior. However, they usually have a grossly inadequate knowledge of the nature of schizophrenia and its treatment. For this reason, prior to starting behavioral family therapy to enhance problem solving, two sessions are devoted exclusively to education about schizophrenia. During these sessions, usually conducted at home, further observation of family interaction is conducted by the therapist.

Education about Schizophrenia

Two sessions at the onset of family treatment are devoted to discussions of the diagnosis, etiology, management, and course of schizophrenia. Family participation is maximized by encouraging the patient to describe his or her symptoms and by encouraging other family members to express their feelings about the illness, including similar experiences they may have suffered. The deficits in the family's knowledge of schizophrenia are the focus of the discussion — in particular, myths and misconceptions about the illness. Families are explicitly told that there are no good scientific data to suggest that schizophrenia is caused by childhood upbringing or family stressors. Biochemical and genetic theories are outlined in a manner comprehensible to the families. Visual aids and clearly written handouts are used to augment discussion.

In the second educational session, a cogent rationale for long-term medication maintenance combined with effective stress management is laid down. The beneficial effects of neuroleptics are outlined, along with their limitations. Side effects are clearly described (including potentially irreversible effects, such as tardive dyskinesia), and methods of coping with these unwanted effects are discussed. Prodromal warning signals of impending relapse are defined by the patient and his or her family so that families know when to seek help. The high rate of relapse with its attendant social disruption in patients who do not continue medication is contrasted with the low relapse rate and minimal social disruption associated with continued regular low-dosage neuroleptic therapy. The value of serial plasma-level estimations in monitoring the medication is discussed. Patients are warned of the adverse effects of street drugs on their illness. They are exhorted to avoid all use of amphetamines, PCP, or hallucinogenic drugs; a warning is also issued about potential negative effects of alcohol and marijuana, particularly about the synergistic effects of these with neuroleptics.

Education about schizophrenia is an ongoing part of the family management program to which the therapist may return from time to time to revise aspects, sort out misunderstandings, or prompt medication compliance. Often families will bring magazine or newspaper articles to the attention of the therapist. Care is taken to evaluate such reports in terms of specifically documented effectiveness of any new, seemingly better therapies, so as to avoid raising expectations falsely. A striking feature of the educational sessions is the large amount of disclosure about symptoms that the patient frequently has never reported while in the hospital or attending an outpatient clinic. A high rate of psychotic episodes described by other family members suggests that future genetic studies might show a higher family incidence of schizophrenia if data were collected following a similar educational program. The two sessions provide an excellent cognitive framework for helping the patient and his or her family to understand the illness, as well as for reducing tension and changing attitudes.

A two-part questionnaire is administered before and after these sessions to measure the amount of information acquired and integrated. Although the instrument is heavily weighted against a predominantly low-socioeconomic-class population with limited reading skills, preliminary results have been impressive. While half of all respondents knew the diagnosis of schizophrenia before treatment, 95% were able to agree on a primary diagnosis of schizophrenia after the educational sessions. A 50% increase in scores on a series of multiple-choice questions was noted, with most patients and their families showing a knowledge level within the range obtained by mental health professionals on the same series of questions. Almost all the acquired knowledge was retained at least 9 months earlier. A few patients and family members did not show much change on the written examination; these were usually persons with limited reading skills in English. Members of one Hispanic family, who appeared deficient on the questionnaire ratings, recalled the discussion about the genetic risks of schizophrenia after the birth of the patient's baby a year later. They spontaneously asked the therapist to review the genetic studies, which demonstrated that the original intervention had indeed been beneficial.

Communication Training

The manner in which family members communicate their thoughts and feelings can and usually does have a major impact on the course of schizophrenia. At times of crisis, ineffective patterns of communication can impede coping efforts and can even contribute to an exacerbation of florid symptoms. On the other hand, effective communication can reduce family tension, enhance coping efforts, and lessen the likelihood of symptomatic exacerbations. One of the main advantages of working with the entire family is the opportunity to intervene and alter dysfunctional patterns of communication. In family management training, special attention is given to examining the ways in which families communicate. A careful behavioral analysis is performed in the early stages of treatment for each family, focusing on how each family member communicates positive and negative feelings, listens to others, and makes requests for behavioral change. Intervention strategies are then tailored to each family's specific deficits in communication skills.

Several aspects of communication are routinely addressed with all families. These include the importance of nonverbal aspects of communication, such as voice tone, eye contact, facial expression, body posture, and distance; the importance of being clear and specific rather than vague or global; and the desirability of using the "I-stance" ("I would worry less if you'd give me a call if you're going to be out past midnight"), rather than giving advice or telling others what they should, ought, must, or have to do ("Why don't you ever call? You should always call if you're going to be out late. You should know that by now . . . "). One of the most powerful interventions is the repeated rehearsal of difficult family situations. Improved communication can be shaped in rehearsal through the use of instruction, modeling, coaching, social reinforcement, and performance feedback. Family members are given homework assignments to practice these skills with other family members or with persons outside the family.

The clinical benefits of improving family communication skills are clear. In families having a member with schizophrenia, the baseline communication skills are frequently very poor. There may be little or no communication of positive feelings, such as praise or appreciation. Parental communications with the patient may be laden with hostile, intrusive, or guilt-inducing statements that raise the tension level in the home. Requests for behavioral change are often made in such fashion as to make the recipient even *less* likely to honor the request (e.g., "Why don't you ever clean up your room?"). Teaching families effective communication skills helps to lower tension in the home and to set the stage for effective problem solving.

In families having a member with persistent psychotic symptoms or serious behavioral disturbance, considerable feelings of frustration, anger, or guilt may contribute to high levels of tension. In such cases, teaching clear, direct communication skills can be particularly beneficial. It is important to get family members to communicate to one another feelings of appreciation or pleasure regarding specific things the other person has done, even if it means overlooking, for the time being, other bothersome or annoying behaviors. Global expressions of positive feelings ("You've been really helpful lately") are probably not as effective as specific expressions ("That was nice of you to take me to the store this morning; it really helped me out"). Emphasis on frequent communication of positive feelings helps contribute to a general atmosphere of support and a lowering of tension in the home.

It is also important to communicate negative feelings, such as anger, hurt, disappointment, or sadness, in an effective manner. Generalized expressions of negative feelings (e.g., "How can you stand to lie around all day doing nothing?") are not only ineffective in engendering behavioral change, but also tend to give rise to feelings of anger or resentment and may cause the undesired behavior to become even more entrenched. Expressions of negative feelings for specific behaviors, coupled with requests for behavioral change (e.g., "It makes me mad when you stay in bed past noon. I would appreciate it if you would try to get up out of bed by 10:00 A.M. or so.") are much more effective and can readily be taught to families via behavioral rehearsal.

A final communication skill that can be taught to families is "active listening." Often when a person is feeling bad, simply having a good listener present helps to make matters better. Family members can be taught to listen attentively, and ask clarifying questions and reflect content through behavioral rehearsal and modeling by the therapist. Many families have very poor listening skills, and this deficit represents one of the major obstacles to effective coping. The therapist can certainly step in at times of crisis and, using his or her listening skills, assist the family in their coping efforts; however, the family that acquires these skills as part of family therapy is better equipped to deal with stressful events without being dependent on extrafamilial professional assistance.

Structured Problem Solving

Because schizophrenia is a stress-related illness, one of the very basic advantages to using a family therapy approach is the opportunity to enable family members to make better use of the family as a resource for coping with stressful life events. At the core of family management training is a structured problem-solving method that is taught to families to improve their coping with major crises, as well as with the lesser problems of day-to-day living. It involves six steps.

STEP 1: IDENTIFY A SPECIFIC PROBLEM

This involves listening actively to each member's description of the problem and seeking clarification when necessary, while trying to avoid premature giving of advice or reassurance. Here it is important to explore the problem fully before going on to the next step. For example, one family worked diligently on listing various places where a very shy son could go to socialize and meet potential girlfriends, when the real problem the son was seeking help for was how to improve his social skills and overcome the incapacitating anxiety he experienced in social settings.

STEP 2: LIST ALTERNATIVE SOLUTIONS

When the problem has been identified, the entire family is encouraged to "brainstorm" and generate a list of possible solutions. No discussion is permitted regarding the merits of each suggestion; all are recorded without prejudgment. This encourages reticent family members to express their views. At least five or six solutions are required as a safeguard against a domineering family member's announcing the "obvious" best solution and thwarting participation by all family members.

STEP 3: DISCUSS PROS AND CONS OF EACH SOLUTION

Each suggested solution is discussed in turn, and its advantages and disadvantages are listed.

STEP 4: CHOOSE THE BEST SOLUTION(S)

On the basis of the preceding discussion, the family decides upon the best solution or combination of solutions. It may be hoped that this will be a consensus decision, though it need not necessarily be so.

STEP 5: PLAN HOW TO IMPLEMENT THE SOLUTION

Successful execution of the selected strategy usually requires careful planning. In some cases, a dry-run practice may help the family prepare for potential difficulties. This may take the form of overt behavioral rehearsal or merely talking through procedures step by step. Little details, such as using bus schedules or telephone services, having adequate finances, understanding how to complete certain forms, and so forth, may doom implementation of the chosen solution if they are not considered in the planning.

STEP 6: REVIEW EFFORTS

At some later time, the family members are invited to review their efforts to implement the agreed-upon solution. Any genuine attempt to implement the solution deserves family praise, even if a successful outcome is not achieved. Failure of any attempt is examined in terms of the partial success achieved. Family members are encouraged to use their knowledge of the results to construct a more effective strategy for future occasions. Care is taken to point out that many problems are very difficult to solve and require repeated problem-solving efforts.

In training families in this approach, the therapist may initially provide clear direction for the family. He or she may demonstrate or instruct the family in active listening skills, suggest possible solutions, and help them evaluate and prepare effective strategies. As soon as the family begins to master the approach, the therapist's involvement is gradually withdrawn. Ideally, the therapist's role eventually becomes that of "outside consultant" or troubleshooter. Families are given homework assignments to practice problem solving between family therapy sessions.

The clinical benefits of teaching families this problem-solving method are considerable. One obvious advantage is that a problem of an individual can be shared with the rest of the family, and the intellectual, emotional, and financial resources of the entire family can be directed into a problem-solving effort. A second advantage is the opening up of family communication channels. The participation by all family members that typically occurs during structured problem-solving sessions contributes to a greater sense of emotional support and family unity, and offers a stark contrast to what in many families was a prior state of fragmentation and emotional isolation. In those cases where problem-solving efforts fail to solve the problem completely, it is a collective failure of the family, and scapegoating or finger pointing is somewhat less likely to occur. A final advantage relates to a clinical phenomenon that is quite striking. The problem-solving method, by its very nature as a structured, task-oriented process, dramatically lowers the level of tension in the family, even when members are discussing emotionally charged issues. Time after time, therapists have noted how families have been able to tackle difficult problems, such as the use of illegal street drugs, continuing unemployment, and intrusive parental behaviors, in a low-key, productive manner. Problems such as these, which have a potential for rending families asunder, can usually be addressed in family problem-solving sessions with very satisfactory results.

Other Behavioral Strategies

Few families have a wide enough repertoire of coping skills to deal effectively with the many problems associated with schizophrenia. While the problem-solving approach provides a structure that helps facilitate family creativity in developing novel solutions, the mental health professional can assist the family by sharing his or her behavioral management expertise with them. Within the problem-solving framework, such issues as administering medication, reducing side effects, coping with persistent delusions or hallucinations, and knowing when to seek professional assistance can be discussed in a straightforward fashion. When a patient remains significantly handicapped by persistent symptoms, family members become the primary caregivers. Attention can be directed to teaching practical management strategies similar to those employed by skilled psychiatric nurses.

One such strategy is to teach families about contingency contracting, an arrangement in which two family members negotiate an exchange of mutually desired behaviors, with a formally worded contract drawn up and signed by each party. Thus, a mother who wanted her husband to take her shopping negotiated a contract for him to "accompany me shopping for 1 hour per week" in return for her cooking "the dinner of your choice Wednesday evenings." Such contracts are particularly useful when neither person is very likely to perform the desired behaviors without the agreed-upon quid pro quo.

Another skill that can be imparted through family therapy is the often difficult process of setting firm limits regarding unacceptable behaviors. Frequently a firm statement of the acceptable limits of a family member's behavior can be crucial in maintaining a reasonable home environment. In one family, the brother of the patient persisted in telling him that he was not mentally ill, but instead needed to be spiritually healed via an exorcism. The parents were encouraged to make a specific statement to the brother that they did not believe that faith healing or an exorcism would help the brother and that taking him to a spiritualist for these purposes was unacceptable to them.

Social skills training can be used in family therapy to practice handling a variety of difficult extrafamilial situations. If a family member is seeking employment but feels very anxious about going for a job interview, the family can help bolster his or her confidence by role-playing job interview situations and providing the individual with a chance to practice or to try out different approaches prior to the actual job interview. Family members can also be taught simple anxiety management procedures, such as requesting a "time out." For example, if a family member is feeling too tense or upset to discuss a problem at that moment, he or she might be encouraged to say something like "Could we discuss this after dinner? I'm feeling too upset right now and would prefer to discuss it later." Excusing oneself from a social situation that is proving to be stressful is another example of a time-out procedure. Situations like these can be rehearsed during family therapy sessions so that the skills are learned prior to the actual situation.

A major problem associated with schizophrenia that has been receiving more attention in recent years is postpsychotic depression. Clinicians treating patients with schizophrenia are aware that moderate to severe depressive episodes occur in at least half of these cases. The family can be of tremendous assistance in managing these depressive episodes on an outpatient basis. In addition to emotional support and encouragement, family members can perform supportive functions, such as encouraging the patient to eat meals with the family, inducing him or her to spend a reasonable amount of time out of bed and around other people, monitoring medications if there is a suicide risk, and so forth. Steps such as these are necessary only during the acute phases of serious depressions. Family measures can often avert hospitalization with all its attendant costs, including financial burden, institutional dependency, and diminished self-esteem.

Another clinical advantage to working with the family pertains to patients who are poor compliers with the pharmacological aspects of treatment. In such cases the therapist can muster the support of other family members to encourage the patient to take his or her medications regularly. Where bothersome side effects, such as drowsiness or extrapyramidal symptoms, are contributing to poor compliance, family problem solving focused on reducing or coping with the side effects may lead to improved medication taking.

Living with a person suffering from schizophrenia can place a considerable burden on the family. This is particularly true for single-parent families, which are often quite socially isolated. Assisting these families in developing extrafamilial sources of support is an important task in treatment. For example, one family consisted of a 30-year-old patient and his markedly overinvolved mother. In a family problem-solving session aimed at helping the mother relieve her feelings of tension and depression, one of the solutions suggested was for her to find part-time employment. When this in fact occurred a few weeks later, she began to develop outside relationships and sources of satisfaction. This in turn led to fewer overinvolved behaviors and a general lowering of tension in the home. The son soon began to function better as well.

A Therapy Session

Each therapy session is structured around teaching the family effective problem solving. The content of the problem issues is less relevant than the problem-solving process. However, there are times when serious current problems interfere with the learning process and must take precedence during the sessions. At these times, the therapist may find it necessary to take a more active role in the family's problem solving, particularly in the early sessions. But at all times he or she remains aware of the family's potential and attempts to facilitate the members' own efforts. The session consists of three parts: (1) review of progress; (2) problem-solving training; (3) planning generalization. Each session is 1 hour long. No restriction is placed on the proportion of each session devoted to each part. When sessions are conducted in the family home, some additional time may be spent in a social setting where time permits. Many families provide drinks and snacks before the session. This enables the therapist to observe the family interacting in a more naturalistic mode and has been considered valuable in most cases, as in the following case example.

Mr. and Mrs. Baron lived with their 25-year-old son Gene. Daughter

Judy, aged 30, spent some time at home, but since her engagement 4 months ago lived predominantly at her fiancé's apartment. All four household members attended evening sessions regularly, with Brian (Judy's fiancé) attending on occasions. After nine sessions, the family members were making good progress in learning the problem-solving approach. However, Mr. Baron continued to find fault with Gene in a rather hostile, critical manner. Mrs. Baron tended to support her husband's critical remarks, but frequently appeared miserable and withdrawn. She described tantrums that her husband displayed that were similar to Gene's. The father's tantrums were provoked by situations in which another family member did not do exactly what he or she had said (e.g., the mother was late home from shopping; Gene did not mow the lawn). Gene's tantrums were provoked by his parents' or sister's not providing him with attention when he wanted to talk about an issue that concerned him, (e.g., how to get a girlfriend, dealing with the boss at work, buying a new car). The mother became fearful whenever her husband or son had tantrums; she subsequently avoided contact with them and appeared depressed. Judy supported her mother at these times and expressed her disapproval of her father's and brother's behavior.

When the therapist arrived at the Baron home he was greeted by the father, who appeared angry and muttered at the doorway, "He's been bad, really bad, I don't know what we can do." The therapist briefly acknowledged this comment and told the father that he would like to meet with Gene privately to review the situation. He asked the father and mother to check their journal entries for the past week while they were waiting and went to Gene's bedroom, where he was waiting. Gene reported that during the week his boss had asked him to work an extra night shift when a fellow employee did not report for work. He was tired and wanted to watch a baseball game on television but thought he would be fired if he refused. He stayed on the job for 2 hours and then walked off without telling his boss. On Gene's arrival home, the father angrily told him that he should not have left the job. Gene began shouting at his father that he wanted to quit the job anyway and that he would kill himself. The father shouted back; after a half hour of hostile interaction, the mother told them both to stop and go to bed. They calmed down a little, and the father suggested that Gene call his boss, apologize, and explain his grievances. Gene did not accept his father's advice; he refused to go to work the next day. The father phoned the boss and told him Gene had taken ill the previous night and was unable to work that day. The boss said that he was annoyed with Gene's behavior but was willing to have him continue the work when he was fit again.

Both Gene and his parents had reported this event in their daily journal records. Gene had not yet returned to work 3 days after the event. Mr. and Mrs. Baron and Judy (who had arrived for the session 5 minutes late) did not identify any other problems in the family over the past week. The therapist inquired what problem-solving attempts the family had made since the father's phone call to the boss. They said that the father had asked Gene when he planned to return to work, and when Gene responded that he did not intend to, the father reminded him that if he did not work he would not be able to make the payments on his new car. No further discussion had ensued. The mother said she had tried to cheer Gene up by cooking his favorite foods and telling him that it would be all right.

The therapist chose to work with this problem in the training session, because it appeared to be an unresolved crisis that threatened to overwhelm the family's current problem-solving ability. However, because the family had shown the ability to follow the six-step problem-solving procedure in the preceding session, he adopted the role of coaching from the sidelines. Gene elected to keep notes on the problem resolution process on the problem-solving guide sheet (see Figure 10.1), which outlines the six steps with spaces for brief comments. The family was instructed to begin solving the problem without assistance from the therapist.

In this instance, the problem was readily defined by the family as "Gene's return to work next week." The next step involved listing all the alternatives, "good" or "bad," that might help resolve the problem. They included the following:

1. Going back to job and apologizing to the boss.
2. Quitting the job.
3. Asking for a transfer to another office.
4. Staying at home and phoning in sick.
5. Looking for a better job.
6. Telling the boss that he is not willing to work overtime.

The father and Gene dominated the listing of alternative solutions; the mother and Judy spoke very little. The therapist prompted the father to invite suggestions from his wife and daughter, and reinforced every suggestion with "Good" or "That's another possibility." On two occasions Gene and Mrs. Baron commented that one proposed solution was "the best one." The therapist instructed them to avoid judgment until all the possible solutions had been exhausted. However, at this point the family members were unable to structure an effective discussion of the pros and cons on each proposed solution in turn. Gene immediately chose to look for a better job, and when the father agreed, no further discussion appeared forthcoming. At this point the therapist invited Gene to describe the desired response pattern of evaluating the solutions. Gene said it was to decide the best solution, but when prompted to read the guide sheet, he corrected himself and instructed the family to evaluate the positive and negative features of each solution in turn.

With this accomplished, and with further assistance from the therapist,

---

Step 1: What is the problem?
Talk about the problem, listen carefully, ask questions, get everybody's opinion.
Then write down *exactly* what the problem is.

_____

_____

Step 2: List all possible solutions.
Put down *all* ideas, even bad ones. Get everybody to come up with at least one
possible solution.

  1. _____
  2. _____
  3. _____
  4. _____
  5. _____
  6. _____

Step 3: Discuss each possible solution.
Go down the list of possible solutions and discuss the advantages and disadvantages of each one.

Step 4: Choose the best solution or combination of solutions.

_____

_____

Step 5: Plan how to carry out the best solution.

  Step 1. _____
  Step 2. _____
  Step 3. _____
  Step 4. _____

Step 6: Review implementation and praise *all* efforts.

Figure 10.1. Problem-solving guide sheet.

the family readily attained a consensus that "returning to work and telling
the boss that he is not willing to work overtime" was the best solution.

The therapist then assisted the family in making specific plans about how
Gene was to accomplish this. These included the following:

Step 1. Phoning the boss and telling him that he was planning to
be at work on Sunday night.

Step 2. Arriving at work 30 minutes early to talk to the boss.

Step 3. Rehearsing with his father what he would say to the boss.

Step 4. Planning to ask for a transfer if the boss proved unwilling
to accept the plan.

The session ended with the therapist asking Gene to prepare a detailed account of the implementation of the plan for discussion at the subsequent session. The therapist praised the efforts of the family in their problem solving during the session. A family meeting, without the therapist, was scheduled by the family for the following Sunday; at that time, the implementation of the work-related issue would be a major topic, along with solving any other problems that should arise.

A CONTROLLED OUTCOME STUDY

In order to test the efficacy of behavioral family therapy as the basis of the family management of schizophrenia, a controlled outcome study was designed (Falloon, Boyd, McGill, Razani, Moss, & Gilderman, 1982). It was not feasible to compare the program with a no-treatment control. The most appropriate comparison appeared to be a therapy program that provided similar intensive support, with optimal medication and crisis intervention. Ideally, the control therapy would have excluded family participation; however, exclusion of family contact and support would have been incompatible with the excellent community management we sought to emulate. For these reasons, the comparison therapy was based on individual problem-solving therapy, with family contact and support when indicated.

The design of the study called for the random assignment of 39 index patients and their families to one of two treatment conditions: family therapy (20 cases) and individual therapy (19 cases). Two patients dropped out in the first month of family therapy and one dropped out of the individual therapy, leaving 18 closely matched patients and families in each group. Treatment assignment occurred when the patients were stabilized on optimal doses of medication following an acute episode of schizophrenia. The initial phase of treatment in the study involved weekly sessions for 3 months, tapering off to biweekly sessions until the 9-month point, when once-monthly booster sessions were initiated. A total of 40 sessions were provided over a 2-year period. Therapists were assigned a similar number of cases in both conditions and were available for additional crisis sessions at all times throughout the study. Case management continued throughout any periods of hospital admission or day treatment.

An extensive battery of dependent measures was administered to each patient (and his or her family) before treatment and after 3, 9, and 24 months of treatment to assess the following independently (and usually blindly): communication and problem-solving behavior, family burden, psychopathology, and social adjustment. In addition, monthly ratings of the index patient's psychopathology, compliance with medication, plasma levels of medication, and serum prolactin levels were made every month. Ongoing data regarding life events and associated family coping behavior were collected via biweekly semistructured interviews with family members.

Patient Selection

All patients who entered the study had a diagnosis of schizophrenia or delusional psychosis on the PSE/Catego criteria (Wing *et al.*, 1974). Most of the patients had symptoms of "nuclear" schizophrenia, indicating the presence of one or more of Schneider's (1959) first-rank symptoms. One-third of the sample had experienced their first episode of schizophrenia just prior to selection for the study. However, another one-third were long-standing cases.

In addition to a definite diagnosis of schizophrenia, index patients were between 18 and 45 years of age, and lived with or in daily contact with at least one natural parent. At least one household member was required to display features of high EE on a CFI, or the family tension was considered extremely high in the absence of high EE. In all cases, English was the language spoken predominantly in the home.

Treatment Conditions

Regardless of treatment condition, certain aspects of treatment were the same for all patients. Specifically, a vigorous attempt was made to maintain all patients on an optimal dosage of neuroleptic medication throughout the 2-year program. Owing to its relative lack of severe side effects and the availability of laboratory assay of plasma levels, chlorpromazine was our drug of choice. In cases where poor compliance persisted, intramuscular fluphenazine decanoate was used. In other cases where tolerance to chlorpromazine was poor, fluphenazine hydrochloride, haloperidol, and thiothixene were used.

Pharmacological aspects of treatment were managed by a psychiatrist or clinical pharmacist who was blind to psychosocial treatment assignment. Once-monthly assessments of the patients' psychiatric status were undertaken by these blind assessors, using the Brief Psychiatric Rating Scale (BPRS) and a Target Symptom Rating (a rating of two or three specific schizophrenic symptoms that were characteristically evident at the time of each patient's exacerbations of schizophrenia). Blood samples were drawn at these monthly visits for assay of drug plasma levels and prolactin.

Another aspect of the treatment program that was common to all patients was rehabilitation counseling. All patients were allocated four 1-hour sessions with an experienced rehabilitation counselor to discuss vocational or educational plans, leisure-time activities, and other areas pertaining to their psychosocial rehabilitation.

Patients assigned to family therapy received their sessions in their homes, whereas patients assigned to individual therapy were seen in the clinic.

Assessment Procedures

Two major hypotheses were tested in this study. First, we wished to determine whether behavioral family therapy was more effective than individual therapy in forestalling or preventing major exacerbations of schizophrenia. Secondly, we wanted to find out whether behavioral family therapy is effective in enhancing the social performance of persons with schizophrenia. In attempting to define exacerbations of schizophrenia, we realized that current concepts of "relapse" are very loosely defined and lack adequate psychometric standardization to be useful in a refined outcome study. For these reasons, we defined "relapse" in a purely clinical manner: specifically, a return to florid symptomatology in a previously symptom-free patient, or a marked exacerbation of existing schizophrenic symptoms of at least a week's duration. Toward this end, target symptoms were defined for each patient, based on his or her acute symptom picture. The symptoms chosen were clearly schizophrenic (e.g., delusions of control, thought interference, auditory hallucinations). Such symptoms as social withdrawal, blunted affect, bizarre behavior, or agitation were avoided, because these can occur in nonschizophrenic conditions as well. Target symptoms were rated by the blind prescribing doctor on a 7-point severity scale. The maximum levels of target symptoms experienced by patients in the two treatment groups are compared in Table 10.1.

Social role functioning was assessed through self-report and interview methods. The Social Adjustment Scale, a self-report questionnaire developed by Weissman and her colleagues (Weissman, Prusoff, Thompson, Harding, & Myers, 1972) was used, as well as the Social Behavior Assessment Schedule (Platt, Weyman, Hirsch, & Hewett, 1980). The latter is an interview schedule that assesses the severity of the patient's behavioral disturbance, impairment in social role performance, and disruptive influence on the household functioning, as well as the relative's distress concerning impaired behavior. These ratings were conducted by a blind assessor.

A further series of assessments concerned observable changes in family problem-solving behavior. Two behavioral assessments were conducted at baseline and at the end of 3 and 24 months of treatment in order to measure changes in family communication and problem solving. The first of these is the Consensus Rorschach (Singer, 1968), in which family members are scored for their communication deviance and healthy communication while carrying out a discussion about their perceptions of a colorful Rorschach card. The second is the Family Confrontation Test procedure which was derived from the work of Goldstein and his colleagues at UCLA (Goldstein, Judd, Rodnick,

Table 10.1. Results of Psychiatric Assessment of Schizophrenia in Patients Completing 9 Months of Randomly Assigned Treatment in Family and Individual Management Conditions

Criteria	Family	$(n = 18)$	Individual	$(n = 18)$
Clinical exacerbations of symptoms (clinical judgment)	1	(6%)	8	(44%)**
Target Symptom Rating (blind rating)				
Pretreatment baseline mean	2.22		2.15†	
Maximum level of monthly ratings	2.25		4.10***	
Symptom "remission" at 9 months (blind rating of PSE)	10	(56%)	4	(22%)*
Community tenure				
Hospital days (mean)	0.83		8.39	
Patients admitted	2	(11%)	9	(50%)*
Total admissions	2		16	

†$t = 0.21$, $p > .05$.
*$p < .05$ (2×2 contingency tables).
**$p < .01$ (2×2 contingency tables).
***$t = 3.80$, $p < .001$.

Alkire, & Gould, 1968). In this procedure, a family is asked to discuss a current "hot" issue for 10 minutes and to try to arrive at a solution. A transcript of the discussion is rated for problem-solving skills and emotional communication.

There is some evidence suggesting that the rating for emotional communication may be an interpersonal analogue of the EE concept (Miklowitz, Goldstein, Falloon, & Doane, 1984). The CFI and its EE index were not employed as an outcome variable in this study, because evidence of the stability of the index over time was insufficiently strong when the study was designed.

A final measure of family change in the natural environment involved an assessment of the coping behavior of family members, contingent upon life changes and stressors. Information obtained from biweekly contact with family members concerning changes in the family were rated by a blind assessor for the coping behavior evident in attempts to minimize the stressful impact of these events. This global rating encompassed concepts of EE, social networks, cognitive appraisal, and behavioral problem solving.

Results

The results of this study clearly support the efficacy of behavioral family therapy in the management of schizophrenia after 9 months of controlled community care.

CLINICAL OUTCOME

There were significantly fewer clinician-rated major exacerbations of florid schizophrenia in the family therapy condition, as Table 10.1 indicates. Blind assessors concurred with this judgment, rating the maximum levels of target schizophrenic symptoms significantly lower in the family-treated group. More family patients were in total remission of all schizophrenic symptoms at the 9-month assessment.

It might be assumed that the absence of florid psychopathology of schizophrenia might be exchanged for a high level of neurotic symptoms, depressions, and the withdrawn and apathetic "negative" syndrome. This was not the case; family-treated patients experienced fewer episodes of depression and lower ratings of "negative" symptoms.

Hospital care was minimal for family-treated patients at the 9-month follow-up. But individually treated patients also spent considerably less time in the hospital than in a comparable period before their index admission prior to entering the study. Therapists provided continued case management throughout hospital admissions and expedited discharge.

SOCIAL FUNCTIONING

Although notable improvements of social achievement in the forms of enhanced work status, sociability, dating, and mating were not achieved, 13 of the 18 family therapy patients either improved or maintained their overall role functioning performance, compared to only 7 of the 18 individually treated cases ($p < .05$) (see Table 10.2). Similar improvements were noted on scales of behavioral disturbance. Work functioning remained the only area of substantial impairment. At a time of high unemployment, jobs were unavailable to

Table 10.2. Social Outcome at 9 Months

Criteria	Family ($n = 18$)	Individual ($n = 18$)
Patients' role performance		
Improved/same	16 (89%)	9 (50%)*
Deteriorated	2	9
Family burden (global)		
None/minimal	15 (83%)	7 (38%)**
Moderate/severe	3	11

Note. Ratings derived from the Social Behavior Assessment Scale (Platt, Weyman, Hirsch, & Hewett, 1980).

*$p < .05$ (2×2 contingency tables, one-tailed).

**$p < .01$ (2×2 contingency tables, one-tailed).

many patients who were ready to work, and a dearth of sheltered workshops frustrated our attempts to find alternative work activity or vocational training. Several patients attended educational courses, and several others worked daily at volunteer jobs. In contrast, several individually treated patients showed deterioration in their social functioning, and few improved substantially.

Similar results, favoring family management, were obtained on the self-report measure.

FAMILY FUNCTIONING

The behavioral assessments of problem-solving skills showed that two-thirds of the family therapy sample had learned to conduct structured problem solving, unaided by the therapist. These results were similar to therapist assessment of problem-solving effectiveness on homework tasks in the home environment.

A preliminary coding of critical, intrusive, and guilt-inducing statements revealed significant reductions in these statements concomitant with the more effective problem-solving behavior. On the other hand, a substantial increase in these negative emotional responses was noted in the individually treated families. Significant increases in problem-solving statements were observed only in the families who received behavioral family therapy.

These laboratory ratings were supported by naturalistic data indicating that families that had received family treatment showed more effective coping behavior in handling stressful life changes over the 9-month follow-up period.

Thus, it may be concluded that behavioral family therapy was effective in promoting more effective problem-solving functions in families, as well as in eliminating emotional responses analogous to those contributing to the EE index.

The distress and dissatisfaction expressed by family members concerning the index patients' social functioning and behavioral disturbance appeared substantially reduced, even in families where considerable impairment was still evident in the patients' behavior. This suggested that family members had developed a more tolerant attitude toward deviant behavior—a factor that may have resulted in better coping responses. A greater understanding of schizophrenia resulting from the family education sessions probably contributed to these changes of attitude, which were not noted in individually treated families. As a result, the global rating of family burden was significantly lower in the family therapy condition at 9 months (see Table 10.2).

THE COST OF TREATMENT

Throughout the study, details of direct and indirect services provided to all study patients were recorded in order to compare the costs of the two methods of treatment. At the end of the first year of treatment, the costs of family treatment were 20% less than the individual approaches. This result was obtained despite doubling the actual costs of each family session to account for the added time required to make home visits. The added days of hospitalization and extra attention for crisis management that were associated with individual therapy exceeded the extra expense of the home-based family approach.

Conclusions

It may be concluded that an intensive behavioral family therapy approach was effective in enhancing the problem-solving behavior of families in dealing with stressful life situations. It is postulated that this improvement in the ability of the family to cope with stressors was associated with a reduced risk of exacerbation of schizophrenia and subsequent hospital admission. Moreover, family problem solving assisted index patients in improving their social role functioning and reduced distress in other family members. Not only was the course of the illness improved, but the quality of patients' lives and those of their family members was substantially enhanced.

These gains continued throughout the second year of community management, with few exacerbations and further improvement in social functioning. While compliance with drug treatment was better in family-treated patients, adequate medication was taken by all patients throughout the 9 months of intensive follow-up. Indeed, family therapy patients ingested somewhat less (approximately 100 mg per day, in chlorpromazine equivalents) of the neuroleptic drugs to remain stable than patients having individual supportive therapy did. Therefore, the dramatic effectiveness of the family therapy is unlikely to have been a function of greater efficacy of pharmacotherapy.

This behavioral family therapy method has not been subjected to field trials. The operational clarity of the behavioral interventions has allowed us to develop a specific training manual (Falloon, Boyd, & McGill, 1984). In combination with a workshop program, the training of clinicians in this method has begun. With thousands of family caregivers and patients searching for support in avoiding the potential ravages of schizophrenia, the need to expedite dissemination of this cost-effective family management approach is clear.

CULTURAL, BIOLOGICAL, AND ETIOLOGICAL ASPECTS OF EXPRESSED EMOTION

11

The Distribution of Expressed Emotion Components in Different Diagnostic Groups and Cultures

A number of samples of relatives have now been interviewed with the CFI from a variety of cultures and diagnostic groupings of patients. There is considerable interest in comparing the distribution of EE components between these samples, because such a comparison throws light on two major issues: the question of the equivalence of emotional expression across cultures, and the question of whether the relatives of schizophrenics show characteristic emotional attitudes.

CRITICISM AMONG RELATIVES OF SCHIZOPHRENICS

The component of criticism lends itself most readily to an analysis of distribution because it has the widest range; Critical Comments scores have varied from 0 to 61 in the samples collected so far. The distribution of Critical Comments scores among relatives of schizophrenics from the various studies undertaken to date is shown in Figures 11.1–11.5.

The distribution of Critical Comments scores among relatives of schizophrenic patients from the first study, by Brown et al. (1972), is L-shaped, with one-third expressing no criticism and an extended tail reaching up into the highest scores recorded (see Figure 11.1). The comparable distribution from the next study, by Vaughn and Leff (1976a), is very similar (see Figure 11.2). Data on relatives of schizophrenic patients are also available from two contrasting cultural settings: California in the United States, and Chandigarh in North India. The Chandigarh material has been collected as part of a project organized by the World Health Organization (WHO), called the Determinants of Outcome of Severe Mental Disorder. The study is financed jointly by WHO, the U.S. National Institute of Mental Health (NIMH), and 12 field research centers (FRCs) in Aarhus (Denmark); Agra and Chandigarh (India); Cali (Colombia); Dublin (Ireland); Honolulu, Hawaii, and Rochester, New York (US); Ibadan (Nigeria); Moscow (USSR); Nagasaki (Japan); Notting-

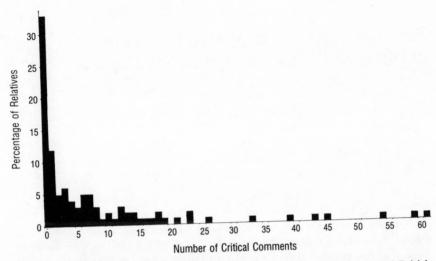

Figure 11.1. The distribution of Critical Comments scores for relatives of British schizophrenic patients (Brown, Birley, & Wing, 1972).

ham (UK); and Prague (Czechoslovakia). All of the FRCs participate in a "core" epidemiological and clinical study, and subgroups of centers carry out a number of special substudies aiming to test specific hypotheses about the course of schizophrenia, its social sequelae, and its associations with other diseases. Chandigarh was chosen as one of the centers in which to conduct

Figure 11.2. The distribution of Critical Comments scores for relatives of British schizophrenic patients (Vaughn & Leff, 1976a).

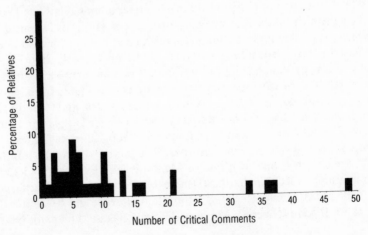

a study of relatives' EE and its relationship to the course of schizophrenia in patients making contact with the psychiatric services for the first time.

The data from the Chandigarh center (Menon *et al.*, 1984) are derived from two different environments—a Western-style city and surrounding villages representing a traditional rural culture. The material has been combined for presentation in Figure 11.3, but interesting differences appear when the urban and rural relatives are considered separately. The shape of the distribution of Critical Comments scores in the combined sample is also that of an L, but the relative proportions of the two limbs of the L are quite different from those of the English samples. A significantly higher proportion (56%; $p < .001$) made no critical comments, while only 12% scored 6 or more and would be considered high in EE by current English standards. The highest score was 14, contrasted with 49 in Vaughn and Leff's (1976a) sample and 61 in the sample of Brown *et al.* (1972). This marked difference in distribution is reflected in a much lower mean Critical Comments score, 1.83 compared with 7.49 for the two English samples combined. Within the Chandigarh sam-

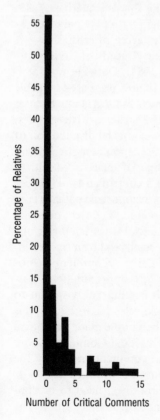

Figure 11.3. The distribution of Critical Comments scores for relatives of Chandigarh schizophrenic patients (Menon *et al.*, 1984).

ple, significant differences in the expression of criticism existed between urban and rural relatives. None of the 31 rural relatives scored 6 or more on Critical Comments, compared with 12 out of 73 urban relatives. The mean Critical Comments score for urban relatives, 2.42, was significantly higher ($p < .01$) than the corresponding figure of 0.58 for rural relatives. We can thus conclude that the expression of criticism by Chandigarh relatives was much more muted than that by their English counterparts, and that within the Chandigarh sample rural relatives were even more restrained than urban relatives.

These interesting cultural differences are complemented by the data from the California sample (Vaughn *et al.*, in press). The distribution of Critical Comments scores for these relatives is shown in Figure 11.4. The shape of this distribution is quite different from that of the other samples of relatives of schizophrenics considered so far. Instead of being L-shaped, it approximates a normal distribution, but with an abbreviated lower tail. Only 4% of the sample made no critical comments, while 53% scored 6 or more, a significantly ($p < .05$) higher proportion than in the combined English samples. Despite this, the mean Critical Comments score of the California relatives, 6.86, does not differ significantly from that of the English relatives, 7.49, because the virtual absence of uncritical California relatives is balanced by the lack of relatives expressing an extremely high degree of criticism.

Preliminary data are also available from Hogarty's study of EE in Pittsburgh (G. E. Hogarty, personal communication, 1983). Data are not sufficiently detailed to construct a histogram, but the figures presented in Table 11.1 indicate that the distribution of Critical Comments scores is much closer to that of the California sample than of either of the earlier British samples.

It would be natural to attribute these differences in the distribution of Critical Comments scores to cultural variations in the expression of criticism, were it not for data from yet another English sample of relatives of schizophrenic patients. These data were obtained from a controlled trial of prophylactic neuroleptic medication in first-admission schizophrenic patients conducted by the MRC Clinical Research Centre in London (T. Crow, personal communication, 1983). If a patient included in the trial was living with one or more relatives, the CFI was administered to the relative(s) by a trained interviewer, who then rated EE. The distribution of Critical Comments scores for this sample of relatives is shown in Figure 11.5; it approximates a normal distribution with an abbreviated lower tail. It is remarkably similar to the corresponding distribution shown by the Los Angeles relatives, and has almost identical statistical characteristics: 5% of the sample made no critical comments, 58% scored 6 or more, and the mean Critical Comments score was 7.26. A statistical comparison of the critical comments made by the various samples of relatives of schizophrenic patients is shown in Table 11.1.

A number of explanations, other than cultural ones, need to be considered as possibly accounting for the similarities and differences among the

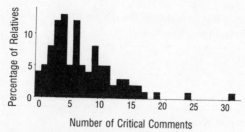

Figure 11.4. The distribution of Critical Comments scores for relatives of California schizophrenic patients (Vaughn *et al.*, in press).

samples of English-speaking relatives. The MRC Clinical Research Centre sample was composed entirely of first-admission patients, while these comprised only 54% of the two earlier London samples combined. However, when the first-admission patients were extracted from the two earlier samples and their relatives' Critical Comments scores were plotted, an L-shaped distribution resulted that was no different in shape from that of the whole group. Furthermore, only 17% of the Los Angeles patients were in their first admission, so that this characteristic cannot account for the similar distribution to the MRC Clinical Research Centre sample.

Social class is another obvious feature to focus on, but unfortunately social class data are no more enlightening than the first-admission data. No differences were found in the distribution of social class between the Los Angeles and the earlier London samples (Vaughn *et al.*, in press), while the Clinical Research Centre sample showed a significantly different distribution ($p < .0025$) from that of the Los Angeles relatives. Furthermore, within the Clinical Research Centre sample, social class bore only a negligible relationship to Critical Comments scores ($r = .26$).

Another possibility concerns the epoch of the studies. The earlier British studies were completed in the 1960s and early 1970s. The American work and the Clinical Research Centre study have been conducted in the 1980s. Is it possible that relatives' attitudes have altered between the two waves of research? This issue can only be addressed by the collection of data on further contemporary samples of British relatives of schizophrenic patients.

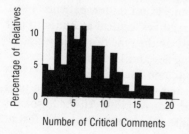

Figure 11.5. The distribution of Critical Comments scores for relatives of British schizophrenic patients (T. Crow, personal communication, 1983).

Table 11.1. Statistical Characteristics of the Distribution of Critical Comments made by Relatives of Schizophrenic Patients

Study Population	Number of Relatives	% No Critical Comments	% 6+ Critical Comments	Mean Number of Critical Comments
London (Brown, Birley, & Wing, 1972)	126	33	37	7.16
London (Vaughn & Leff, 1976a)	45	29	44	8.22
Chandigarh (Menon et al., 1984)	104	56	12	1.83
Los Angeles (Vaughn et al., in press)	109	4	53	6.86
Pittsburgh (G. E. Hogarty, personal communication, 1983)	356	10	46	6.65
London (T. Crow, personal communication, 1983)	92	5	58	7.26

CRITICISM AMONG RELATIVES OF PATIENTS WITH OTHER CONDITIONS

Having seen how the expression of criticism by the relatives of schizophrenic patients differs across cultures, we can turn our attention to the relatives of patients with other conditions. Three samples of relatives are currently available: spouses of depressed neurotic patients from London (Vaughn & Leff, 1976a), parents of anorexic patients from London (G. Szmukler, personal communication, 1983) and spouses of obese women from California (Havstad, 1979). The distributions of Critical Comments scores from these samples are displayed in Figures 11.6–11.8).

These three distributions do not resemble those of the relatives of schizophrenic patients, but do show a likeness as a group. This is reflected in the statistical characteristics of the distributions, which are shown in Table 11.2. The relatives of neurotic depressives had a much higher mean score on Critical Comments than the other two groups, because of a small number of relatives with very high scores. However, in all other respects, the three samples were very similar. The closest resemblance was between the husbands of the obese California women and the parents of the anorexic London patients, most of whom were women. This suggests that relatives' critical attitudes to patients with eating problems are little affected by the type of relationship, or by the cultural differences between Los Angeles and London.

Here we digress briefly to present the outcome results of Havstad's (1979) study of obese women. Her sample consisted of 28 married women who answered local newspaper advertisements in Los Angeles. All the husbands were working, and all the families were white. The women had each lost at

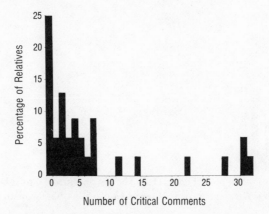

Figure 11.6. The distribution of Critical Comments scores for relatives of British depressed neurotic patients (Vaughn & Leff, 1976a).

least 15 pounds in weight during the previous year, and had maintained their target weight for a mean period of 8.5 months.

The CFI was given to the husbands in a modified form, in which the section on events leading to hospitalization was replaced with a section on the wife's weight history. The rater was trained to a high level of interrater reliability on all EE scales.

Follow-up took place 4–5 months after the initial interview, and "relapse" was defined as a gain of 20% or more of the amount of weight lost between the interview and the follow-up. The amount of weight lost referred to the reduction during the most recent diet to target weight.

Of the 28 subjects, 14 relapsed during the follow-up period, according to these criteria. A correlation matrix was constructed of all the variables measured. The only measure found to be significantly related to relapse was

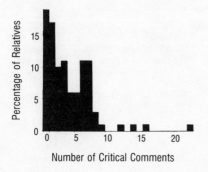

Figure 11.7. The distribution of Critical Comments scores for parents of British anorexic patients (G. Szmukler, personal communication, 1983).

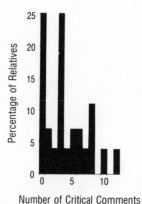

Figure 11.8. The distribution of Critical Comments scores for spouses of California obese women (Havstad, 1979).

the number of critical remarks made by the spouse ($r = .56$, $p < .01$). The best separation between relapsed and nonrelapsed women was achieved when a Critical Comments cutoff score of 3 or above was used. With this cutoff point, 13 out of 18 (72%) relapsed in the high-criticism group, compared with 1 out of 10 (10%) in the low-criticism group ($p < .01$). It will be recalled that the best separation between relapsed and nonrelapsed depressed neurotic patients in Vaughn and Leff's (1976a) study was achieved with a cutoff score of 2 on Critical Comments. If this level is applied to Havstad's data, a significant difference is also found between relapsed and nonrelapsed obese women, 68% compared with 11% ($p < .025$). Hence there are considerable similarities between the influence of relatives' critical attitudes on the course of depressive neurosis and on weight maintenance in obese women.

Table 11.2. Statistical Characteristics of the Distribution of Critical Comments Made by Relatives of Nonschizophrenic Subjects

Study Population	Number of Relatives	% No Critical Comments	% 6+ Critical Comments	Mean Number of Critical Comments
Depressive neurotics, London (Vaughn & Leff, 1976a)	32	25	34	7.19
Anorexics, London (G. Szmukler, personal communication, 1983)	72	19	32	3.88
Obese women, Los Angeles (Havstad, 1979)	28	25	29	3.71

HOSTILITY AND CRITICISM

Having presented the findings of Havstad's study of EE and obesity, we continue with the distribution of EE components.

The prevalence of hostility in the various samples of relatives of schizophrenics echoes the distribution of criticism, as one would expect from the close relationship between these two components of EE. In the two earlier London samples, hostility was almost always associated with a high degree of criticism and was shown by 18% of relatives. The same relationship pertained in the California sample: No hostile relative scored less than 6 on Critical Comments. As a result, the greater proportion of critical Los Angeles relatives is paralleled by a significantly ($p < .05$) higher proportion expressing hostility (28%). An identical proportion of Pittsburgh relatives expressed hostility. The proportion of Chandigarh relatives scoring high on Hostility was 16%, very similar to the comparable figure for London relatives. However, its relationship to criticism appears to be different. Whereas only a handful of English-speaking relatives who voiced hostility scored less than 6 on Critical Comments, this was true of 29% of hostile Chandigarh relatives. Of the 17 relatives in the Chandigarh sample who expressed hostility, only one made fewer than three critical remarks, and this relative was from the rural area. This distribution of hostility suggests that a score of 3 on Critical Comments may be a more appropriate cutoff point for high criticism in Chandigarh relatives than the Anglo-American threshold of 6.

Hostility was not confined to the relatives of schizophrenic patients. It was also found in the nonschizophrenic samples, occurring in 19% of relatives of neurotic depressives, 14% of the husbands of obese women, and 6% of the parents of anorexics. Only the last group of relatives stands out from all the others as showing a low degree of hostility. In each of the samples, hostility bears the same relationship to criticism as in the schizophrenic material. Among the relatives of neurotic depressives, hostility was confined to the six relatives with the highest Critical Comments scores, which ranged from 14 to 32. The four hostile husbands of obese women scored 8 or more on Critical Comments, while all the parents of anorexics who were rated as hostile scored 6 or more on Critical Comments. Thus the numerical relationship of Hostility scores to Critical Comments scores remains remarkably constant across cultures and diagnostic groups, with the sole exception of the relatives of Chandigarh schizophrenics, whose expression of criticism was much more restrained than that of any other sample.

EMOTIONAL OVERINVOLVEMENT AMONG PARENTS

The third element of EE that is linked to relapse of schizophrenia, emotional overinvolvement, was found much more commonly in parents than in spouses. For this reason, it was virtually absent from Vaughn and Leff's

(1976a) sample of relatives of neurotic depressives, only four of whom were parents, and also from Havstad's sample of husbands of obese women. This leaves only the parents of anorexics as a valid comparison with the various samples of relatives of schizophrenics. Among the schizophrenic groups, 21% of British parents, 15% of California parents, and 29% of Pittsburgh parents scored 4 or 5 on the Emotional Overinvolvement scale, a nonsignificant difference. The comparable proportion for the parents of anorexics was 8%, which is significantly lower than the proportion of Vaughn and Leff's parents of schizophrenics ($p < .05$). If the lower cutoff point of 3 on this scale is employed, the proportions showing overinvolvement become 18% of parents of anorexics and 36% of parents of schizophrenics, a nonsignificant difference.

The importance of this finding is that it provides evidence for the first time that overinvolved attitudes are not confined to the parents of schizophrenics, although whether they are equally pathogenic for anorexic patients depends on follow-up data that are not yet available.

Within the sample of relatives of schizophrenics, cultural differences emerge when the North Indian material is compared with the Anglo-American data. Of the 67 parents in the Chandigarh sample, none scored more than 3 on Emotional Overinvolvement, and only three individuals (4%) scored 3. This is, of course, a highly significant difference from the comparable figure of 36% among Vaughn and Leff's parents of schizophrenics ($p < .001$).

OVERVIEW

When we take an overview of these various samples, it is apparent that no component of EE that is linked with the outcome of schizophrenia is confined to the relatives of schizophrenic patients. Each component is found among relatives of one or more of the nonschizophrenic samples that have been studied. In particular, hostility was rated as consistently present across all diagnostic groups and cultures. These findings indicate that the emotional attitudes measured represent nonspecific stress factors in the pathogenesis of schizophrenia. The specificity must lie in the schizophrenic patient's reaction to stress; we believe in the nature of the biologically determined vulnerability.

When we consider the cultural differences in EE, those that distinguish California from London relatives are interesting, though not unexpected. The Los Angeles relatives expressed a significantly higher amount of criticism and more hostility than the London relatives, but an equivalent degree of overinvolvement. However, outstanding differences divide the Chandigarh relatives from the Anglo-Americans. The North Indian relatives showed a fraction of the amount of criticism and overinvolvement of their Western counterparts, although, interestingly, they are equally as hostile as the London relatives. Whether this is paralleled by a better outcome for schizophrenia remains to be seen, but in itself it opens up a fascinating perspective on cultural influences on the expression of emotion. It is clearly necessary to conduct further studies of EE in diverse cultures, encompassing a wider range of non-Western peoples and a selection of urban and rural settings.

12

Expressed Emotion, Life Events, and Prophylactic Medication

The intervention studies described in Section III have provided solid evidence for the causal role of relatives' EE in relapse of schizophrenia. However, EE is not the only source of stress in the social environment that has been identified as relevant to schizophrenic patients. Life events have attracted the attention of investigators for many years now. They may be conceived of as sudden happenings in the person's immediate social environment, which are often unexpected and usually demand some alteration in the person's psychological adjustment or life style. For this reason they have been termed "psychosocial transitions."

CLASSIFICATION OF LIFE EVENTS

Research on life events is beset by pitfalls, but these have now been clearly charted and techniques have been developed to avoid them. It is all too easy to be caught up in circular reasoning, as in this common example: Prodromal behavior that heralds an attack of illness gives rise to a life event — for example, loss of job — which is then misidentified as a precipitant of the episode of illness. Two principles have been proposed by Brown and Birley (1968) to reduce the likelihood of this error to a minimum. One precaution is to be conservative in dating the onset of an episode of illness — that is, to place it as far back in time as is consistent with the history in order to include most, if not all, of any prodromal period. The other is a technique of classifying life events according to the probable contribution of the patient's own behavior. Thus, events are classified as "dependent" behaviors of the patient stemming from the illness (these events are excluded from further consideration), "possibly independent," and "independent." "Possibly independent" events are those that are within the patient's control but that have not been brought about by any unusual behavior on the patient's part (e.g., changing jobs). "Independent" events are those that are clearly outside the patient's control. Exclusive concern with independent events reduces the likelihood of tautologous associations to a minimum. For that reason, we only include data concerning independent events in this chapter.

LIFE EVENTS AND EE FOR SCHIZOPHRENIC AND DEPRESSED NEUROTIC PATIENTS

The data to be presented were collected in the course of two studies, already described in detail in previous chapters. The first was the naturalistic study of the association between relatives' EE and outcome in schizophrenic and depressed neurotic patients (Vaughn & Leff, 1976a). The second was the trial of social intervention in families of schizophrenic patients (Leff *et al.*, 1982). In both studies, life events were recorded by using Brown and Birley's (1968) schedule and were evaluated with their manual. This specifies criteria to be used in deciding whether an occurrence qualifies as a life event, and whether it is possibly independent or independent. In the case of each life event, contextual information was collected and was used later to assess the probable emotional impact of the event on the subject.

In the naturalistic study, the period assessed for life events was the 3-month period before the onset of symptoms. This period was chosen on the basis of earlier studies by Brown and his colleagues. There were usually no difficulties in pinpointing the onset of schizophrenic episodes, but depressive illnesses often began in a more insidious way. In such cases the onset was placed as far back in time as possible, for the reasons already given. Various items of each patient's history were also collected, including whether maintenance medication was prescribed prior to admission and an estimate of the patient's reliability in taking it.

In presenting the relationship between life events and relatives' EE, we draw on the material discussed in Chapter 6, which indicated that the level of critical comments predictive of relapse proved to be lower in depressed neurotic patients than in schizophrenics. The proportions of patients experiencing at least one independent event in the 3 months before onset of illness are shown in Table 12.1.

When the conventional criteria for assigning relatives to high-EE and low-EE groups are applied, a significant difference in the experience of life events appears among patients with schizophrenia. Relatively few patients in high-EE homes experienced an independent life event in the 3 months prior to onset of an episode, compared with the majority of patients living with low-EE relatives. When the same criteria are used for the relatives of depressed patients, the proportions experiencing a life event appear virtually identical in the two kinds of homes. However, when a cutoff score of 2 or more on Critical Comments is applied, a significant difference in the experience of life events emerges between patients living with high-criticism and low-criticism

Table 12.1. Proportions of Patients with at Least One Independent Event in the 3 Months before Onset

Relatives' EE or Criticism	Schizophrenics	Depressive Neurotics
High EE[a]	6/21 (28.6%)**	7/11 (63.6%)
Low EE	11/16 (68.8%)**	12/19 (63.2%)
Total	17/37 (46.0%)	19/30 (63.3%)
High criticism[b]	–	16/21 (76.2%)*
Low criticism	–	3/9 (33.3%)*
Total	–	19/30 (63.3%)

[a]6+ score on Critical Comments and/or 4+ score on Emotional Overinvolvement.

[b]2+ score on Critical Comments.

$*p = .036.$

$**p = .018.$

relatives. It is striking that this difference is in the opposite direction to that found among schizophrenic patients. We can interpret this as indicating that over a 3-month period before onset of illness, either an independent life event or living with a high-EE relative is sufficient to precipitate an episode for schizophrenic patients, while for depressed neurotic patients the *combination* of a life event and a critical relative is pathogenic in the majority of cases.

In their pioneering work on life events, Brown and Birley (1968) found that the crucial period of vulnerability preceding onset of illness for schizophrenic patients was 3 weeks, as opposed to the 3 months that appeared for depressives (Brown & Harris, 1978). Therefore we analyzed our data for the 3 weeks preceding onset of illness. This analysis is presented in Table 12.2.

It can be seen that the only groups that differed in their experience of life events over this 3-week period were the schizophrenic patients living with high-EE and low-EE relatives. Furthermore, the difference between these two groups over the 3-week period before onset was considerably greater than that pertaining to the 3-month period. This confirms the finding of Brown and his colleagues that the pathogenic effect of independent life events has a different time course in schizophrenia and in depressive neurosis, being 3 weeks in the former and 3 months in the latter. Not only is the time course of the impact of life events different, but, as we have shown above, the relationship between life events and relatives' emotional attitudes differs between the two diagnostic groups. Consideration of these findings leads us to conclude that the specificity of time courses and interrelationships among social factors can be utilized to test the validity of diagnostic distinctions in psychiatry. This could be a very important aspect of the study of social factors, since there are few existing criteria for the validation of psychiatric diagnoses.

We discuss some further implications of the findings for depressed neurotic patients before presenting additional data concerning schizophrenia. The majority (70%) of depressed neurotic patients studied were living with high-criticism relatives, and most of these (76%) had experienced at least one independent event in the 3 months before they fell ill. The patients living with low-criticism relatives had a low rate of life events, and could thus be considered as suffering from unprecipitated depression. We must remind the reader that patients with depressive delusions and/or hallucinations were deliberately excluded from this study so that our depressives would provide the maximum contrast with the schizophrenic sample. Thus the small group of depressed neurotic patients for whom life events and critical relatives do not appear to act as pathogens may represent a portion of an "endogenous" category, extending from the psychotic into the neurotic end of the clinical spectrum.

For the other depressed neurotic patients, the conjunction of an independent life event and a difficult marital relationship appeared to be potent in inducing their condition. This finding is in accord with that of Brown and Harris (1978), who identified the lack of an intimate relationship as one of the factors rendering women vulnerable to life events. Such a relationship was almost always with a sexual partner and provided a woman with someone to confide in. It is likely that our measure of criticism in spouses and Brown *et al.*'s assessment of the lack of an intimate are both reflecting similar aspects of unsatisfactory marriages. It remains to be demonstrated that the conjunction of a life event and an unsatisfactory marital relationship is indeed a *causal* constellation in depression. Since independent events are by definition virtually uncontrollable, the most practical strategy would be to attempt to im-

Table 12.2. Proportions of Patients with at Least One Independent Event in the 3 Weeks before Onset

Relatives' EE or Criticism	Schizophrenics	Depressive Neurotics
High EE[a]	1/21 (4.8%)*	3/11 (27.3%)
Low EE	9/16 (56.3%)*	7/19 (36.8%)
Total	10/37 (27.0%)	10/30 (33.3%)
High criticism[b]	—	8/21 (38.1%)
Low criticism	—	2/9 (22.2%)
Total	—	10/30 (33.3%)

[a]6+ score on Critical Comments and/or 4+ score on Emotional Overinvolvement.

[b]2+ score on Critical Comments.

*$p = .0007$.

prove unsatisfactory marriages in patients prone to depression and to look for an effect in the course of the illness. There is a close parallel between this endeavor and the studies of intervention in the families of schizophrenic patients presented in Section III of this book.

THE ROLE OF MAINTENANCE DRUG THERAPY

The naturalistic study we conducted (Vaughn & Leff, 1976a) enabled us to work out the relationships between life events and relatives' EE, but failed to illuminate the place of maintenance drug therapy in the scheme. This is because these assessments of social factors were made at the point of admission for relapse or first onset of illness, and few patients are found to be on regular maintenance drugs at this juncture. Maintenance with antidepressants for neurotic depressives is not usually considered to have the same therapeutic potency as maintenance with prophylactic antipsychotic drugs for schizophrenia, and we do not dwell any longer here on the drug data for depressed patients. Maintenance drug therapy is a crucial factor in schizophrenia relapse, but very few patients in our sample were judged to be taking medication regularly (only 6 out of 37). Even with these 6, the judgments about compliance with prescribed drug regimens were made retrospectively; this raises doubt about their reliability.

We had to wait for the completion of our trial of social intervention in the families of schizophrenics (Leff *et al.*, 1982) to obtain reliable data on drug therapy, along with contemporaneous assessments of life events and relatives' EE. This trial has been described in detail in Chapter 9. We should remind the reader that virtually all the patients in the trial were maintained on long-acting injections of antipsychotic medication. This was so for 21 of the 24 patients living with high-EE relatives; the other 3 took oral neuroleptics regularly as prescribed. A history of life events was obtained at the 9-month follow-up for 23 of the 24 patients (1 refused the interview). A number of the relatives in these families had become low in EE at follow-up; most of these were from the experimental group, but a few were from the control group. As a consequence, 14 patients were still living with high-EE relatives at follow-up. Six of these had relapsed while on medication, and the other eight remained well.

These two groups were compared with respect to a large number of demographic and historical data, as well as the 38 syndromes derived from the PSE. No significant difference emerged from these comparisons. The life events data for these patients are shown in Table 12.3.

When all independent events were considered, the groups did not differ significantly. Each event had been rated for contextual threat by Dr. P. Bebbington, using the method developed by Brown (1974). Severity of threat is rated on a 4-point scale, with 1 representing the severest and 4 the mildest

Table 12.3. Independent Life Events in the 3 Weeks before Relapse or Interview in Medicated Patients from High-EE Homes

Relapse Category	Number	Any Life Event	Threatening Life Event[a]
Relapse	6	5 (83.3%)	5 (83.3%)*
No relapse	8	3 (37.5%)	2 (25.0%)*

Note. "High-EE" defined as 6+ score on Critical Comments and/or 3+ score on Emotional Overinvolvement.

[a]Rating of 3 or below on Brown's (1974) scale.

*p = .049.

form of stress. In fact, events rated as 4 are not considered to involve any degree of threat. All events preceding relapse were rated as 3 or below, indicating different degrees of threat, whereas one of the well patients had experienced an event rated as 4. When this is excluded, a significant difference emerges between the two groups, as can be seen in Table 12.3. It is noteworthy that all events recorded for the patients in the naturalistic study were given a threat rating of 3 or below. Both studies together indicate that no schizophrenic patient who relapsed had experienced only a trivial or nonthreatening event in the preceding 3 weeks. This suggests that the threatening nature of life events is a crucial aspect of their role in precipitating episodes of schizophrenia.

It is of considerable interest to compare the high-EE patients in the intervention study who relapsed while on medication with those in the naturalistic study whose relapse occurred in the absence of prophylactic drugs. To make a valid comparison, it is necessary to make a minor adjustment, since the criteria for assignment to a high-EE group had changed slightly between the two studies. We had lowered the threshold for Emotional Overinvolvement scores from 4 to 3; however, this only meant reassigning one family in the naturalistic study from the low-EE to the high-EE group. As a result, the number of high-EE patients in this study who developed a schizophrenic episode while off drugs became 16. Of these only one experienced an independent event in the 3 weeks before onset. This proportion (6.3%) is strikingly different from the corresponding proportion (83.3%) among high-EE patients who relapsed while on drugs in the intervention study. The difference between these two proportions is highly significant (exact $p = .0013$).

RELATIONSHIP AMONG LIFE EVENTS, EE, AND DRUG THERAPY: OVERVIEW

On the basis of the data we have accumulated from these two studies, we can formulate statements about the relationship among life events, relatives' EE, and maintenance on neuroleptic drugs for schizophrenic patients. Those individuals living with relatives in the community are vulnerable to two main varieties of stress: acute stress in the form of threatening life events, and the chronic stress involved in living with a high-EE relative. In patients who are unprotected by medication, one or the other form of stress is sufficient to precipitate an episode of illness. Thus unmedicated patients in high-EE homes do not show a concentration of life events preceding onset, whereas those in low-EE homes do. Patients on regular medication are protected against one or the other type of stress, but not against a combination of acute and chronic stresses. Thus medicated patients in high-EE homes have a marked concentration of life events preceding a relapse.

What about medicated patients living with low-EE relatives? Since prophylactic drugs give adequate protection against one or the other form of stress, and these patients are exposed only to life events and not to high-EE relatives, relapse should not occur. In fact, the eight patients in the intervention study whose relatives changed from high to low in EE and who were maintained on long-acting injections all remained well during the 9-month follow-up. In the naturalistic study, the nine low-EE patients on prophylactic medication had not relapsed at the 9-month or at the 2-year follow-up (Leff & Vaughn, 1981).

So far we have not taken account of the protective effect of low face-to-face contact, demonstrated both in the series of naturalistic studies and in the intervention study. The number of patients from the latter study whose relatives remained high in EE throughout and who experienced a threatening life event in the 3 weeks before relapse or interview was small. However, among the eight patients concerned, the two who remained well were in low contact with their relatives, compared with only one of the six who relapsed. These numbers are too small to be of statistical significance, but they do suggest that low face-to-face contact with a high-EE relative may reduce the stressful effect sufficiently for patients on medication to survive the added impact of a threatening life event.

The relationships between these various social factors and preventive medication have been formulated above in a series of statements, behind which lie a number of assumptions that are worth spelling out in detail. One is that the chronic stress of living with a high-EE relative has an effect on the schizophrenic patient equivalent to the acute stress of a threatening life event. Another assumption is that maintenance on antipsychotic medication provides adequate protection against either life events or a high-EE relative, but not against both in combination. It is possible, however, that if the patient is in low contact with a high-EE relative, medication may exert a sufficient buffering effect to protect him or her from threatening life events. Since a threatening event is bound to occur at some point in the patient's life, relapse is only a question of time for those living in high contact with a high-EE relative, regardless of regular medication.

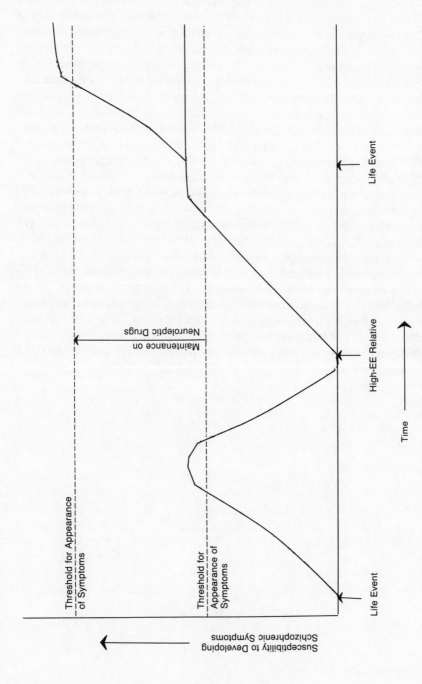

Figure 12.1 A graphic representation of the schizophrenic patient's susceptibility to environmental stress.

193

A further assumption made above is that the acute stress of a life event and the chronic stress of living with a high-EE relative are additive in their effect on the patient. These assumptions can be depicted graphically, as shown in Figure 12.1. The curves represent an individual patient's susceptibility to develop schizophrenic symptoms. The baseline levels are above those for the general population, and may be elevated even further by either the occurrence of a threatening life event or living with a high-EE relative. The curve rises steeply following a life event, or more gradually in response to a high-EE relative, until it reaches the level at which schizophrenic symptoms appear. High face-to-face contact with a high-EE relative may increase the gradient of the rise, or, alternatively, the final level of susceptibility reached.

Maintenance treatment with neuroleptic drugs raises the threshold level for appearance of symptoms above the peaks of susceptibility consequent on either a threatening life event or a high-EE relative. However, the new elevated threshold is exceeded when a life event is experienced by a patient living with a high-EE relative, whose susceptibility is already at an intermediate level.

This conceptual scheme accommodates the findings we have presented for schizophrenic patients living with relatives. It is admittedly speculative, but it does give rise to testable hypotheses. For example, it predicts that the susceptibility to develop symptoms, however measured, will fall more rapidly in patients hospitalized following a life event than in those who relapse in response to the chronic stress of living in a high-EE home. Some evidence for this hypothesis has been provided by psychophysiological studies; it is presented in Chapter 13.

13

Expressed Emotion and the Psychophysiology of Schizophrenia

In Chapter 12, we developed a model for integrating the pathogenic effects of EE and life events with the prophylactic effect of medication in schizophrenia. It follows from the model that research into the biological basis of schizophrenia should include assessments of these environmental factors. An early study by Venables and Wing (1962) used skin conductance measures as an index of physiological arousal, and revealed that socially withdrawn, chronic schizophrenics appear to be highly aroused. Since then, an extensive literature has grown on the orienting response in schizophrenia and other psychiatric disorders. Öhman (1981) recently reviewed this literature and concluded that electrodermal activity was related to vulnerability to schizophrenic episodes. In this chapter, we present studies that were undertaken of a possible link between environmental factors identified as influencing the course of schizophrenia, and electrodermal activity in patients.

THE FIRST STUDY: PATIENTS IN REMISSION AT HOME

The first of these studies developed out of our replication of the EE work (Vaughn & Leff, 1976a). This line of research indicated that schizophrenic patients were sensitive to critical and overinvolved attitudes in their relatives. It also showed that high social contact with high-EE relatives increased the risk of relapse. An explanation of this was formulated in terms of the concept of physiological arousal. This was admittedly a somewhat vague notion of the patient's central state of excitability, but it could be defined clearly by applying predetermined criteria to measures of skin conductance. The relationship of these peripheral autonomic measures to central nervous system activity remains conjectural, but at least this formulation allowed us to make sense of the findings from our various studies.

We hypothesized that environmental stress, in the form of either life events or relatives' EE, could increase arousal in schizophrenic patients. In itself, this hyperarousal might be no different from that induced in normal people by stress. However, in individuals vulnerable to schizophrenia, a certain level of hyperarousal could trigger the onset of a psychotic episode. This hypothesis requires two links to be established: an association between environmental stress and hyperarousal, and an association between hyperarousal and psychotic symptoms. In this chapter, we concentrate on the former link.

When we initially thought about studying psychophysiological responses in schizophrenic patients, the standard procedures were all designed to be carried out under strict control in a laboratory. We had considerable reservations about this approach, which rested on the assumption that the laboratory was a neutral environment, to which each subject reacted in a similar way. This assumption seemed unlikely to apply to schizophrenic patients. One could imagine paranoid patients becoming highly suspicious of the laboratory procedures and personnel. Patients with delusions of control might even incorporate the testing apparatus into their delusions. We have encountered at least two psychotic patients who misinterpreted the subject's chair as being an electric chair in which they were going to be wired up for execution.

These considerations led us to conclude that, far from being a neutral, standardized environment, the laboratory has an extremely varied psychological impact on the range of psychiatric patients tested therein. Rather than using an environment involving an unknown degree of stress, it seemed preferable to test the patients in an environment whose stressful nature was known and, indeed, calibrated. We are, of course, referring to the patients' families. Since we had already assessed the relatives on the EE index, we knew which of them were likely to pose a psychological threat to the patients. There was another reason for testing the patients in the context of their families, and that was the opportunity it afforded for studying the effect of face-to-face contact on the patients.

For these reasons, a study was designed that involved measuring psychophysiological variables in the patients while they were in their home environment (Tarrier, Vaughn, Lader, & Leff, 1979). This required the development of mobile equipment and the agreement of patients and their relatives to be visited at home by a research psychologist. The schizophrenic patients included in our EE replication (Vaughn & Leff, 1976a) formed the research population, and were contacted by letter about 2 years after their initial assessment in that study. Of the 37 possible patients, 21 were available and agreed to take part. Twenty-one age-and-sex-matched normal subjects with no history of psychiatric illness were recruited as a control group and underwent tests identical to those administered to the patient group.

The procedure was as follows. After the experimenter arrived at a subject's home, the subject was asked to sit and relax while the portable polygraph for measuring continuous sweat gland activity and heart rate was assembled. Sweat gland activity was measured as skin resistance, and was recorded from the thumb using a standard method. Another device was attached to the wrist of the other hand and measured heart rate. The subject's blood pressure was taken at the beginning and end of the recording session. Recordings were made for the first 20 minutes with only the experimenter present. At the end of this period, the subject's key relative was invited into the room, and a further 20 minutes of recordings were taken. The aim behind this design was to determine whether the patient reacted physiologically to face-to-face contact with the relative.

The experimenter knew which were the control subjects, because it was impossible to keep this hidden from him, but he was unaware whether the patients' relatives were high or low in EE. Before the test, each patient was given two questionnaires — one to ascertain the amount of face-to-face contact in a typical week, and the other to determine the nature and quantity of medication taken. After the test, both patient and relative were asked a list of questions in order to identify the occurrence of any independent life event in the preceding 3 weeks (see Chapter 12). For the patients, this procedure was carried out in the home on three occasions with an average of 3 months between each test. The control subjects were tested only once.

Differences among the three groups emerged in respect to each of the psychophysiological measures employed, but the clearest findings were associated with the rate of spontaneous fluctuations of skin conductance, and we concentrate exclusively on these. A "spontaneous fluctuation" was defined as a nonspecific response with an amplitude of at least 2% of the baseline. The mean number of spontaneous fluctuations per minute for each of the three groups on the first occasion of testing is plotted out in Figure 13.1.

Over the whole 30-minute period analyzed, the patient groups had higher rates of spontaneous fluctuations per minute than the control group (means: high-EE = 5.9, low-EE = 5.6, controls = 2.8; $p < .0001$). The changes in this measure over time reveal interesting differences among the three groups. Although they all started at about the same level, the control group showed a steady decline in spontaneous fluctuation rate over the 30-mintue period, with only a transient rise in response to the entry of the relative. This decline can be interpreted as an index of habituation, the physiological process of adaptation to a novel stimulus. By contrast, neither group of patients showed any sign of habituation during the first 15 minutes[1] of recording. Their spontaneous fluctuation rate was as high at the end of this period as it was at the beginning. Although this failure to habituate is abnormal, it is not characteristic of schizophrenics, since it has been observed in patients with acute anxiety states (Toone, Cooke, & Lader, 1981).

The entry of the relative into the room was marked by a rise in the spontaneous fluctuation rate in all three groups. However, this response was

---

1. The first 5 minutes of recording were omitted from the analysis to exclude a settling down period, while the last 5 minutes were excluded to equalize the time periods before and after relatives' entry.

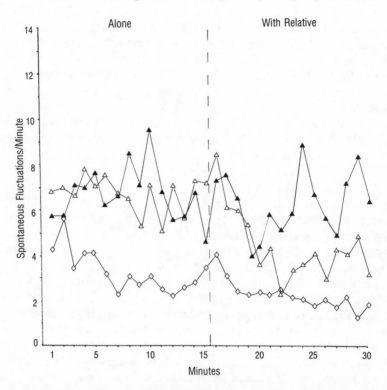

Figure 13.1. Mean number of spontaneous fluctuations of skin conductance per minute for schizophrenic patients and controls. High-EE patients ($n = 11$) are represented by solid triangles, low-EE patients ($n = 10$) by outline triangles, and controls ($n = 21$) by outline diamonds. (From "Bodily Reactions to People and Events in Schizophrenia" by N. Tarrier, C. Vaughn, M. H. Lader, and J. P. Leff, 1979, *Archives of General Psychiatry*, *36*, 311–315. Copyright 1979, American Medical Association. Reprinted by permission.)

significantly greater in the high-EE patients than in the low-EE patients or the controls. Following the entry of the relative, the high-EE patients sustained a high rate of spontaneous fluctuations, and had still shown no sign of habituation by the end of the second 15-minute period. A different response was shown by the low-EE patients to their relatives: Once they were in face-to-face contact, the spontaneous fluctuation rate fell steeply over the next 5 minutes to reach the same level as that of the control subjects. Whereas the high-EE and low-EE patients were indistinguishable in respect to their spontaneous fluctuation rate in the first 15 minutes, the low-EE patients had a significantly lower rate ($p < .01$) in the second 15 minutes. This was interpreted as evidence for a calming and reassuring effect of the low-EE relatives on the patients, enabling them to adapt to the novelty of the testing situation.

Hence we have evidence from the patients' psychophysiological reponses of different psychological effects for high-EE and low-EE relatives. Schizophrenic patients in remission appear to find it difficult to adapt to a new situation. High-EE relatives do nothing to help the patients cope with such a situation, whereas the presence of low-EE relatives seems to exert a calming effect on the patients, allowing the normal physiological process of habituation to occur.

It is of great interest that this differential influence of high-EE and low-EE relatives on the patients' spontaneous fluctuation rate was only apparent on the first occasion of testing. On the subsequent two occasions, both groups of patients showed a normal habituation response from the beginning of the recording. This suggests that the novelty of the experience had worn off by the second time around; the experimenter, the apparatus, and the procedure were now familiar to the patients. It is worth emphasizing that it was only when the patients were highly aroused by the first experience of testing that it was possible to demonstrate a differential effect of high-EE and low-EE relatives.

We mention above that a history of life events was taken for the 3 weeks preceding each recording session. We found that seven of the patients had experienced an independent life event in the period before one of the sessions. On the other two occasions for each patient, no such event had occurred. It was possible, therefore, to use the patients as their own controls, comparing their skin conductance recordings on the occasions preceded by a life event with those following an event-free period. This comparison is displayed in Figure 13.2.

The two sets of recordings did not differ for the first 15 minutes, during which the patient was alone with the experimenter. However, after the entry of the relative, there was a dramatic rise in the spontaneous fluctuation rate on the testing occasions preceded by a life event. This rise was sustained throughout the remaining 15 minutes and differed significantly ($p < .05$) from the rate recorded on event-free occasions. It is evident from this that, following the occurrence of a life event, the presence of the relative increases the patient's arousal more sharply than on event-free occasions. Thus there is an interaction between the arousing effects of a recent life event and of the relative's presence, so that in combination they increase the rate of spontaneous fluctuations shown by the patient.

This finding is in line with the model proposed in Chapter 12, with the qualification that the model specifies that the relative must be high in EE in order to exert an arousing effect on the patient. Unfortunately, the number of patients experiencing a life event was too small to be subdivided into high-EE and low-EE groups, and thereby to permit a meaningful analysis. Nevertheless, the means for each group are worth presenting, as they are suggestive of an interpretation.

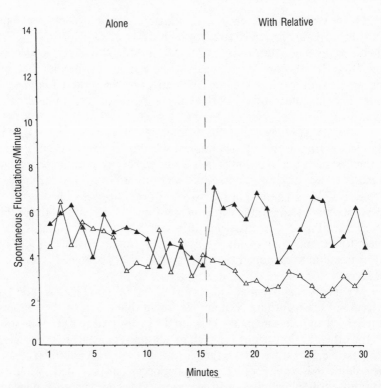

Figure 13.2. Mean number of spontaneous fluctuations of skin conductance per minute for patients on occasions preceded by a life event (solid triangles, $n = 7$) and for the same patients on occasions when no life event had occurred (outline triangles). (From "Bodily Reactions to People and Events in Schizophrenia" by N. Tarrier, C. Vaughn, M. H. Lader, and J. P. Leff, 1979, *Archives of General Psychiatry, 36,* 311–315. Copyright 1979, American Medical Association. Reprinted by permission.)

It can be seen from Table 13.1 that the only group with a mean increase in spontaneous fluctuations over the second 15 minutes of the session was that of the patients in high-EE homes who had experienced a recent life event. This suggests that the rise in the spontaneous fluctuation rate following the entry of the relative that is evident in Figure 13.2 is largely if not totally attributable to patients living with high-EE relatives, as predicted by the model. The group showing the greatest decrease in arousal over time was comprised of patients in low-EE homes without a recent life event. The remaining two groups were intermediate between these extremes. Although the differences among the means of these groups are not significant, the relationship of these means to one another is in accordance with the model. The presence of a high-EE relative or the recent occurrence of a life event increases a patient's arousal from a baseline level, exhibited by those event-free individuals who resided in low-EE homes. The highest level of arousal was found in patients who were exposed to a combination of a high-EE relative and a recent life event.

THE SECOND STUDY: PATIENTS IN AN ACUTE EPISODE IN THE HOSPITAL

The findings of this first study were encouraging enough for us to carry on with this line of inquiry. The patients studied by Tarrier *et al.* (1979) were all in remission, and many of them had not experienced a schizophrenic episode for over a year. It seemed important to use the same measurement procedure with patients who were experiencing an acute attack of illness, and the intervention study reported in Chapter 9 afforded an ideal opportunity for this. Not only would we be able to assess psychophysiological functioning in acutely ill patients, but the follow-up would yield data bearing on a crucial issue. If we were indeed able to change the level of EE in some relatives from high to low, would we see a commensurate alteration in the patients' psychophysiological responses to the relatives?

The concentration on acutely ill patients necessitated major changes in the research procedures. All the patients were hospitalized, so that it was not possible to carry out the recording sessions in their homes as in the previous study. Therefore it was planned to make the recordings in a special studio available in the hospital grounds. A key relative would be brought in to each session as before, so that we would be addressing the question of whether the physical environment of the home was essential to elicit the phenomena already observed, or whether the presence of the relative was sufficient, regardless of the venue.

The use of the studio conferred the additional advantage of videotape facilities, and each session that included the relative was recorded. A split-screen technique was employed so that the amount of direct eye contact between patient and relative could be assessed (Kuipers, Sturgeon, Berkowitz, & Leff, 1983).

Table 13.1. Mean Change in the Number of Spontaneous Fluctuations over 15 Minutes following Entry of the Relative

EE Status	Life Event	No Life Event
High	+ 17.5	− 7.2
Low	− 2.3	− 15.3

There was also a difference between the earlier study and the later one (Sturgeon, Turpin, Kuipers, Berkowitz, & Leff, 1984) in the composition of the patient population. The first piece of work used patients from a naturalistic study (Vaughn & Leff, 1976a), who were not selected for any characteristics of the home environment. The second study was based on the patients in the intervention project (Leff *et al.*, 1982), who were included because of being *in high contact* with their relatives. This is an important distinction between the two samples, and it has a potential bearing on the interpretation of the findings.

The design of the intervention study included a follow-up 9 months after discharge from the hospital. This provided the opportunity to record the patients' psychophysiological responses when in a state of clinical remission. At that stage, they would be more nearly comparable with the patients tested by Tarrier and his colleagues.

First, we present the results of testing the patients during an acute episode of schizophrenia, while they were still hospitalized. Before the first recordings could be undertaken, a number of research procedures had to be completed with the patients and relatives. These procedures took up more time than anticipated, so that the mean duration of stay in hospital before the recording took place was as much as 33 days for the low-EE patients and 46 days for the high-EE patients, a nonsignificant difference. This delay affects the interpretation of our findings and is discussed later.

The number of spontaneous fluctuations of skin conductance per minute was determined from the recordings, and the means for the two groups of patients were plotted out as shown in Figure 13.3. In all, 30 patients from the intervention study took part in satisfactory recording sessions; 11 of these were from low-EE homes and 19 from high-EE homes. The most striking finding was that the mean rate of spontaneous fluctuations of the high-EE patients was about double that of the low-EE patients *throughout* the 30 minutes of recording. This is a highly significant difference ($p = .006$) and contrasts with the findings of Tarrier *et al.* (1979) on patients in remission. The question of whether this difference related to a more severe clinical picture in the high-EE patients might well be raised. In fact, there was no evidence for this. The PSE data from the clinical examination were processed by the Catego program (Wing *et al.*, 1974) to yield 38 syndromes. The high-EE and low-EE patients did not differ significantly with respect to the presence or absence of any one of the syndromes. Furthermore, the average number of syndromes present was 12.6 in the high-EE patients and 12.7 in the low-EE patients.

Another important respect in which the Sturgeon *et al.* (1984) study differed from the Tarrier *et al.* (1979) study is that the rate of spontaneous fluctuations for both patient groups declined throughout the 15 minutes both before and after the relative's entry ($p = .049$). This decline became even more

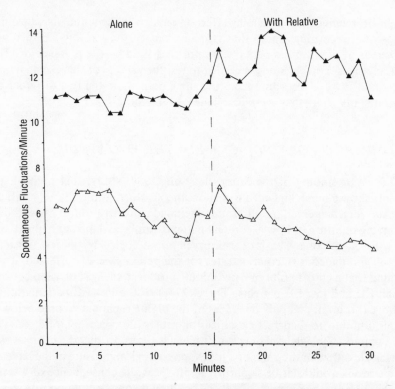

Figure 13.3. Mean number of spontaneous fluctuations of skin conductance per minute for schizophrenic patients during an acute episode. High-EE patients (*n* = 19) are represented by solid triangles, and low-EE patients (*n* = 11) are represented by outline triangles. (From "Psychophysiological Responses of Schizophrenic Patients to High and Low Expressed Emotion Relatives: A Follow-Up Study" by D. Sturgeon, G. Turpin, L. Kuipers, R. Berkowitz, and J. Leff, 1984, *British Journal of Psychiatry, 145*, 62–69. Reprinted by permission.)

pronounced following the entry of the relative (*p* = .027), but this also applied to both groups of patients. Hence the differential response of patients to low-EE and high-EE relatives that Tarrier and his colleagues found was not replicated in this study of acutely ill patients. This might be attributed to the difference in clinical state of the patients in the two studies. However, as we point out, the patients in the later study showed the same pattern of responding to relatives at follow-up, when in remission, as during the acute episode. Alternatively, the difference could be a consequence of the venue of testing, reflecting a difference in the patients' sensitivity to relatives in the strange setting of the hospital as opposed to the familiarity of their own homes. To explain the findings on this basis, it would have to be argued that high-EE relatives have a calming effect on patients in the unfamiliar surroundings of a recording studio that is equivalent to that of low-EE relatives, whereas in their homes patients are not reassured by the presence of high-EE relatives. Further study is needed to test the validity of this explanantion; it would involve recording from the same patients in the two different environments while they were in a state of remission.

COMPARISON OF FINDINGS FROM THE TWO STUDIES

The major finding of the Sturgeon *et al.* (1984) study, that high-EE patients show a much higher rate of spontaneous fluctuations than low-EE patients when acutely ill, requires more detailed consideration. It raises the intriguing question of how accurately patients can be assigned to high-EE and low-EE homes on the basis of their psychophysiological responses. When the mean spontaneous fluctuation rates for the patients were considered, it was found that a cutoff point of 6 per minute produced the best division between high-EE and low-EE patients. Three (27%) of the low-EE patients scored above this level, and only one (5%) of the high-EE patients scored below it. This amounts to a correct classification rate of 26 out of 30, or 83%. This is a remarkably high level of accuracy when we consider that the *relatives* were being classified on the basis of a psychophysiological measure in the *patients*. This result would not be so surprising if it was the consequence of a stable quality (X) in the patients, of which the spontaneous fluctuation rate was an index, and which provoked high-EE attitudes in relatives (Situation A in Figure 13.4).

This explanation, however, is virtually ruled out by the finding of Tarrier *et al.* (1979) that the spontaneous fluctuation rate of patients in remis-

Figure 13.4. Possible relationships between patients' psychophysiological responses and relatives' EE.

SITUATION A

Relatives	Patients
High-EE ⟵	Quality X ⟶ High spontaneous fluctuation rate
Low-EE ⟵	No quality X ⟶ Low spontaneous fluctuation rate

SITUATION B

Relatives		
High-EE ⟶	Patients ⟶	High spontaneous fluctuation rate
Low-EE ⟶	Patients ⟶	Low spontaneous fluctuation rate

sion did not differ between high-EE and low-EE homes. This observation induces us to favor the view that the higher spontaneous fluctuation rate in acutely ill patients from high-EE homes was a direct consequence of the psychological effect of their relatives on such patients (Situation B in Figure 13.4). A comparison of the mean rates for patients from the two studies is displayed in Table 13.2; it clarifies the position.

It is evident that the low-EE patients hospitalized for an acute episode of schizophrenia had mean spontaneous fluctuation rates that were very similar to those of the low-EE patients from the first study, who were tested in remission. The fact that high-EE patients were found to have much higher spontaneous fluctuation rates during an acute episode than when they were in remission suggests that this measure increases in parallel with exacerbations of schizophrenia. However, if this is so, why does it not apply to the low-EE patients?

The answer to this puzzle may lie in the delay between admission for an acute episode and the recording session. As mentioned above, this averaged 5 weeks for the low-EE patients. It is conceivable that by the time the psychophysiological measures were recorded, the level had already dropped back from a peak to the baseline found during remission. Of course, this argument would only be applicable to the low-EE patients. Indeed this is a sequence of events that is predicted by the model presented in Chapter 12—namely, that a rise in some biological measure that leads to an episode of schizophrenia in low-EE patients would be transient. By contrast, any similar rise shown by high-EE patients would last for much longer. Clearly, in order to test this hypothesis, it is necessary to hold a recording session as soon after admission as possible. Data of this kind are not currently available.

Our recent measurements show that high-EE patients have high spontaneous fluctuation rates as long as 7 weeks after admission. This observation raises the question of how long such rates take to fall to the levels found by Tarrier *et al.* (1979) in high-EE patients in remission. Some indication of the answer can be derived from the recordings made at the 9-month follow-up in the intervention study.

It is regrettable that the follow-up was by no means as comprehensive as we had planned. We were more successful in gaining the cooperation of the high-EE relatives in the experimental group, with whom we had worked quite intensively, than of those in the control group, to whom we had offered no help. Follow-up recordings were made of nine experimental high-EE patients and four control high-EE patients. In addition, we tested six low-EE patients. Figure 13.5 shows the recordings of the high-EE patients at follow-up, compared with those of the same patients at the initial session.

There was very little difference in the spontaneous fluctuation rates of the low-EE group between the two occasions. This is reflected in the follow-up mean of 5.9 for the whole session, the comparable figure for the initial

Table 13.2. Mean Rate of Spontaneous Fluctuations in the Two Studies

Study	Relatives	First 15 Minutes	Second 15 Minutes	Whole Session
Tarrier, Vaughn, Lader, & Leff (1979) (patients in remission)	High-EE	6.2	5.8	5.9
	Low-EE	6.7	4.4	5.5
Sturgeon, Turpin, Kuipers, Berkowitz, & Leff (1984) (patients in acute episode)	High-EE	11.1	11.9	11.5
	Low-EE	5.8	5.0	5.4

session being 5.4. This is only to be expected, since even in the acute episode, the low-EE patients had a mean rate of spontaneous fluctuations that was no higher than that of patients in remission. Therefore one would not anticipate any further reduction in the rate over time. The high-EE patients at follow-up produced a record that was lower at every point than it was during the acute episode. The mean rate at follow-up was 7.9, which represents a substantial drop from the level recorded during admission; however, the difference fails to reach significance, probably because of the small numbers involved.

Thus the follow-up study provides evidence of a slow fall in the spontaneous fluctuation rate of high-EE patients over a 9-month period following discharge. The study by Tarrier *et al.* (1979) indicates that by 2 years after an acute episode, high-EE patients reached a level of spontaneous fluctuations equal to that of low-EE patients. However, our patients differed from those in the earlier study in one important respect. The earlier sample represented a mixture of intensities of face-to-face contact, whereas the more recent sample was exclusively composed of patients in high contact with their relatives.

We have suggested, in presenting the model in Chapter 12, that high contact might increase the rate of rise in vulnerability and/or the final level reached. If the spontaneous fluctuation rate is taken to indicate vulnerability, then it might also be true that high face-to-face contact retards the decline in this rate following an acute episode of illness. If so, then it could have taken considerably longer for the high-EE, high-contact patients in the intervention study to subside to a baseline rate of spontaneous fluctuations than the mixed-contact group studied by Tarrier *et al.* (1979).

There is also some evidence for the proposition that high contact increases the spontaneous fluctuation rate reached during an acute episode of illness. A small group of high-EE patients in low contact with their relatives has been studied in a subsidiary project. Psychophysiological recording sessions, into which the relatives were introduced, were conducted exactly as in the intervention study, while the patients were hospitalized for treatment of an episode of schizophrenia. The mean spontaneous fluctuation rate of this group of six low-contact patients for the whole recording session was 7.3. This is well below the rate exhibited by high-contact patients, 11.5, although the difference fails to reach significance. Once again, this is likely to be a consequence of the small numbers involved.

Throughout the exposition of our psychophysiological studies, we have tacitly assumed that the spontaneous fluctuation rate is a direct index of vulnerability to schizophrenic episodes. To what extent is this true? We can look for an answer to this question in the effect of the intervention study on the patients' psychophysiological responses. Since the intervention was successful in lowering EE in a proportion of experimental relatives, and since this was paralleled by a significant reduction in the relapse rate of experimental patients, some effect on the patients' psychophysiology should be demonstrable.

Figure 13.5. Mean number of spontaneous fluctuations of skin conductance per minute. High-EE patients during an acute episode ($n = 13$) are represented by solid triangles, and the same patients at 9-month follow-up are represented by outline triangles.

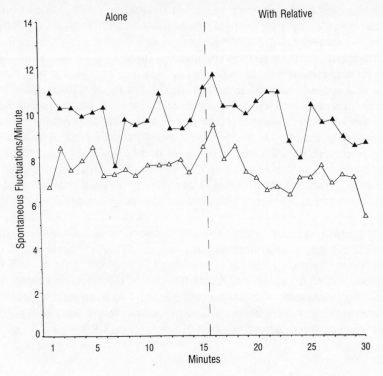

This possible effect was sought for by a variety of statistical analyses, the main one being a multivariate analysis of variance. The interpretation of the findings is somewhat clouded by the small number of families participating in the follow-up recordings, particularly from the control group. Nevertheless, no significant effect of the therapeutic intervention on the patients' spontaneous fluctuation rate emerged from these analyses. We must conclude from this that the striking reduction in vulnerability to schizophrenic relapse that was produced by the intervention program was not reflected in the patients' psychophysiological responses.

This disappointing result forces us to consider the possibility that the patients' spontaneous fluctuation rate may be a red herring, having nothing directly to do with schizophrenic relapse. This possibility was examined in another multivariate analysis of variance, which included skin conductance data from initial and follow-up interviews, the EE status of the relatives as rated at these two points, and whether the patients remained well or relapsed during the follow-up period. A number of significant effects emerged from this analysis. A high spontaneous fluctuation rate initially was significantly linked with high EE ratings, both initially ($p = .003$) and at follow-up ($p = .003$). In addition, a high rate of spontaneous fluctuations at the initial session was linked with relapse during the follow-up period ($p = .014$). This analysis suggests that a high spontaneous fluctuation rate recorded during an acute episode of schizophrenia is related *independently* to high-EE relatives and to subsequent relapse of the illness.

Hence we cannot discard the spontaneous fluctuation rate as an unimportant epiphenomenon. On the other hand, it cannot be regarded as a direct index of a patient's current state of vulnerability to an episode of schizophrenia, although it evidently has some predictive value for the future. Further work with these measures is clearly indicated. Skin conductance recordings need to be made on a variety of patients very shortly after admission for an acute episode of schizophrenia. Larger numbers of patients need to be tested in studies of intervention with high-EE families, particularly at follow-up. Furthermore, patients living with persistently high-EE relatives need to be followed up for psychophysiological recordings over considerably longer periods.

It is gratifying and exciting that this combination of a social and biological approach to schizophrenia has paid off. Biological measures in the patients have been found to reflect measures of stressors in their social environment — both life events and high-EE relatives. However, we suspect that at best the spontaneous fluctuation rate will prove to be an indirect measure of vulnerability to schizophrenia. Our own inclination is to search for a more direct index in the psychophysiology of the cerebral cortex.

14

Expressed Emotion and Related Measures
of Family Functioning

The measure of EE undoubtedly taps some aspect of family relationships that is predictive of the course of schizophrenia. It is not the only measure of this kind. Each group of early family theorists claimed to have identified an aspect of family relationships that was specific to the relatives of schizophrenics and played an etiological role. For T. Lidz and his colleagues (T. Lidz *et al.*, 1957), the key aspect was a disturbed parental relationship with the consequent formation of transgenerational alliances. Bateson, Haley, and their group (Bateson *et al.*, 1956) identified "double-bind" communication as the pathogenic factor, while for Wynne and Singer (1963), it was "communication deviances." Of these three groups, only Wynne and Singer produced a manual of operational definitions that allowed scientific replication of their work to be attempted. In fact, a British attempt at replication failed to repeat their original finding that communication deviances could be used to discriminate almost perfectly between the parents of schizophrenics and the parents of neurotic patients (Hirsch & Leff, 1971). Our clinical experience with the families of schizophrenic patients suggests that each of the abnormalities mentioned above is encountered in some, but by no means all, families. Furthermore, scientific studies of marital "schism" and "skew" and of the "double bind" have shown that they are by no means confined to the families of schizophrenic patients (Hirsch & Leff, 1975).

Thus it appears that each family feature that was claimed by its discoverers to play an etiological role in schizophrenia has proved to occur in only a proportion of the families of schizophrenics, and has also been found in families of other psychiatric diagnostic groups. In this respect, of course, there are close parallels with relatives' EE. High-EE features are found in about half the families of schizophrenic patients; as we have seen, they also occur among the relatives of depressed neurotic patients, the parents of patients with anorexia nervosa, and the spouses of obese women. The wide distribution of high-EE features across the diagnostic spectrum in psychiatry does not weaken their pathogenic significance for the recurrence of schizophrenic symptoms, however. For the same reason, such concepts as marital "skew" and "schism," "double bind," and "communication deviance" should not be discarded. Rather, there is great interest in discovering what their overlap with relatives' EE might be. There are two reasons for pursuing this line of inquiry. First, it is worth determining whether these apparently different measures are in fact tapping the same aspect of disturbed family relationships or whether they are to some extent complementary. If they are complementary, then it is possible that a combination of measures might give a better prediction of outcome in schizophrenia than one measure alone. The second possible advantage is the possibility of developing a brief method of assessing families, which could become a more practical clinical tool than EE.

Work of this nature is currently being conducted. Measures of EE, communication deviance, and affective style (Doane *et al.*, 1981) are being employed in parallel in the same families. Patients with schizophrenia and with depressive neurosis are also being compared (A. Strachan, personal communication, 1984). Findings from this study are not yet available, but a less extensive study has been completed and is of considerable relevance, as it consists of a comparison between EE and direct observation of family interaction (Valone, Norton, Goldstein, & Doane, 1984).

COMPARISON OF EE MEASURES AND OBSERVATIONS OF INTERACTION

The standard EE measure is an *indirect* way of assessing the emotional climate in a family, since it involves only a relative. It has been assumed that the emotions expressed by the relative in the interview are indicative of the way in which the relative behaves toward the patient over long periods of time. This assumption is not entirely untested, since in our recent study (Leff *et al.*, 1982), joint interviews were held with each relative and patient, and observations of their behavior were made (Kuipers *et al.*, 1983). In the study by Goldstein's group in California (Valone *et al.*, 1984), an attempt was made to identify those aspects of intrafamilial behavior that might be related to high-EE attitudes. Valone *et al.* included in their study 52 adolescents whose families had sought help for their offspring at the UCLA Outpatient Clinic. Selection criteria were an intact family and the absence of current or previous symptoms of psychosis in the adolescent. Each parent was separately interviewed with the UCLA Parent Interview and audiotaped; from these audiotapes, EE ratings were made by trained raters. Since the UCLA Parent Interview differs in some respects from the CFI, it was necessary for the raters to ignore certain of the parental responses for the purposes of rating EE.

In addition to the EE assessment of the parents, each adolescent took part in two videotaped dyadic interactions with his or her mother, and two interactions with the father. Following these four dyadic interactions, the adolescent participated in two triadic discussions involving both the mother and the father. In the study under discussion, only the first dyadic interaction with each parent and the first triadic study were analyzed. To set up the interaction, a problem of relevance to the family under study was identified, using a modification of Strodtbeck's (1954) Revealed Differences technique. Family members were instructed to discuss the problem, to express their feelings and ideas about it, and to attempt to resolve the issue. The discussion was transcribed from audiotapes and analyzed for parental affective style.

A number of categories of affective comments were defined. These included Benign Criticism and Harsh Criticism (which comprise Personal Criticism), Guilt Inducement, and Critical Intrusive Comments, all of which appear from their description to be aspects of Critical Comments and Hostility on the EE index. Another category, Neutral Intrusive Statements, has something in common with the symbiotic aspect of Emotional Overinvolvement on the EE index, while the last kind of affective comment, Support Statements, appears to overlap with the EE measures of Warmth and Positive Remarks.

The transcripts were coded by two raters who were blind to the initial status of the families, and highly satisfactory levels of interrater reliability were achieved for each category of affective style. A number of significant associations were found between the EE status of parents and their style of affective behavior in direct family interactions. High-EE parents expressed significantly more benign criticisms toward their offspring than low-EE parents ($p < .0001$), the major contribution to this difference being high-EE mothers in dyadic interactions and high-EE fathers in triadic interactions. High-EE parents also manifested more harsh criticisms than low-EE parents in dyadic and triadic interactions ($p < .01$). The two kinds of parents did not differ in their expression of either neutral intrusive statements or support statements.

The authors of this study did not look for associations between individual EE components and categories of affective style, but this is almost certainly because only 2 of the 42 high-EE parents were rated high on Emotional Overinvolvement; the others scored high on Critical Comments, Hostility, or both. Hence, we can conclude that the differences found between the high- and low-EE parents in the expression of benign and harsh criticisms are directly related to the EE ratings for Critical Comments and Hostility. The results of this study provide strong evidence for the assumption that the EE measures of Critical Comments and Hostility are reflected in the actual behavior of high-EE relatives toward patients.

ANALYSIS OF FAMILY INTERACTIONS

We now consider two other recent pieces of work that have employed family measures other than those already discussed and have related them to the outcome of schizophrenia. In both instances, the measures have something in common with EE. In the first study, Angermeyer (1982), like Valone and his colleagues, used direct observation of family interaction to assess the emotional climate in a family. He also used Strodtbeck's (1951) Revealed Differences technique to stimulate discussion, but employed a quite different technique of analysis. The subjects were male schizophrenics with two parents available, and the family triads were involved in discussions at the time at which each patient was about to be discharged from the hospital. The family interaction occurred over a 30-minute period while a family was left on its own.

Each discussion was audiotaped and transcribed, and the transcriptions were processed using the Content Analysis Scales developed by Gottschalk and Gleser (1969). Six forms of anxiety and four forms of hostility are delineated in this scale; the categories are influenced by psychoanalytic theory, learning theory, and linguistics. The ratings are made on verbal content alone, although the presence of a variety of defensive and adaptive mechanisms is used to infer the existence of suppressed and repressed feelings. Each subject's score was corrected for the number of words spoken. All transcripts were scored by two raters independently and blindly. Satisfactory levels of interrater reliability were reached on all scales, the lowest correlation being .78 for Mutilation Anxiety.

Only first-admission patients were included; a total of 30 families entered the study over 2½ years. The diagnosis of schizophrenia was made on the basis of symptoms elicited with the PSE. The patients were followed up for 2 years, and any readmission to a psychiatric hospital was ascertained. Our approach to outcome was different, as it was based on relapse of schizophrenia, regardless of readmission. Despite this, the outcome figure for Angermeyer's (1982) sample (43% rehospitalized over 2 years) was almost identical to ours (44% relapsed over 2 years) (Leff & Vaughn, 1981). The rehospitalized patients did not differ from the rest of the sample with regard to clinical state at admission or level of premorbid social adjustment.

Several of the ratings made of family interaction were found to relate to hospitalization of the patients during the subsequent 2 years. Mothers of rehospitalized patients showed significantly more guilt anxiety ($p < .01$), shame anxiety ($p < .05$), and inwardly directed hostility ($p < .05$) than mothers of patients who were not readmitted. The fathers of readmitted patients, however, showed more outwardly directed hostility ($p < .05$) and more ambivalent hostility ($p < .05$) than their counterparts in the non-readmitted group. The patients themselves also differed in the amount of hostility expressed: The readmitted patients showed less inwardly directed and ambivalent hostility than those who stayed out of the hospital. A stepwise discriminant analysis was carried out; it revealed that the emotional ratings of mothers rather than those of fathers were primarily responsible for the differentiation between parents of readmitted and nonreadmitted patients.

In addition to analyzing the mean score on each scale for the whole discussion period, Angermeyer also looked for changes over time by calculating means for each 5-minute segment. He found that for most of the emotional scales, readmitted sons and their mothers tended to vary together over time, showing a symmetrical relationship. By contrast, mothers of sons who stayed out of the hospital tended to vary in an opposite direction to their sons, displaying a complementary relationship. A similar, but less marked, pattern was found among fathers.

Angermeyer (1982) interprets these findings as evidence for a relationship between the emotional atmosphere in the family of a male schizophrenic patient and the patient's subsequent career. There is an obvious equivalence between the outwardly directed hostility and the ambivalent hostility of the German fathers studied by Angermeyer and the elements of criticism and hostility in EE as measured in our studies. The parallel between the German mothers' emotional expression and that of their counterparts in the English studies is not as clear. Angermeyer speculated that the guilt and anxiety of the mothers in his study would lead them to become overinvolved with and overprotective of their sons. It is certainly true that overanxiety represents one component of the element of overinvolvement in EE. However, it cannot be assumed that guilt necessarily leads to overprotective behavior, although we have certainly found this to be so in a number of cases.

The contrast found by Angermeyer between the symmetrical and complementary relationships of the emotional scales in the families of readmitted and non-readmitted patients echoes differences we have observed in coping styles of high-EE and low-EE relatives. A symmetrical relationship on the Outwardly Directed Hostility scales means that as a son becomes more aggressive, so do his parents. This is reminiscent of the confrontational style of high-EE relatives (see Chapter 8), who provoke arguments with the patients. By contrast, low-EE relatives avoid confrontations and would be expected to show decreasing hostility as a patient becomes more hostile; this would lead to a complementary relationship on the scales. The same is true of anxiety, since we have evidence that low-EE relatives are able to reassure and calm aroused patients (see Chapter 13); once again, this would produce a complementary relationship in the anxiety scales. An opposite effect would be expected with high-EE relatives, whose anxiety would rise in accord with the patients'.

Thus, although Angermeyer used a different outcome measure from that used in the EE studies, there are considerable similarities between his results and ours, suggesting that the indirect approach of measuring relatives' EE is closely related to direct observations of family relationships in an experimental setting.

USE OF A SELF-REPORT QUESTIONNAIRE

The second recent study sheds light on a different aspect of the EE work — namely, the possibility of tapping the same elements of family relationships with a self-respect questionnaire. This instrument, the Parental Bonding Instrument (PBI), was designed as a refined measure of the two dimensions isolated in factor-analytic studies as reflecting fundamental parental characteristics, care and protection (Parker, Tupling, & Brown, 1979). The PBI is a simple self-report measure, taking about 10 minutes to complete; it requires subjects to score parents as they remember them in their first 16 years. It produces scores for parents' Care and Protection. Parker *et al.* consider that parents who score low on Care and high on Protection resemble high-EE relatives.

The PBI was employed in a study of newly admitted schizophrenic patients and a group of controls, matched for sex, social class, and age, who were attending several general medical practices in Sydney, Australia (Parker, Fairley, Greenwood, Jurd, & Silove, 1982). The patients were requested to complete a PBI for each parent on two occasions: shortly after admission, and later on when their clinical state had improved. All but a few patients were able to complete the PBI forms when first requested; satisfactory forms were obtained for 72 out of 93 subjects.

The patients were followed up for 9 months after discharge, the outcome measure being readmission, as in Angermeyer's study. Of these patients, 25 (35%) were discharged to their parents' homes, but many of these did not remain there during the follow-up period. Forty one (60%) had some degree of contact with their parents after discharge, and they were far more likely to be readmitted than patients not contacting their parents (49% vs. 13%; $p < .01$).

The first question to be addressed is whether the patients' mental state on admission might have distorted their responses on the PBI. Comparison of the mean PBI scores on the two occasions of testing showed significant (all $p's < .001$) correlation coefficients as follows: maternal Care, .77; maternal Protection, .73; paternal Care, .58; paternal Protection, .69. These figures suggest some influence of the patients' mental state on their PBI scores, which were more marked for the perceived attitudes of their fathers than for those of their mothers.

When compared with the matched controls, the patients achieved significantly lower scores for maternal and paternal Care, and significantly higher scores for paternal Protection. As a consequence, a significantly higher proportion of patients' fathers than of controls' fathers fell into the low-care-high-protection category. It was found that patients assigning one or both parents to this category were significantly younger at initial psychiatric hospitalization than the rest of the sample.

Analysis of the readmission data showed that only the second PBI scores, produced when the patients had improved clinically, were predictive of outcome. Of the 34 patients reporting one or both parents as low in care and high in protection, 16 (47%) were rehospitalized, compared with 7 (23%) of the remaining 23 ($p < .05$). When only the 24 patients who were discharged to live with their parents were considered, there was no significant difference between the groups with regard to rehospitalization. However, a significant difference emerged when all 39 patients who had had contact with parents after discharge were included. The rehospitalization rates for this group were as follows: low-care–high-protection parents, 15 (65%) of 23; others, 5 (31%) of 16 ($p < .05$).

Parker *et al.* (1982) interpret these findings as showing that PBI scores enable schizophrenic relapse to be predicted in patients who are in contact with their parents. There should be some reservation in equating relapse with rehospitalization, but apart from that, their interpretation of the predictive accuracy of the PBI seems justified. However, a doubt remains about the nature of the link between PBI scores and rehospitalization. As noted above, these authors found a significant association between a patient's age at initial hospitalization and assignment of one or both parents to the low-care–high-protection category. They also found that current age of the patient was not related to readmission. However, they neglected to test the relationship between age at first admission and readmission. Thus the possibility remains that patients who are first admitted at an early age are both likely to perceive their parents as low in care and high in protection and to be rehospitalized.

Even if this interpretation were to be proved incorrect, the PBI does not achieve as clear-cut a separation between good and poor outcome as does relatives' EE. The 9-month relapse rate in high-EE homes is slightly more than 50%, comparable to the rehospitalization rate in Parker's *et al.* low-care–high-protection homes. However, the rate in low-EE homes is no more than 15%, less than half that in Parker's other categories of homes. This suggests that the overlap between low care–high protection and high EE is only partial, and that a significant proportion of high-EE relatives would be assigned to other categories by patients using the PBI. It would clearly be informative to compare EE ratings and PBI scores for the same relatives, and this is a procedure that Parker and his colleagues endorse. Until that is done, we can only speculate on the correspondence between perceived low care–high protection and the individual components of EE.

CONCLUSION

The studies reviewed in this chapter have shown that the criticism and hostility elements of EE are indicative of relatives' actual behavior toward patients, that other measures of direct family interaction are predictive of hospitalization in schizophrenia, and that a simple self-report questionnaire can significantly predict rehospitalization. This is an encouraging beginning, but it is evident that a great deal more work needs to be done on establishing the behavioral equivalents of individual EE components, as well as on defining the degree of correspondence between EE and other measures of family functioning.

15

Expressed Emotion and the Etiology of Schizophrenia

We emphasize in the introduction to this volume that our strategy has been to study established cases of schizophrenia and to examine the subsequent course of the illness with the aim of identifying important social influences. We consider that strong evidence has been put forward for a causal role in the relapse of schizophrenia for independent life events and relatives' expressed emotion. In the case of independent life events, the evidence is just as strong for their influence on first episodes of schizophrenia as on relapses. This is because of the concept, built into the assessment of life events, of independence of any behavior of a patient. This qualification ensures that any events identified as occurring in the period before the first onset of schizophrenia could not have been brought about by behavior of the patient that may herald the illness.

The same is not true of relatives' EE. Whereas a life event is a discrete happening that can be pinpointed in time, it is not possible to be at all accurate in dating the emergence of critical and overinvolved attitudes. Furthermore, from a retrospective inquiry, one cannot rule out the possibility that such attitudes were a direct response to altered behavior of the patient that preceded the appearance of identifiable symptoms. Only a long-term prospective study of preschizophrenic individuals would satisfactorily answer this question, and although studies of this kind are proceeding, they have not yet yielded the data required. Short of this ideal, there are other, less satisfactory kinds of data, which nevertheless are worth considering since they are the best currently available.

THE CHILD GUIDANCE CLINIC STUDIES

Information that is least contaminated by a retrospective bias comes from child guidance clinic records in the United States. Such clinics were set up in America in the 1920s and represent a source of material that was collected before the subsequent psychiatric careers of the children were known. Of course, some of the children grew up to be healthy adults, while others developed a variety of psychiatric problems. Among the latter, a small proportion presented with schizophrenia. O'Neal and Robins (1958) conducted a 30-year follow-up of 526 children who had attended a child guidance clinic. They identified 28 of this sample who subsequently developed schizophrenia,[1] and matched them for age and area of residence with 57 control clients who were found to be psychiatrically healthy at follow-up. A number of significant differences emerged relating to abnormal behavior in the preschizophrenic children. They showed significantly more pathological lying, physical aggression, eating disorder, phobias, tics, and mannerisms than their healthy controls. Only a single difference between the groups concerned the parent–child relationship: The preschizophrenic children were more often dependent on their mothers than the controls, as shown by a fear of letting their mothers out of sight.

The same research strategy was used by Waring and Ricks (1965), who reviewed the records of 18,000 clients seen at Judge Baker Child Guidance Clinics (Boston, Massachusetts) prior to a time that any of them became schizophrenic. From these, the records of 50 children were identified who were hospitalized for schizophrenia an average of 6 years later. This sample was matched with 50 control children who were not subsequently admitted to a psychiatric hospital. Matching was in terms of age, sex, IQ, social class, ethnic background, and presenting symptoms at the clinic. The clinic workers had paid special attention to family factors that at the time were considered important in psychiatric disturbance. In analyzing this material, Waring and Ricks employed the concepts of "emotional divorce" (Bowen, Dysinger, & Basamania, 1959) and marital "schism" and "skew" (Fleck, Lidz, & Cornelison, 1963; T. Lidz *et al.*, 1957). Subjects were defined as chronic schizophrenics (in a hospital at the time of follow-up), released schizophrenics, (currently out of the hospital), and nonpsychiatric controls.

It was found that the type of marriage most closely associated with subsequent schizophrenia in a child was characterized by emotional divorce, in which parents lived under the same roof but in a state of mutual withdrawal. This situation was present in 35% of the chronic schizophrenic group, but in only 4% of the controls ($p < .01$). Skewed and schismatic marriages were no more common in the preschizophrenic group than the controls. In scrutinizing the family environment, Waring and Ricks (1965) discerned symbiotic relationships in which a child was socially isolated and unduly helpless at home, making no attempt to escape. Excessive dependence of this kind was found to be significantly more common among the chronic schizophrenics than the controls.

---

1. In contrast to most American psychiatrists, this group has consistently applied a narrow definition of schizophrenia.

Ricks and Nameche (1966) added further evidence on this point, such as a parent's bathing a child even in adolescence, isolating the child from its peers, and not allowing the child privacy. Nameche, Waring, and Ricks (1964) also reported that 65% of 20 chronic schizophrenics identified in their sample had never been separated for even one night from their parents by the time they were seen at the clinic; this figure contrasts with 23% for the released schizophrenics, and was attributed by the authors to parental reluctance to let a child go.

These findings cannot be generalized to all parents of schizophrenics, since the preschizophrenic children in these studies were disturbed enough to have been referred to a child guidance clinic. Disturbances of this severity are probably shown by a minority of preschizophrenic children. With this reservation, we can conclude that three features distinguish the family life of some preschizophrenic children from that of matched controls: a poor marital relationship; overprotection of a child by the parents, particularly the mother; and excessive dependence of the child on the parents.

We do not take the simplistic view that these relationships are the result of a one-way influence by the parents on the child. Evidence is accumulating that from birth onward the preschizophrenic child often manifests minor developmental abnormalities, which may well provoke parental anxiety and overprotection (see Pollin & Stabenau, 1968; Pollin, Stabenau, Mosher, & Tupin, 1966). From child guidance clinic records, Nameche *et al.* (1964) determined that preschizophrenic children were often in need of special care, had been felt to be sickly or weak, or seemed to require special treatment by their mothers. From our point of view, it is immaterial that both parents and child may contribute to a mutually interdependent relationship. If the quality of the relationship before the onset of schizophrenia has something in common with one or both key elements of EE, then there is the possibility of altering it with therapy. The intervention studies have demonstrated that the vulnerability of schizophrenic patients to relapse can be significantly reduced by a combination of maintenance on medication and therapeutic alteration of the family environment. There is every reason to suppose that if critical or overinvolved attitudes were present before the first onset of schizophrenia, they would be at least as amenable to therapeutic intervention then as they would be later on in the illness. Thus, if it were possible to identify a preschizophrenic child reliably on the basis of some biological index (and that is a big "if"), then tackling overinvolved and critical attitudes of relatives could be an effective means of preventing the appearance of the illness.

In fact, parental overprotection, as identified in the child guidance clinic studies, seems to be identical to the overprotective element of emotional overinvolvement. No equivalent of criticism appears to have been identified in these studies, but there is an overlap between the quality of the parental marriage termed "emotional divorce" and the measure of parental conflict used in the EE studies. In fact, as explained in Chapter 6, parental conflict in families where both parents were present has proven as good a predictor of schizophrenic relapse as critical attitudes toward the patient. Hence the features that have been found in some families of preschizophrenic children have their equivalents among the factors identified in the EE work as determining relapse of the established illness. This continuity over time indicates that these emotional attitudes are not a direct response to the development of schizophrenia in a family member, but antedate its appearance by many years, if not decades.

EVIDENCE FROM CASE HISTORIES

Further evidence for this view, which is admittedly of an anecdotal nature and hence not absolutely reliable, derives from the case histories in the EE studies. A few examples suggesting that overinvolved attitudes often begin very early in a child's life are given here.

Case 1 (Leff et al., 1982)

The mother of the patient was found to be high on Emotional Overinvolvement (a score of 3 on the 5-point scale) at the time of his first admission at the age of 23. His younger brother was psychiatrically normal and well adjusted. Their mother had seen the patient as the more vulnerable of her two sons since early in his childhood, when he had developed a severe chest infection. He had slept in her bed until the age of 15, when she had become anxious about their closeness and had sent him on a trip to America.

Comment: The mother's permissiveness in allowing her son sharing her bed well beyond an appropriate age is evidence of long-standing overprotection. She gave an account of this attitude as being aroused by a severe childhood illness, but it is possible that her attitude was already oversolicitous and had merely crystallized around the illness.

Case 53 (Leff et al., 1982)

The patient, a woman of 25, lived with her mother and the mother's boyfriend; her father had committed suicide in a psychiatric institution. The patient failed to grow at a normal rate as a child and was discovered to have Turner syndrome (XO constitution, giving rise to dwarfism and failure to develop secondary sexual characteristics). When the patient was admitted, her mother was found to score very high on Emotional Overinvolvement (5), as well as to be excessively critical. In the course of meetings of the relatives' groups, which were tape-recorded and transcribed, the mother described her relationship with the patient in the following terms:

"She didn't like her father very much. It's always been me ever since she was born. She was a difficult baby. She screamed and didn't sleep very much as a child, and wherever I went she had to go. Even when she was young, if I went into friends I was being cut out again. You know, the others all played but not her. 'Mum, come in.' It's always been the same with her. Very, very pathetic.

"Being small, like, I think really I've overprotected her. She's always thought I'd be there, which I was, of course, and she's kind of gone on thinking, 'If I don't do it, Mum'll do it,' which I would anyway. I can't say I wouldn't, because I would."

Any effort the mother made to help her daughter become independent was countered by the following objection:

"It's a bit more complicated, because she can come back at you and say, 'well, it's not going to make me grow, Mum. It's not going to give me periods. I'm not going to be able to have babies.' And then you start getting very upset. She just uses me sometimes."

Comment: These quotations illustrate the patient's dependence on her mother from an early age, as well as the mother's overprotection, of which she was well aware. It is clear that the mother responded to the patient's failure to grow normally by being overprotective, and that the patient nurtured this attitude by playing on the mother's guilt.

Case 26 (Vaughn & Leff, 1976a)

The patient, a young man of 23, was living with his parents at the time of his first admission. When interviewed, the mother scored high on all three of the EE scales: Emotional Overinvolvement (4), Critical Comments, and Hostility. Although not overprotective where her son's social life was concerned, she reported many attempts to exert a controlling influence through her nagging and "If only you listened to me" advice: for example, "Can't you buy more decent shoes than that? They look ugly!" and "You should look at what you buy before it goes in the bag. If you want some grapes, just tell me and I'll buy it." She resented the patient's reluctance to heed such advice, calling him "ungrateful" and a "spoiled puzzle." She made repeated references to the parents' past self-sacrifice and willingness to do anything for their only child:

"I started working at home, but never leaving the child anywhere, always looking after the child – he had everything he wanted. . . . There is not a child who had a more easy life than he had! He had more than I had, and more than his father had."

After showing the interviewer many old photographs of the patient as a baby and small child, the mother said:

"You see, we [have] done everything possible for the child—every dream, every wish he had, we made it possible. If I could reach the moon for him, I would do so. So really, I can't tell you what made him like this."

In reported conversations she addressed the patient as "boy" and "child," and she referred to him in these terms throughout the interview.

Comment: It seems that this mother behaved in an excessively devoted and self-sacrificing way toward the patient from a very early age. When he became an adult, she could not let go; she found it difficult to accept his expressions of independence and autonomy and viewed them only as signs of rejection. She spoke as if he were still a small child, and her behavior suggested that in her own mind he remained a child.

Case 16 (Vaughn et al., in press)

This family was unusual in that both parents scored highly on Emotional Overinvolvement (4). Their son, aged 35 and divorced, had experienced his first schizophrenic breakdown 6 years before. Both the mother and the father viewed his subsequent deterioration as particularly tragic because of his considerable early promise; he was described as a model child and a student of many talents prior to his failure at college. Both parents' accounts were notable for a preoccupation with the distant past and for the quantity and content of positive remarks concerning the patient when young. The mother, for example, spoke of her son in the following terms:

"When he was born I was given an injection to stave off miscarriage. I wonder if this was a cause. I love him so much, I hate to say this—maybe I should have had it. All he did was suffer. He gave me a lot of joy, mostly heartache. So after that he was born. He was beautiful, absolutely beautiful! To look at he was perfect. The most beautiful child.

"I want to tell you, at 15 he saved a man's life . . . heaven watch over my son and save him. He revived him—my son! I've got a few pictures here—just snapshots—so you could know him as he was . . . he was so beautiful, so handsome, and his teeth were like pearls. My broken heart, he was so beautiful!

"His poems, they were so beautiful—his poems were a treasure. He's naturally poetic."

From childhood the patient was absolved of responsibility for any errors of judgment; the mother always blamed others. Thus she excused his arrest for joyriding at the age of 15 by saying, "He was involved with bad children—he didn't know any better." Even after the onset of illness, she continued to view the patient as an exceptional individual: "He's such a wonderful man. His soul is so beautiful and exquisite." She made 20 such remarks during the course of her interview.

The father was remarkably similar to the mother in his descriptions of the patient's youthful traits and accomplishments, as the following passages illustrate:

"Barry was never rude or swearing. Well, maybe once or twice since he was a little boy. When he was small he never uttered a vulgarity at all—I never heard it—and everybody used to love and respect him. They used to come over to our house when he was 8, 9, 10, and say 'He's a diamond in the rough!' That's how everybody respected him. And he was so *lovable*! He was such a beautiful baby, and enthralled whenever you did anything for him. He respected everything.

"Later on, he was a B+ student and everyone loved him. Very well-liked on the block, but always quiet and smiling. But not too quiet . . . I liked to go to a ball game, but that bored him. Once I was given an all-season pass—I got him to go once, that was it. He wouldn't go again. The big thrill of a father is to take his son to a ball game. And he can pitch a ball well! I did want him to become a ball player, but I didn't pressure him. I wanted him to become a pitcher. He can pitch with either hand; [he was] somewhat ambidextrous but right-handed when he ate with his fork and knife.

"He would have made an excellent lawyer. I wish I had a film or tape of him appearing in a traffic small claims court downtown . . . only 16 years old, but the way he spoke up to the judge so dramatically! The judge even said, 'I ought to sit on the bench where you're sitting, and you sit here.' He got applause! He was so . . . for 16 years old!—I was astounded! He has all the capabilities."

These detailed anecdotal accounts were delivered with a powerful sense of the moment; it was difficult for the interviewer to realize that each pertained to events that had occurred more than 20 years before. The father also emphasized the closeness of his relationship to the patient when the patient was a child. Relevant remarks included, "When he was a baby, I worked on the graveyard shift, and used to carry him everywhere on my shoulder," and "Three months in 1948, when he was 5, that's the longest I can remember being away from him."

Comment: Many of the elements of emotional overinvolvement that characterized the mother's and father's respective attitudes toward the patient in the present were also featured in their descriptions of the past: extravagant praise, some lack of objectivity, and overconcern expressed as an exaggerated emotional response. The overinvolvement shown by each appeared to be deep-rooted and enduring.

Case 34 (Vaughn et al., in press)

The patient was an only child of 22 with a long psychiatric history, her first admission having occurred at the age of 14. Her mother was extremely agitated and distressed at interview and scored highly on Emotional Overinvolvement (4), Critical Comments and Hostility. She supplemented an excessively detailed and melodramatic account of the patient's life from birth with equally detailed written notes (with dates) prepared before the interview. She dwelled on her daughter's childhood illnesses, believing them to have special significance for the onset of later psychiatric complaints. In response to the question "When did you first notice something wrong with your daughter?", she said:

> "Why is it that when a baby is 1½ months old and you're giving it a bath, have it fully protected, and its little feet are dangling in very little water, and you have a real soft washcloth, washing her little legs, right? All of a sudden the child goes limp. What happened? I don't know. It scared me to death . . . I ran out of the house screaming! . . . It was a hard birth, a breech birth, and the doctor who delivered her was no more interested in that child than in the moon. Anyway, I had to take her to doctors often during that first year. . . . She's always seen doctors . . . I just made an appointment, dashed in to see them. It was always 'Oh, there's nothing wrong with her.' But you can't tell me there wasn't, because how come does a baby gain weight for a week and then the next week lose it all?
>
> "She had X-rays of her kidney tubes at the age of 9. Thank goodness she didn't have any operation on that. Her two tubes were all right, no clogging, praise the Lord for that! You see, Dr. Guy did not put her in the hospital. He did the tests there in his office, and I'll bet you a $1000 that that's what happened with her nerves."

From an early age, the patient had few friends and relied on her mother for company. She was very demanding, and the mother went to extreme lengths to be accommodating: "Anything to keep her happy." For example, when the patient (aged 13) complained that her parents made too much noise while eating their food, the mother moved into a trailer near the house to sleep and to work: "She had the run of the house then, it was all right."

The mother also revealed a long-term preoccupation with quite minor aspects of her daughter's behavior. When the patient was 14, the mother was so concerned by the angle of her legs as she slept that she sought the advice of a friend, with bizarre results:

> "My friend's 4-year-old and my daughter did the same kind of things. My friend helped a lot. I said to her, 'Look, her legs are always coming up towards her chin when she's in bed. What can I do? I can't sleep that way!' So this lady said, 'Well, you just take nylon stockings and tie her legs to the posts in the bed.' And that's what I did. And that's how she slept."

Comment: The mother's account provided considerable evidence of an exaggerated emotional response to the patient from birth. Excessive detail about the distant past and her reported reactions at the time, together with some excessively overprotective and self-sacrificing behavior when the patient was young, all suggest the long-standing presence of emotional overinvolvement in a marked form.

These case reports add clinical evidence to the child guidance clinic studies. Taken together, they suggest that overprotective and overinvolved parental attitudes often develop very early on in a child's life. However, definitive data can only come from longitudinal prospective studies of children at high risk for schizophrenia, which are currently in progress.

Epilogue

The reader will have noticed the diversity of topics in Section IV of the book, compared with the other parts. This accurately reflects the way in which research on EE, having developed in a single direction over two decades, has taken a prismatic form in the last few years. Until the end of the 1970s, the work was pursued entirely within the MRC Social Psychiatry Unit, but recently the techniques and themes have been taken up enthusiastically by researchers in a number of countries. This development has enriched the work with an influx of invaluable data and fresh ideas. From the new starts that have been made, it is possible to predict the directions in which research is likely to move over the next decade.

Further naturalistic studies of the association between relatives' EE and the course of schizophrenia will be undertaken in non-Western countries. These will reveal whether the expression of criticism, warmth, and overinvolvement is generally as muted in the Third World as suggested by the data from Chandigarh. They will also determine whether variation in EE contributes to the manifestly better outcome of schizophrenic patients in these countries as compared with the West.

The work on EE and course of illness will be extended to other diagnostic groups; manic–depressive psychosis is an obvious choice. It is possible that patients with this condition who are poorly controlled with lithium are exposed to the stress of high-EE homes, paralleling the findings for schizophrenic patients who relapse on maintenance neuroleptics.

Different approaches to intervention in the families of schizophrenic patients will undoubtedly be evaluated, using EE as a target measure. Intervention studies of this kind will also be attempted with other diagnostic groups for whom relatives' EE has been identified as a determinant of course of the illness. A controlled trial of marital therapy with the high-EE spouses of depressed patients is crying out to be done.

The relationship between EE and other well-established assessments of family interaction will be worked out in detail, and a brief method of identifying high-EE relatives will be developed for use in clinical settings. Increasingly, patients are being discharged from hospitals to live in sheltered accommoda-

tions with professional and lay caretakers. The role of EE in these extrafamilial social groups is certain to come under scrutiny.

Finally, measurement of EE will be incorporated in a variety of biological
investigations into schizophrenia, both physiological and biochemical, and
thereby will reduce the heterogeneity of patient samples. This is likely to lead
to a clearer definition of the biological abnormality in schizophrenia.

This book has been written at an exciting time in EE research. We can
look back over a line of solid and painstaking work, which has begun to influence ways of looking at the families of psychiatric patients and of working
with them clinically. We can look forward to an expansion and diversification
of research that is likely to illuminate many of the dark corners of psychiatry.

References

Angermeyer, M. C. (1982). The association between family atmosphere and hospital career of schizophrenic patients. *British Journal of Psychiatry, 141*, 1–11.

Antelman, S. M. & Caggiula, A. R. (1980). Stress-induced behavior: chemotherapy without drugs. In J. M. Davidson & R. J. Davidson (Eds.), *The psychobiology of consciousness*. New York: Plenum Press.

Baker, B. & Merskey, H. (1982). Parental representations of hypochondriacal patients from a psychiatric hospital. *British Journal of Psychiatry, 141*, 233–238.

Baldwin, A. L., Kalhorn, J., & Breese, F. H. (1949). The appraisal of parent behavior. *Psychological Monographs, 63*, 4 (Whole No. 299).

Barnes, B. (1982). *T. S. Kuhn and social science*. London: Macmillan.

Barton, R. (1959). *Institutional neurosis*. Bristol, England: John Wright & Son.

Bateson, G., Jackson, D. D., Haley, J., & Weakland, J. (1956). Toward a theory of schizophrenia. *Behavioral Science, 1*, 251–264.

Beck, A. T. (1967). *Depression: Clinical, experimental and theoretical aspects*. New York: Harper & Row.

Berkowitz, R., Eberlein-Vries, R., Kuipers, L., & Leff, J. (1984). Educating relatives about schizophrenia. *Schizophrenia Bulletin, 10*, 418–429.

Berkowitz, R., Kuipers, L., & Leff, J. (1981). Keeping the patient well: Drug and social treatments of schizophrenic patients. *Psychopharmacology Bulletin, 17*, 89–90.

Berkowitz, R., & Leff, J. (1984). Clinical teams reflect family dysfunction. *Journal of Family Therapy, 6*, 78–89.

Bleuler, M. (1968). A 23-year longitudinal study of 208 schizophrenics and impressions in regard to the nature of schizophrenia. In D. Rosenthal & S. Kety (Eds.), *The transmission of schizophrenia* (pp. 3–12). Oxford: Pergamon Press.

Bowen, M., Dysinger, R. H., & Basamania, B. (1959). The role of the father in families with a schizophrenic patient. *American Journal of Psychiatry, 115*, 1017–1020.

Brown, G. W. (1959). Experiences of discharged chronic schizophrenic mental hospital patients in various types of living group. *Millbank Memorial Fund Quarterly, 37*, 105–131.

Brown, G. W. (1960). Length of hospital stay and schizophrenia: A review of statistical studies. *Acta Psychiatrica Neurologica Scandinavica, 35*, 414.

Brown, G. W. (1967). The family of the schizophrenic patient. In A. Coppen & A. Walk (Eds.), *Recent developments in schizophrenia: A symposium* (Special Publication No. 1). London: Royal Medico-Psychological Association.

Brown, G. W. (1974). Meaning, measurement and stress of life-events. In B. S. Dohrenwend & B. P. Dohrenwend (Eds.), *Stressful life-events: Their nature and effects*. New York: Wiley.

Brown, G. W., & Birley, J. L. T. (1968). Crises and life changes and the onset of schizophrenia. *Journal of Health and Social Behavior, 9*, 203.

Brown, G. W., Birley, J. L. T., & Wing, J. K. (1972). Influence of family life on the course of schizophrenic disorders: A replication. *British Journal of Psychiatry, 121,* 241–258.

Brown, G. W., Bone, M., Dalison, B., & Wing, J. K. (1966). *Schizophrenia and social care: A comparative follow-up study of 339 schizophrenic patients* (Maudsley Monograph No. 17). London: Oxford University Press.

Brown, G. W., Carstairs, G. M., & Topping, G. (1958). Post hospital adjustment of chronic mental patients. *Lancet, ii,* 685–689.

Brown, G. W. & Harris, T. (1978). *Social origins of depression.* London: Tavistock.

Brown, G. W., Monck, E. M., Carstairs, G. M., & Wing, J. K. (1962). Influence of family life on the course of schizophrenic illness. *British Journal of Preventive and Social Medicine, 16,* 55–68.

Brown, G. W., & Rutter, M. (1966). The measurement of family activities and relationships: A methodological study. *Human Relations, 19,* 241–263.

Campbell, D. T., & Stanley, J. C. (1963). Experimental and quasi-experimental designs for research. In N. L. Gage (Ed.), *Handbook of research on teaching.* Chicago: Rand McNally.

Creer, C., & Wing, J. K. (1974). *Schizophrenia at home.* London: National Schizophrenia Fellowship.

Davitz, J. R. (Ed.). (1964). *The communication of emotional meaning.* New York: McGraw-Hill.

Doane, J. A., West, K. L., Goldstein, M. J., Rodnick, E. H., & Jones, J. E. (1981). Parental communication deviance and affective style. *Archives of General Psychiatry, 38,* 679–685.

Ekman, P., & Friesen, W. V. (1968). Nonverbal behavior in psychotherapy research. In J. Shlien (Ed.), *Research in psychotherapy* (Vol. 3). Washington, DC: American Psychological Association.

Etzioni, A. (1960). Interpersonal and structural factors in the study of mental hospitals. *Psychiatry, 23,* 13–22.

Falloon, I. R. H., Boyd, J. L., & McGill, C. W. (1984). *Family care of schizophrenia: A problem-solving approach to the treatment of mental illness.* New York: Guilford Press.

Falloon, I. R. H., Boyd, J. L., McGill, C. W., Razani, J., Moss, H. B., & Gilderman, A. (1982). Family management in the prevention of exacerbations of schizophrenia: A controlled study. *New England Journal of Medicine, 306,* 1437–1440.

Falloon, I. R. H., Watt, D. C., & Shepherd, M. (1978). A comparative controlled trial of pimozide and fluphenazine decanoate in the continuation therapy of schizophrenia. *Psychological Medicine, 8,* 59–70.

Faris, R. E. L., & Dunham, H. W. (1939). *Mental disorders in urban areas.* Chicago: University of Chicago Press.

Fleck, S., Lidz, T., & Cornelison, A. (1963). Comparison of parent–child relationships of male and female schizophrenic patients. *Archives of General Psychiatry, 8,* 1–7.

Freeman, H. E., & Simmons, O. G. (1963). *The mental patient comes home.* New York: Wiley.

Glaser, B. G., & Strauss, A. L. (1967). *The discovery of grounded theory.* Chicago: Aldine.

Goffman, E. (1961). *Asylums.* New York: Anchor.

Goldstein, M. J., Judd, L. L., Rodnick, E. H., Alkire, A. A., & Gould, E. (1968). A method for studying social influence and coping patterns within families of disturbed adolescents. *Journal of Nervous and Mental Disease, 147,* 233–251.

Gottschalk, L. A., & Gleser, G. C. (1969). *The measurement of psychological states through the content analysis of verbal behavior.* Berkeley: University of California Press.

Hamburg, D. A., Sabshin, M., Board, F. A., Grinker, R. R., Korchin, S. J., Basowitz, H., Heath, H., & Persky, H. (1958). Classification and rating of emotional experiences. *Archives of Neurology and Psychiatry, 79,* 415–426.

Hanson, N. R. (1958). *Patterns of discovery: An inquiry into the conceptual foundations of science*. Cambridge, England: Cambridge University Press.

Hanson, N. R. (1971). *Observation and explanation*. New York: Harper & Row.

Hare, E. H. (1956). Family setting and the urban distribution of schizophrenia. *Journal of Mental Science, 102*, 753-760.

Havstad, L. F. (1979). *Weight loss and weight loss maintenance as aspects of family emotional processes*. Unpublished doctoral dissertation, University of Southern California.

Hirsch, S. R., Gaind, R., Rohde, P. D., Stevens, B. C., & Wing, J. K. (1973). Out-patient maintenance treatment of chronic schizophrenic patients with long-acting injections of fluphenazine decanoate: A double-blind placebo-controlled trial. *British Medical Journal, i*, 633-637.

Hirsch, S. R., & Leff, J. P. (1971). Parental abnormalities of verbal communication in the transmission of schizophrenia. *Psychological Medicine, 1*, 118-127.

Hirsch, S. R., & Leff, J. P. (1975). *Abnormalities in parents of schizophrenics* (Maudsley Monograph No. 22). London: Oxford University Press.

Hogarty, G. E., Goldberg, S. C., & the Collaborative Study Group. (1973). Drug and sociotherapy in the aftercare of schizophrenic patients: one-year relapse rates. *Archives of General Psychiatry, 28*, 54-64.

Hogarty, G. E., Goldberg, S. C., Schooler, N. R., Ulrich, R. F., & the Collaborative Study Group. (1974). Drug and sociotherapy in the aftercare of schizophrenic patients: II. Two-year relapse rates. *Archives of General Psychiatry, 31*, 603-608.

Hogarty, G. E., Schooler, N. R., Ulrich, R. F., Mussare, F., Ferro, P., & Herron, E. (1979). Fluphenazine and social therapy in the aftercare of schizophrenic patients. *Archives of General Psychiatry, 36*, 1283-1294.

Hollingshead, A. B., & Redlich, F. C. (1958). *Social class and mental illness: A community study*. New York: Wiley.

Izard, C. E. (1971). *The face of emotion*. New York: Appleton-Century-Crofts.

Johnson, D. A. W. (1976). The expectation of outcome from maintenance therapy in chronic schizophrenic patients. *British Journal of Psychiatry, 128*, 246-250.

Kaplan, A. (1964). *The conduct of inquiry: Methodology for behavioral science*. San Francisco: Chandler.

Krawiecka, M., Goldberg, D., & Vaughn, M. (1977). A standardized psychiatric assessment scale for rating chronic psychotic patients. *Acta Psychiatrica Neurologica Scandinavica, 55*, 299-308.

Kuhn, T. S. (1962). *The structure of scientific revolutions*. Chicago: University of Chicago Press.

Kuipers, L., Sturgeon, D., Berkowitz, R., & Leff, J. (1983). Characteristics of expressed emotion: Its relationship to speech and looking in schizophrenic patients and their relatives. *British Journal of Clinical Psychology, 22*, 257-264.

Laing, R. D. (1967). *The politics of experience*. New York: Pantheon.

Laing, R. D., & Esterson, D. (1964). *Sanity, madness and the family*. London: Tavistock.

Lakatos, I., & Musgrave, A. E. (1970). *Criticism and the growth of knowledge*. Cambridge, England: Cambridge University Press.

Leff, J. P. (1979). Developments in family treatment of schizophrenia. *Psychiatric Quarterly, 51*, 216-232.

Leff, J. P. (1982). Chronic syndromes of schizophrenia. In J. K. Wing & L. Wing (Eds.), *Psychoses of uncertain aetiology: Handbook of psychiatry 3* (pp. 13-16). Cambridge, England: Cambridge University Press.

Leff, J. P., Hirsch, S. R., Gaind, R., Rohde, P. D., & Stevens, B. C. (1973). Life events and maintenance therapy in schizophrenic relapse. *British Journal of Psychiatry, 123*, 659-660.

Leff, J. P., Kuipers, L., Berkowitz, R., Eberlein-Vries, R., & Sturgeon, D. (1982). A controlled trial of social intervention in the families of schizophrenic patients. *British Journal of Psychiatry, 141*, 121–134.

Leff, J. P., & Vaughn, C. (1981). The role of maintenance therapy and relatives' expressed emotion in relapse of schizophrenia: A two-year follow-up. *British Journal of Psychiatry, 139*, 102–104.

Leff, J. P., & Wing, J. K. (1971). Trial of maintenance therapy in schizophrenia. *British Medical Journal, iii*, 599–604.

Lewis, A. (1959). The impact of psychotropic drugs on the structure, function and future of psychiatric services (a) in the hospitals. *Neuropsychopharmacology, 1*, 207–212.

Lidz, R. W., & Lidz, T. (1949). The family environment of schizophrenic patients. *American Journal of Psychiatry, 106*, 332–345.

Lidz, T. (1967). The family, personality development and schizophrenia. In *The origins of schizophrenia* (Excerpta Medica International Congress Series No. 151) (pp. 131–138). Amsterdam: Excerpta Medica.

Lidz, T., Cornelison, A. R., Fleck, S., & Terry, D. (1957). The intrafamilial environment of schizophrenic patients: II. Marital schism and marital skew. *American Journal of Psychiatry, 114*, 241–248.

Martin, D. (1955). Institutionalization. *Lancet, ii*, 1188.

Mayer-Gross, W., Slater, E., & Roth, M. (1954). *Clinical Psychiatry*. London: Cassell.

Medawar, P. (1969). *Induction and intuition in scientific thought*. London: Methuen.

Menon, K., Leff, J., Kuipers, L., Bedi, H., Ghosh, A., Day, R., Korten, A., Ernberg, G., Sartorius, N., & Jablensky, A. (1984). The distribution of expressed emotion components among relatives of schizophrenic patients in Aarhus and Chandigarh. Submitted to *British Journal of Psychiatry*.

Miklowitz, D. J., Goldstein, M. J., Falloon, I. R. H., & Doane, J. A. (1984). Interactional characteristics of expressed emotion in the families of schizophrenics. *British Journal of Psychiatry, 144*, 482–487.

Minuchin, S., & Fishman, H. C. (1981). *Family therapy techniques*. Cambridge, MA: Harvard University Press.

Nameche, G., Waring, M., & Ricks, D. (1964). Early indicators of outcome in schizophrenia. *Journal of Nervous and Mental Disease, 139*, 232–240.

Ødegaard, O. (1946). Marriage and mental disease. *Journal of Mental Science, 92*, 35–59.

Ødegaard, O. (1953). New data on marriage and mental disease. *Journal of Mental Science, 99*, 778–785.

Öhman, A. (1981). Electrodermal activity and vulnerability to schizophrenia: A review. *Biological Psychiatry, 12*, 87–145.

O'Neal, P., & Robins, L. N. (1958. Childhood patterns predictive of adult schizophrenia: A 30-year follow-up study. *American Journal of Psychiatry, 115*, 385–391.

Parker, G. (1979). Parental characteristics in relation to depressive disorders. *British Journal of Psychiatry, 134*, 138–147.

Parker, G. (1981). Parental representations of patients with anxiety neurosis. *Acta Psychiatrica Neurologica Scandinavica, 63*, 33–36.

Parker, G., Fairley, M., Greenwood, J., Jurd, S., & Silove, D. (1982). Parental representations of schizophrenics and their association with onset and course of schizophrenia. *British Journal of Psychiatry, 141*, 573–581.

Parker, G., Tupling, H., & Brown , L. B. (1979). A parental bonding instrument. *British Journal of Medical Psychology, 52*, 1–10.

Platt, S., Weyman, A., Hirsch, S., & Hewett, S. (1980). The Social Behavior Assessment Schedule (SBAS): Rationale, contents, scoring and reliability of a new interview schedule. *Social Psychiatry, 15*, 43–55.

Pollin, W.. & Stabenau, J. (1968). Biological, psychological and historical differences in a series of monozygotic twins discordant for schizophrenia. In D. Rosenthal & S. Kety (Eds.), *The transmission of schizophrenia* (pp. 317–332). Oxford: Pergamon Press.

Pollin, W., Stabenau, J. R., Mosher, L., & Tupin, J. (1966). Life history differences in twins discordant for schizophrenia. *American Journal of Orthopsychiatry, 36*, 492–509.

Reason, P. & Rowan, J. (Eds.). (1981). *Human inquiry*. Chichester: Wiley.

Richardson, S. A., Dohrenwend, B. S., & Klein, D. (1965). *Interviewing: Its forms and functions*. New York: Basic Books.

Ricks, D. F., & Nameche, C. (1966). Symbiosis, sacrifice and schizophrenia. *Mental Hygiene, 50*, 541–551.

Riskin, J., & Faunce, E. (1972). An evaluative review of family interaction research. *Family Process, 11*, 365–456.

Rosenthal, D., & Kety, S. S. (Eds.). (1968). *The transmission of schizophrenia*. London: Pergamon Press.

Rutter, M., & Brown, G. W. (1966). The reliability and validity of measures of family life and relationships in families containing a psychiatric patient. *Social Psychiatry, 1*, 38.

Salzinger, K. & Pisoni, S. (1960). Reinforcement of verbal affect responses of normal subjects during the interview. *Journal of Abnormal and Social Psychology, 60*, 127–130.

Schneider, K. (1959). *Clinical psychopathology*. New York: Grune & Stratton.

Singer, M. T. (1968). The consensus Rorschach and family transaction. *Journal of Projective Technique and Personality Assessment, 32*, 348–350.

Singer, M. T., & Wynne, L. C. (1963). Differentiating characteristics of the parents of childhood schizophrenics, childhood neurotics, and young adult schizophrenics. *American Journal of Psychiatry, 120*, 234–243.

Singer, M. T., & Wynne, L. C. (1965). Thought disorder and family relations of schizophrenics: IV. Results and implications. *Archives of General Psychiatry, 12*, 201–212.

Singer, M. T., & Wynne, L. C. (1966). Communication styles in parents of normals, neurotics, and schizophrenics. *Psychiatric Research Reports, 20*, 25–38.

Staddon, J. E. R. (1971). Darwin explained: An object lesson in theory construction. *Contemporary Psychology, 16*, 689–691.

Stevens, B. S. (1969). *Marriage and fertility of women suffering from schizophrenia or affective disorders* (Maudsley Monograph No. 19). London: Oxford University Press.

Strodtbeck, F. L. (1951). Husband–wife interaction over revealed differences. *American Sociological Review, 16*, 468–473.

Strodtbeck, F. L. (1954). The family as a three person group. *American Sociological Review, 19*, 23–29.

Sturgeon, D., Kuipers, L., Berkowitz, R., Turpin, G., & Leff, J. (1981). Psychophysiological responses of schizophrenic patients to high and low expressed emotion relatives. *British Journal of Psychiatry, 138*, 40–45.

Sturgeon, D., Turpin, G., Kuipers, L., Berkowitz, R., & Leff, J. (1984). Psychophysiological responses of schizophrenic patients to high and low expressed emotion relatives: A follow-up study. *British Journal of Psychiatry, 145*, 62–69.

Tarrier, N., Vaughn, C., Lader, M. H., & Leff, J. P, (1979). Bodily reactions to people and events in schizophrenia. *Archives of General Psychiatry, 36*, 311–315.

Toone, B., Cooke, R., & Lader, M. (1981). Electrodermal activity in the affective disorders and schizophrenia. *Psychological Medicine, 11*, 497–508.

Valone, K., Norton, J. P, Goldstein, M. J., & Doane, J. A. (1983). Parental expressed emotion and affective style in an adolescent sample at risk for schizophrenia spectrum disorder. *Journal of Abnormal Psychology 92,*. 399–407.

Vaughn, C. (1977). Interaction characteristics in families of schizophrenic patients. In H. Katschnig (Ed.), *Die andere seite der schizophrenie*. Vienna: Urban & Schwarzenberg.

Vaughn, C. E., & Leff, J. P. (1976a). The influence of family and social factors on the course of psychiatric illness: A comparison of schizophrenic and depressed neurotic patients. *British Journal of Psychiatry, 129*, 125–137.

Vaughn, C. E., & Leff, J. P. (1976b). The measurement of expressed emotion in the families of psychiatric patients. *British Journal of Social and Clinical Psychology, 15*, 157–165.

Vaughn, C. E., Snyder, K. S., Freeman, W., Jones, S., Falloon, I. R. H., & Lieberman, R. P. (in press). Family factors in schizophrenic relapse. *Archives of General Psychiatry.*

Venables, P. H., & Wing, J. K. (1962). Level of arousal and the sub-classification of schizophrenia. *Archives of General Psychiatry, 7*, 114–119.

Wardle, C. (1960). *Social achievement and the functional psychosis.* Unpublished thesis.

Waring, M., & Ricks, D. (1965). Family patterns of children who become adult schizophrenics. *Journal of Nervous and Mental Diseases, 140*, 351–364.

Weissman, M. M., Klerman, G. L., Paykel, E. S., Prusoff, B., & Hanson, B. (1974). Treatment effects on the social adjustment of depressed patients. *Archives of General Psychiatry, 30*, 771–778.

Weissman, M. M., Prusoff, B. A., Thompson, W. D., Harding, P. S., & Myers, J. K. (1978). Social adjustment by self-report in a community sample and in psychiatric outpatients. *Journal of Nervous and Mental Disease, 166*, 317–326.

Wing, J. K., Cooper, J. E., & Sartorius, N. (1974). *The measurement and classification of psychiatric symptoms: An instruction manual for the PSE and Catego Program.* Cambridge, England: Cambridge University Press.

Wynne, L. C., & Singer, M. T. (1963). Thought disorder and family relations of schizophrenics. *Archives of General Psychiatry, 9*, 191–206.

Wynne, L. C., Ryckoff, I., Day, J., & Hirsch, S. (1958). Pseudo-mutuality in the family relations of schizophrenics. *Psychiatry, 21*, 205–220.

Wynne, L. C., Singer, M. T., Bartko, J. J., & Toohey, M. L. (1977). Schizophrenics and their families: Research on parental communication. In J. M. Tanner (Ed.), *Developments in psychiatric research* (pp. 254–286). London: Hodder & Stroughton.

Yarrow, M. R. (1963). Problems of methods in parent–child research. *Child Development, 34*, 215–226.

Znaniecki, F. (1934). *The method of sociology.* New York: Farrar & Rinehart.

Author Index

Alkire, A. A., 168
Angermeyer, M. C., 212, 214
Antelman, S. M., 16

B

Baker, B., 44
Baldwin, A. L., 19
Barnes, B., 25
Bartko, J. J., 151
Barton, R., 2
Basamania, B., 217
Bateson, G., 1, 151, 209
Beck, A. T., 72
Berkowitz, R., 125, 130, 131, 142, 151, 201, 202
Birley, J. L. T., 9, 10, 20, 24, 152, 186–188
Bleuler, M., 94
Bone, M., 95
Bowen, M., 217
Boyd, J. L., 165
Breese, F. H., 19
Brown, G. W., 13, 17–20, 22, 24, 26–30, 34, 37, 44, 64, 77–90, 92–97, 119, 134, 151, 152, 175, 177, 186–189, 190
Brown, L. B., 214

C

Caggiula, A. R., 16
Campbell, D. T., 23
Carstairs, M., 9, 10, 12, 19

Cooke, R., 197
Cooper, J. E., 79
Cornelison, A. R., 151, 217
Creer, C., 95
Crow, T., 178

D

Dalison, B., 95
Davitz, J. R., 29
Day, J., 151
Doane, J. A., 119, 168, 210
Dohrenwend, B. S., 27
Dunham, H. W., 11, 16
Dysinger, R. H., 217

E

Eberlein-Vries, R., 125, 131
Ekman, P., 29
Esterson, D., 1
Etzioni, A., 2

F

Fairley, M., 214
Falloon, I. R. H., 97, 111, 165, 168, 171
Faris, R. E. L., 11, 16
Faunce, E., 27
Fishman, H. C., 45
Fleck, S., 151, 217
Freeman, H. E., 15, 95

233

Subject Index